SPANISH DRAMA OF
THE GOLDEN AGE

by

MARGARET WILSON

Lecturer in Spanish in the University of Hull

1966
THE QUEEN'S AWARD
TO INDUSTRY 1966

PERGAMON PRESS

OXFORD · LONDON · EDINBURGH · NEW YORK
TORONTO · SYDNEY · PARIS · BRAUNSCHWEIG

Pergamon Press Ltd., Headington Hill Hall, Oxford
4 & 5 Fitzroy Square, London W.1
Pergamon Press (Scotland) Ltd., 2 & 3 Teviot Place, Edinburgh 1
Pergamon Press Inc., Maxwell House, Fairview Park, Elmsford,
New York 10523
Pergamon of Canada Ltd., 207 Queen's Quay West, Toronto 1
Pergamon Press (Aust.) Pty. Ltd., 19a Boundary Street,
Rushcutters Bay, N.S.W. 2011, Australia
Pergamon Press S.A.R.L., 24 rue des Écoles, Paris 5°
Vieweg & Sohn GmbH, Burgplatz 1, Braunschweig

Copyright © 1969 Margaret Wilson
First edition 1969
Library of Congress Catalog Card No. 74–78906

Printed in Great Britain by A. Wheaton & Co., Exeter

08 013954 X (flexicover)
08 013955 8 (hard cover)

TO THE MEMORY OF

ANNIE ROSE NUTTALL

INEZ ISABEL MACDONALD

AND

FLORENCE SPENCER STREET

CONTENTS

PREFACE

I WAS first prompted to write this book by the number of my colleagues in Arts Faculties who knew the names of Lope de Vega and Calderón but little else about them, and who wanted some guide to a clearly important but little-known field of European drama. There has hitherto been nothing in English to which one could conveniently refer them, and I very much hope that this work will meet that need. At the same time I hope it may also be of use to university students of Spanish and teachers of Spanish literature to sixth forms. Recent criticism on the *comedia* is mainly in article form and may not be easily accessible to them; and they might in any case find it difficult to build up a complete picture from isolated studies of individual authors and works. I have tried to give such a picture of the *comedia* as a whole, and of its development through the century of its existence.

For the sake of readers without a knowledge of Spanish I have translated all quotations, giving the Spanish text first in the case of plays, but not prose and other writings where the original language is of no special significance. Titles are translated on their first appearance, except for those which are proper names, or self-explanatory.

The field I have attempted to cover is a vast one, not merely in the quantity of the drama itself, but also in the amount of criticism it has called forth. This is a sphere in which it is almost certainly true to say that knowledge has doubled itself in each of the last two decades. Faced with so much material I have had to be selective, and I am well aware that my selections may be open to question. Had space and time been unlimited I should have liked to include more minor dramatists and to analyse many more plays; and my apologies are due to a number of critics of whose views and findings it has not been possible for me to give account.

No one, I think, could nowadays claim specialist knowledge of the whole field, and I have necessarily relied greatly on the works of other scholars. For instance, the Introduction and those parts of Chapter 11 dealing with stage presentation are drawn entirely from N. D. Shergold's splendid *History of the Spanish Stage*, and my indebtedness to A. A. Parker, E. M. Wilson, A. E. Sloman and others in my chapters on Calderón will be clearly apparent. It may very well be too that over the years of my study of the *comedia* certain views of others may have become a part of my own thinking without my being aware of it, and for any such unacknowledged debts I apologize in advance. Generally speaking, however, the analyses and estimates of the plays I deal with are my own; and while it is not to be expected that they will all meet with the complete agreement of other Hispanists, I hope they will be found to include a fair measure of broadly acceptable independent criticism.

My practice has been to refer to particular points of criticism, and editions of single plays, in the appropriate chapters or the notes thereto. These will thus offer guidance on further reading to those interested in individual works. The bibliographies are restricted to collections of plays and general critical studies.

Over and above my gratitude to all those scholars on whose work I have drawn and who have so much enriched my understanding and enjoyment of the *comedia*, I must express my sincere thanks to Professor A. A. Parker and Professor F. W. Pierce for their repeated encouragement, and to Professor R. B. Tate, Professor G. W. Ribbans and Mr. C. B. Morris for reading my text and making many valuable suggestions for its improvement. As head of the department in which I have been working for the last five years Mr. Morris has shown me the utmost consideration and helpfulness, and this, together with Miss Pat Foster's careful and willing assistance with the typing of the manuscript, has greatly eased my task. Lastly, there are two debts of a more personal nature which I gratefully acknowledge. My friend Dr. Renee C. Winegarten first convinced me that I ought to try to write this book, and has gone on believing that I could do it, long as it has taken me; and the same support has come from my husband, Dr. Harold H. Borland, whose help and advice have been constantly sought, and unfailingly and ungrudgingly given.

Hull
July 1968

INTRODUCTION
THE THEATRES

ON ALMOST any afternoon in the early seventeenth century, if it were not in Lent, a play would be performed in each of the theatres of Madrid. There were only two of them at the time, and like most of their English counterparts they were housed not in roofed buildings but in yards. The theatres themselves were even known as *corrales*, the Corral del Príncipe and the Corral de la Cruz. They stood respectively in the streets which still bear those names today, close to each other and barely five minutes' walk from the Puerta del Sol. Modern audiences at the Teatro Español in the Calle del Príncipe see plays performed on the same site as their predecessors of the 1600's.

What would most surprise these modern playgoers if they could observe a seventeenth-century audience would be the segregation of the sexes, in all but the most expensive seats. The yards were not by this time those of inns, as often in London, but courtyards surrounded by houses. The windows of these houses along the side walls served as boxes, occupied by the gentry and town officials, and here men and women did mix. But in the lateral rows of seats below these, and in the central pit where the groundlings stood, there were only men. Women entered through a separate door and sat in enclosures at the back of the *corral*, opposite the stage, expressively called the *cazuelas*, or stewpots. These were at ground and first floor levels. At second floor level there was another enclosure, the *tertulia*, for the clergy, who were thus directly above the *cazuelas* and protected from any contact with their occupants.

The stage took up the fourth side of the theatre. It was a platform stage with no proscenium arch or front curtain. A curtain stretched across the back provided the actors with a green-room and exits and entrances, and like the Elizabethan arras could be partially drawn back to supply an inner room or alcove when the action required it. Above the stage the gallery which ran round the *corral* at first-floor level could be brought into service as an upper storey, or even a mountain. Although costumes were fairly elaborate, scenery where it existed at all was simple, and the spectators were prepared to use their imagination. In particular, since performances took place in daylight and in the open air there was no means of creating darkness, and the many night settings in the drama of the time could only be conveyed by the text and by the actors wearing appropriate clothing. Yet the darkness is often so much a part of the atmosphere and of the action that it must be assumed that the audience was capable of supplying it mentally.

There was a charge for admission to the theatre itself, and a further sum to be paid if one occupied a seat. The takings were distributed in a way which is somewhat unexpected: the surprising fact is that the permanent public theatres of Madrid really came into being as fund-raisers for charity. Already by the 1570's some of the confraternities devoted to good works had sensed in the growing popularity of the drama a possible source of regular income for the hospitals they ran, and from the following decade they were the owners and beneficiaries of Madrid's two theatres. Much of the administration was put into the hands of lessees. These were originally little more than caretakers to whom certain perquisites such as the sale of refreshments had been farmed out; but in the seventeenth century they became virtually theatre managers, with responsibility for hiring the acting companies and for the finances of the whole enterprise. They met the running costs and also paid to the hospitals a proportion of each day's takings, in addition to the considerable fixed sum which their lease had cost them.

Eventually the ownership and control of the theatres passed to the Town Council, who compensated the hospitals by means of an annual subsidy. But the charitable connection had been of great importance in the development of the theatre and in its resistance to moral opposition. It was one of the justifications for the frequency of performances, which some people found excessive. They had originally been given only on Sundays and holidays; then permission was granted to hold them on two week-day afternoons, then on three, and finally all limitation was abandoned. With a performance most days, and a relatively small population, plays naturally had a much shorter run than is usual today. They were often subsequently performed in the provinces, but the habitués of the Madrid *corrales* probably demanded a new play at least once a week.

Who were these habitués? Virtually, it seems, the whole population of the city. Members of the enclosed religious orders would not be there (though they sometimes saw plays performed in their convents), but the secular clergy were catered for in the *tertulia*. Reserved rooms in the houses overlooking the *corrales* were one of the privileges of town officials. Nobles would rent similar "boxes" for a whole season or longer, and the King himself had his own "box" at the Corral de la Cruz. The side benches, the *cazuelas* and the pit were there for the populace, whose catcalls and quarrels constituted part of the entertainment for their superiors. The facts that the quarrels were often over seats, and that a booking office was open in the mornings, indicate that the space available was not always equal to the demand.

Once the audience were settled in their places, the musical prelude played and the prologue recited, what kind of plays did they see? What was the nature of this drama so avidly demanded and so constantly supplied, and by what processes had it evolved? Who were the playwrights who devised it? What are its merits, and its interest for the student of literature today? These are the questions which this book will try to answer.

General Works

RENNERT, H. A., *The Spanish Stage in the Time of Lope de Vega* (2nd ed., New York, 1963).

SHERGOLD, N. D., *A History of the Spanish Stage from Medieval Times until the End of the Seventeenth Century* (Oxford, 1967).

1

THE BEGINNINGS

THE Spanish plays written during the century which ran from
the start of the career of Lope de Vega in the 1580's to the death
of Calderón in 1681 may be said to constitute a genre of their
own. It is a genre which shares a number of features with Elizabethan drama, but could never be confused with it. Although
it developed partly through contacts with Italy and with classical
drama, it remained essentially non-classical, and made no clean
break with the Middle Ages as did the contemporary theatre
in France. It is therefore with the dramatic activity known to
have existed in medieval Spain that a study of the evolution of
the Spanish national theatre must begin.

In Spain as elsewhere the beginnings of modern drama must
be sought in the Latin tropes, or short illustrative scenes, which
from the eleventh century onwards were performed in church,
in close connection with the Liturgy, to celebrate the festivals
of Christmas, Epiphany and Easter. The parts of Spain where
this early liturgical drama seems to have flourished most are
Catalonia, Valencia and Majorca, that is, those eastern regions
where French influence was strongest. But whereas in France
and England it had by the fourteenth century developed into
long, elaborately staged and highly artistic cycles of "mystery
plays", in Spain this evolution did not take place. "Mysteries"
do eventually appear in the Levantine provinces, but only in
the late fifteenth and the sixteenth centuries; and they are still
isolated pieces in honour of a saint or of a festival such as the
Assumption. The *Misterio de Elche*, still annually performed in
that town today, is an example.

In Castile, where contacts with France were fewer, little

evidence of medieval church drama survives. The *Auto de los Reyes Magos* (*Play of the Three Kings*), a twelfth-century fragment from Toledo which is the oldest extant play in Spanish, testifies to the existence of festival pieces in the vernacular at a relatively early date, and Alfonso X (1252–84) speaks of Christmas, Easter and Epiphany plays as regular occurrences at his court, also in Toledo.[1] There is, however, an almost complete dearth of any texts before the late fifteenth century; and when we do meet, for instance, a *Representación del Nacimiento* (*Nativity play*), written by Gómez Manrique between 1467 and 1481, it shows very little advance dramatically on the Epiphany fragment of three centuries earlier.

A tradition which appears to have been much more highly developed in Spain as a whole is that of dramatic ritual, whether religious or secular. It seems certain that there were frequent representations marking some season or occasion, in which song and dance played a more important part than any written text, and in which the audience were involved as worshipping or rejoicing participants, rather than remaining apart as detached observers of an æsthetic performance. The influence of this popular tradition is strong in the dramatic texts of the early sixteenth century, and persists throughout the Golden Age theatre, in which song and dance often play an important part.[2]

To this tradition belong also the open-air celebrations of the feast of Corpus Christi, held from the time of the proclamation of that festival in 1311. Since it was a feast whose import could not easily be illustrated by the acting of any scenes, but one which lent itself perfectly to spectacle in the form of public display and adoration of the Sacrament, it came to be celebrated by outdoor processions and pageants, above all in the Mediterranean provinces. The popularity of such spectacles may well have been one factor helping to inhibit the development of

[1] *Siete partidas* I.115.

[2] See Charlotte Stern, "Fray Íñigo de Mendoza and medieval dramatic ritual", *HR* 33 (1965) 197–245; and "Some new thoughts on the early Spanish drama", *BC* 18 (1966) 14–19.

other types of religious drama. They cannot be called plays at this stage, but were destined to grow into one of the major and most characteristic forms of dramatic activity in Spain.

Far older than the religious drama, however, was the popular entertainment of the ancient world, the mime. Its stock comic characters had amused audiences with their horseplay from Roman times onwards, and there seems little doubt that the mime flourished in Spain, as in other parts of the former Roman empire, throughout the medieval period. The fact that mime performances were largely improvised and unscripted means that little other than pictorial records of them survive; but we can deduce their popularity in medieval Spain from the persistence of the attacks they provoked, and also from certain forms in which their influence seems to have been mingled with that of the religious drama. There were, for instance, the *juegos de escarnio* ("mocking games"), specifically forbidden by the *Siete partidas*, the thirteenth-century code of laws of Alfonso X. These were diversions in which the minor church officials appear to have found an outlet for their suppressed high spirits. They took place in or near the church, but were entirely profane, embodying pagan rites or parodying religious ones. What may perhaps be seen as a more acceptable influence of the mime tradition is apparent by the late fifteenth century, when the shepherds of the Nativity plays have become comic yokels akin to the *stupidus* of the mime.[3] These comic rustics are to acquire a role of great importance in the Golden Age theatre, which in this and other ways has been shown to depend to a surprising extent on the mime tradition.[4]

The picture of dramatic activity in the Middle Ages is completed by the performances regularly given in towns and villages by *juglares* or wandering minstrels, pupper-masters and other itinerant entertainers; and the displays held from time to time, either

---

[3] Cf. E. Auerbach, *Mimesis* (transl. Willard Trask, New York 1957), pp. 138, 139.

[4] See E. Müller-Bochat, "Mimus, Novelle und spanische Comedia", *RF* 68 (1956) 241–70.

in public or at court, to celebrate some royal occasion: tableaux, pageants, masquerades, the recorded details of whose staging bear witness to both love of spectacle and great technical skill.[5]

The sixteenth century was a period of experiment. The influence of Renaissance Italy, while it gave the first impulse to evolution, did not at once transform Spain's theatre as it did her lyric poetry. The beginning of the process is seen in the work of the man who has come to be known as the father of Spanish drama: Juan del Encina. In the 1490's Encina was court poet and music master to the Duke of Alba, and it was in the ducal palace at Alba de Tormes, in the province of Salamanca, that his early plays were performed. (Many of his own musical settings to his verse also survive, and he is probably more widely known nowadays as a composer than as a playwright.) The plays which he wrote for the Duke are mostly short pieces called *églogas*, intended for seasonal celebrations at Christmas, Shrovetide and Easter, and they thus belong to the tradition of the old liturgical drama. They are enlivened by songs and dances and by personal and topical allusions, such as a discussion of the author's chances of being appointed choirmaster of Salamanca Cathedral; and their humorous but kindly treatment of shepherds and other rustics may partly reflect Encina's own acquaintance with the peasants on the Duke's estate. As we have seen, it was out of such figures that one of the stock comic characters of Spanish drama evolved, and by making them speak in *sayagués*, one of the local dialects of the Salamanca region, Encina established this speech once and for all as the conventional mode of utterance for the comic rustic.[6]

So far, however, his work was entirely medieval, in both form and spirit. But about the turn of the century he visited Rome, and while there, or at any rate under the influence of Italian

---

[5] See C. V. Aubrun, "Sur les débuts du théâtre en Espagne", *Hommage à Ernest Martinenche* (Paris, 1939), pp. 293–314.

[6] See Charlotte Stern, "Sayago and *sayagués* in Spanish history and literature", *HR* 29 (1961) 217–37.

literature, he wrote three further eclogues, of a very different kind. The names of their protagonists suggest their origin: Fileno, Zambardo and Cardonio; Cristino and Febea; Plácida and Victoriano; these are the shepherds, not of Salamanca, but of Arcadia. One of the works is based directly on an eclogue by the Italian poet Tebaldeo, and through him their ancestry goes back to Virgil. They deal with subject-matter entirely new to Spanish drama: the suicide of a disdained lover, a would-be hermit's capitulation to love, the resuscitation of a dead shepherdess by the goddess Venus. Here for the first time we meet the spirit and the literary conventions of the pagan Renaissance; Spanish drama has at once become both secular and European.

Yet the effect of the pastoral convention is far from dehumanizing or artificial, and the shepherds of Encina's Italianate eclogues are the first to be clearly endowed with character. They are differentiated, as those of the Nativity plays were not: the long-winded and insufferable Fileno, who insists on drawing the last line of rhetoric out of his woes; the stoic Cardonio; and the kindly but ineffectual Zambardo. For all their culture, these works of Encina are linked to his earlier pieces by humour, charm and a freshness which makes them still very readable today.

After at least one more visit to Rome, Encina took priestly orders. He journeyed to Jerusalem in 1519 to say his first mass there, and afterwards appears to have lived in Spain as an obscure ecclesiastic until his death. Thus in his life as in his work Encina perfectly reflects the Spanish Renaissance, which in most spheres was a transition rather than a clean break: a new awakening to learning and culture, to foreign forms and ideas, and to a broad interest in man; but without any severance from the age-old national and religious roots.

The next step forward was taken very soon, by a man who may well have known Encina in Rome. Torres Naharro was living there in the household of a cardinal. His collected plays, published in 1517 under the title of *Propalladia*, come much closer to the modern concept of drama than anything previously written in Spanish. Instead of short pieces in dialogue form there now appears for the first time real stage action. He classifies his works as *comedias a noticia* (plays of observation) and *comedias a fantasía* (plays of invention). In the former he depicts the activities of soldiers and servants, travellers and innkeepers, and so there appears in the Spanish theatre what is to be one of its constant characteristics, the painting of contemporary customs, often linked with social satire. In the latter, even more important, there is shapely construction involving division into five acts, with exposition, development and climax: in other words, a plot.

It is, of course, still a very rudimentary plot. That of the *Comedia Himenea*, for instance, can be briefly summarized. In the exposition we learn that Himeneo is in love with Febea. In the course of the development the latter accepts and returns his love, and agrees to admit him to her room. The climax consists of the discovery of the pair by Febea's brother, who threatens to kill Febea to preserve the family honour. Himeneo has made his escape, but returns in time to offer to marry Febea, a solution to which the brother readily agrees.

Even this simple plot, however, is much richer in incident and motivation than anything previously known in Spain. Above all it is noteworthy in its use of honour as a mainspring of drama. This is the first appearance of the *pundonor*, or "point of honour", the rigorous code of behaviour which has some part to play in innumerable *comedias*, and is often their principal theme. Naharro's contrivance of plot, moreover, is only one aspect of his sound theatrical technique. He has acquired something which Encina never had: the notion of what makes a good play in terms of exits and entrances, action and dialogue; and his works impress as drama which, while still extremely simple, is humanly and æsthetically satisfying.[7]

[7] Cf. J. E. Gillet: "Perhaps Torres Naharro is the first dramatist in the modern world who recognized (at least in practice) that there was *necessity* in the scheme of drama, the necessity that Aristotle described as that *form* which alone could convert mimicry into a powerful instrument of tension and release, of deliverance and delight." ("*Propalladia*" *and Other Works of Torres Naharro,* Vol. IV, Philadelphia, 1961, p. 563.)

The originality of his achievement must be fully recognized. It is true that he learned to handle the dramatic form in Italy, where the works of Plautus, Terence and Seneca were being imitated, both in Latin and Italian. The use of love intrigues and the role of servants in his plays clearly owe something to Latin comedy. But his debt to Italy should not be overstressed, since at the time when he was writing (1513?–17) the Italian theatre was scarcely in existence. The first attempt at a tragedy in the vulgar tongue is Pistoia's *Panfila*, 1499, but there is no true tragedy before Trissino's *Sofonisba*, 1515. The first original Italian comedies, those of Ariosto, date only from 1508 (*Cassaria*) and 1509 (*I suppositi*); Machiavelli's *Mandragola* was written after 1512. Torres Naharro was the fellow and contemporary of these dramatists, rather than their successor, and accomplished for Spain no less than they did for Italy.

There is one other noteworthy element in his work. In the Preface to his *Propalladia* he outlines the views on drama expressed by Cicero and Horace, and then proceeds to give opinions of his own, thus becoming Spain's first dramatic theorist. His practical recommendations—five acts, the characters to number between six and twelve—are not of great importance. The significant features of his theorizing are, firstly, the very fact of its existence: in the hands of the Italian-domiciled Naharro, Spanish drama has become a self-conscious art form; secondly, the confidence with which his own views are asserted and ranked with those of the ancients; and thirdly, his new concept of the *comedia a fantasía*. This, it is clear, is to be a work of the imagination, not the retelling of an old story. "It is not an imitation, an interpretation and explanation of reality, but an attempt at simply *presenting* it. The dramatist desires to show life-in-the-act, not to make the public vicariously and consciously understand it" (Gillet, *op. cit.*, Vol. IV, p. 567). At this early stage in the development of the Spanish theatre, Torres Naharro, while learning much of his craft alongside his Italian neighbours, already rejects the basis of classical drama.

While Juan del Encina and Torres Naharro were at work in

Italy, nearer home a contemporary of theirs was experimenting on his own. In Portugal from the year 1502 Gil Vicente was court poet to King Manuel I. He was probably like Encina a man of varied talents, for it seems likely that he was court goldsmith too, and that the beautiful monstrance of the Lisbon Museum of Ancient Art is his handiwork. There is something of the same lace-like delicacy about the verses which he wrote for Manuel and his family—many of them short dramatic pieces to celebrate weddings or other royal occasions. He was also capable of a more sustained poetic fantasy. His *Don Duardos*, for instance, is a little idyll based on the romances of chivalry, about a princess, and a prince from a far-off land who comes to claim her as his bride. Wishing to be loved for himself alone rather than for his rank, he pretends to be a gardener, and in a lyrical scene of sensuous romanticism, converses with the princess as she walks in the palace garden.[8]

Don Duardos is punctuated by courtly love lyrics, and the lyric strain is strong in the whole of Vicente's theatre. Song and dance are an essential part of his entertainments, deriving probably from the already popular court masque, which may in turn have had its roots in medieval folk drama and dramatic ritual. In both dialogue and song he is equally at home with the courtly and the popular. Nowhere is the power of his imagination more apparent than in the *Auto de la Sibila Casandra*, in which he develops the simple traditional Nativity play into a clever allegory. Casandra is the sibyl who foretells the birth of Christ, and since the sibyl is often identified with the Queen of Sheba, she is wooed by Solomon. But she is also a peasant girl, and Solomon is the shepherd whom her uncles Abraham, Moses and Isaiah want her to marry. She refuses, because she mistakenly thinks that *she* is the virgin who is to bear the Messiah. The language of all the characters is rustic and collo-quial, and the songs are popular lyrics, probably already well known, or at least elaborated by Vicente on familiar refrains.

[8] See the edition of *Don Duardos* by Dámaso Alonso (Madrid, 1942).

> Dicen que me case yo;
> no quiero marido, no,
>
> ("They say I should get married, but I don't want any husband,")

sings Casandra; and when she is finally convinced by a vision of Mary with the Child, it is again a lyric popular in flavour (though this time Vicente tells us it is his own) in which all join to worship the Virgin, singing and dancing before the Christmas tableau:

> Muy graciosa es la doncella,
> ¡cómo es bella y hermosa!
>
> ("Lovely is the maiden, how fair and beautiful she is!")

Gil Vicente's range extends still further, for chivalresque material of the kind so poetically handled in *Don Duardos*, in his *Amadís de Gaula* is wittily burlesqued;[9] and other works are virtually moralities, voicing outspoken social satire. This is to be found in the trilogy of the *Barcas* (*The Boats*), in which boatloads of souls bound for hell, purgatory and heaven describe the way of life that has determined their fate. The conception is a medieval one, but much of the actual satire belongs clearly to the Reformation period:

> Como! Por ser namorado,
> e folgar c'hũa mulher,
> se há-de um frade de perder,
> com tanto salmo rezado ?   (*Barca do Inferno*)
>
> ("What! Just for being in love and enjoying himself with a woman, is a friar to be damned, after reciting all those psalms?")

Vicente wrote sometimes in Spanish and sometimes, as above, in Portuguese; and he did not evolve any distinct dramatic form. His geographical isolation kept him a little outside the mainstream of development. Yet in widening the scope of drama he shared in a tendency common to the whole Peninsula, where by the time of his death in 1536 a number of new experiments were being made.

The religious theatre still flourished, and *autos*, or one-act plays of the type of Encina's early eclogues, continued to appear,

[9] See the edition of *Amadís de Gaula* by T. P. Waldron (Manchester, 1959).

though with new refinements. Vicente himself invested them with allegory, Diego Sánchez de Badajoz with a theological content; Hernán López de Yanguas brought about a fusion of the shepherds' play with the Corpus Christi pageant, thus initiating a genre known as the *farsa sacramental*. Other more ambitious authors copied from Torres Naharro the techniques of Renaissance drama, and so the first full-length religious plays came to be written. Palau's *Historia de Santa Orosia* (date uncertain) dramatizes a theme from national history and hagiography. Carvajal's five-act *Josefina* (1535), based on the Old Testament story of the life of Joseph, introduces a chorus of Hebrew girls, and so comes nearer to the classical model than any previous Spanish play. Little is known about these authors beyond their names, and their works are not widely read; but they represent the beginnings of an important current in Spanish drama, the full-length dramatization of the life of a saint or biblical character. Such plays are known as *comedias de santos*.

Encina, Naharro and Vicente, like their Italian contemporaries, wrote for private patrons. Their plays were performed in the palaces of kings, nobles or cardinals, and were not destined for the general public. Their immediate successors, however, seem to have been able to write with a wider public in view, since the early sixteenth century sees the birth and growth of the theatre as a commercial institution. Documents of the 1540's refer to companies of paid actors, and a work published in 1552 (Diego Sánchez de Badajoz's *Recopilación en metro*) lists some well-known players of the period. By mid-century there was a flourishing commercial theatre, with which the name of one man in particular was connected. This was Lope de Rueda, a native of Seville and the actor-manager of an itinerant company. He is known to have performed in various parts of Spain, and may even have set up a permanent playhouse in Valladolid. More often he would use temporary stages erected in inn yards or other public places; and such was his reputation that he was often commissioned to perform too in the houses of the aristocracy. In 1554, for instance, a host of the future Philip II employed him to give an entertainment before the Prince when the latter was on his way north to join Mary Tudor in England.

It must have been about this time that his audience on at least one occasion included Cervantes, then a young boy. Many years later, in the 1615 Prologue to his own plays, Cervantes recalls "the great Lope de Rueda" with pleasure, praising his acting ability and the effects he was able to achieve with the most modest equipment: a stage thrown together from a few planks resting on benches, an old blanket hung up behind to provide a dressing-room, and a bundle of costumes and properties that could all be carried in a single sack. This has long been accepted as an eye-witness and therefore reliable account; but Professor Shergold has shown that contemporary documents and the evidence of Rueda's own plays suggest much more elaborate staging and effects. It would not be surprising if Cervantes' memories from sixty years back were inaccurate, and he may have been influenced by subsequent written accounts which exaggerated the primitive quality of Lope de Rueda in order to enhance the achievements of the later stage. It seems probable that in the very early years of the commercial theatre Lope de Rueda already had a company of some twelve to fifteen actors and was able to put on relatively polished performances.

The plays he gave were his own compositions. Cervantes mentions two types: eclogues involving two or three shepherds and a shepherdess, and the *entremeses*, or entr'actes, with which these were interspersed. The *entremés*, which Rueda himself called a *paso* (passage), was a one-act sketch deriving from the mime tradition and relying for its humour on some stock comic type, or simply on racy plebeian dialogue. Rueda wrote these sketches himself, and it is upon the two dozen or so which survive that his reputation as a playwright chiefly rests. But he also wrote full-length plays which Cervantes seems not to have known, in the tradition of Torres Naharro—or perhaps rather in the tradition of the numerous Italian playwrights who had been at work since Naharro's time. Lope de Rueda's four extant plays all rely heavily on Italian originals, and have little dramatic merit. (One of them, *Los engañados*, *The Deceived*, derives via the Italian *Gl'ingannati* from Plautus's *Menaechmi*, that work fertile in literary progeny, and is thus a cousin of *The Comedy of Errors* and *Twelfth Night*.) But it is interesting to see in his output, as in the religious theatre, the development side by side of two types of play: the full-length work of three, four and five acts, deriving via Torres Naharro from Renaissance influences, and the one-act *auto*, *paso* or *entremés*, continuing unbroken the medieval tradition.

The commercial theatre seems to have prospered from its earliest beginnings, and there was soon a large body of dramatists supplying plays in answer to the public demand. One critic has counted the names of thirty-eight known to have been writing before 1540,[10] and research not infrequently brings hitherto unknown sixteenth-century plays to light. Few of them have any merit, or show anything approaching the dramatic skill of Torres Naharro. The reminiscences of his work that do appear are all textual, and would seem to indicate a knowledge of the printed text of the *Propalladia*, rather than familiarity with the effect of his plays as presented on the stage. It must be concluded that these were widely read in Spain, but probably not performed.[11]

In addition to the romantic type of comedy, with its by now usually intricate and sensational plot, there also came from Italy a reinvigoration of the mime tradition in the form of the *commedia dell'arte*. Companies of Italian players regularly toured Spain, as they did France and England, in the second half of the sixteenth century, and their popularity is attested by the fact that the names of certain *commedia dell'arte* actors, such as Ganassa and Bottarga, passed temporarily into the Spanish language to denote the types they commonly represented.[12] This kind of drama not

[10] Cañete, referred to by Menéndez y Pelayo in his preliminary study to the *Propalladia* in *Libros de antaño*, Vol. X (Madrid, 1890), pp. i–cliii.

[11] See J. E. Gillet, "Torres Naharro and the Spanish drama of the sixteenth century", *Homenaje a Bonilla y San Martin*, Vol. II (Madrid, 1930), pp. 437–68.

[12] See N. D. Shergold, "Ganassa and the 'Commedia dell'arte' in sixteenth-century Spain", *MLR* 51 (1956) 359–68.

only influenced public taste, it must certainly have been frequently witnessed by Lope de Vega himself, who clearly learned much from it in respect of plot and dramatic technique.

Religious drama in the latter half of the century continued along the two lines of development earlier indicated. Some hundred of the *autos* of the period are fortunately preserved for us in a collection in the Biblioteca Nacional of Madrid usually known as the *Códice de autos viejos*, and published in four volumes by Léo Rouanet under the title *Colección de autos, farsas y coloquios del siglo XVI* (Barcelona, Madrid, 1901). The collection is chiefly noteworthy, from the point of view of dramatic development, in showing the increasing popularity of allegory and the *farsa sacramental*. In the domain of the full-length play popular *comedias de santos*, often written to celebrate the feast-day of a local patron saint, are found in increasing numbers; but there also appears a learned type of play, foreshadowed by the classical tendencies in Carvajal's *Josefina*. This is due to the link with the school drama. Academic institutions throughout Renaissance Europe were now cultivating a learned or humanistic theatre, directly influenced by that of the ancients, as part of their educational activities. Students would perform as exercises in rhetoric plays written for the purpose by their teachers, such as those of Juan Pérez, or Petreius, Professor of Rhetoric at Alcalá in the 1540's. At first they were always in Latin, but this gradually gave way to the vernacular. Since by the late sixteenth century the Jesuits were the most important body of teachers throughout Europe, it is not surprising that much of the school drama originated in Jesuit colleges and used religious subject-matter. The Spanish Jesuits in particular seem to have been zealous in producing dramatized versions of the life of their founder, St. Ignatius Loyola. These works combined imitation of the classics with many of the popular features which had come down from the Middle Ages, such as the comic rustic. It is worth remembering that the great dramatists of the Golden Age would all in the course of their formal education have witnessed performances of this type of play, and some may even have taken part in them. Their influence on the later theatre cannot be discounted.[13]

It was to be expected that in this century of experiment Spanish dramatists would eventually pay some attention to a genre which had been essayed in Italy fifty years earlier, and which in France was to prevail over all others: that of classical tragedy. This mode does make its appearance in Spain, but only hesitatingly and late. The first neo-classical tragedies are adaptations from the Portuguese: Jerónimo Bermúdez's *Nise lastimosa* and *Nise laureada* (*Nise the Pitiful* and *Nise Crowned*) published in 1577 and based on a play of 1558 by Antonio Ferreira, on Portugal's national tragic heroine Inés de Castro. Cristóbal de Virués writes one strictly classical play, *Elisa Dido*, but in his other tragedies ignores the rules and spreads himself in a novelesque and romantic manner. The action of Lupercio Leonardo de Argensola's *Isabela* and *Alejandra*, while contained in an Aristotelian mould, is equally alien to classical taste. Even on those few authors who took cognizance of the classical theatre, the chief influence was not that of the Greeks but of Seneca. His strain of horror, violence and bloodshed is strong in them, as in Thomas Kyd and the Elizabethans. It was to persist in later Spanish drama when Aristotelian forms were swept aside, and is the one clear legacy of the ancient theatre to the *comedia*.

It is present in high degree in the works of Juan de la Cueva, a Sevillian dramatist who helped to steer Spanish tragedy away from classical forms, and to give it a more national cast. His plays include much that is gory and horrific, but they are also noteworthy for their use of Spanish history, and in particular of material from the medieval ballads. *El reto de Zamora* (*The Challenge of Zamora*), for instance, dramatizes most poignantly the defence of Zamora by the Princess Urraca against siege by her own brother, Sancho I, and the conflict of the young Rodrigo Díaz, later to be known as the Cid, torn between his loyalty to his king and his affection for Urraca. Cueva has an

[13] See J. García Soriano, *Teatro universitario y humanístico de España* (Toledo, 1945).

acute eye for the dramatic situation and the emotive passages in the ballads, some of which he incorporates into his own text; though his sense of dramatic construction is less good, and he fails to scale his material down from epic proportions to those befitting a play.

That his experiments were judged successful is shown, first by the publication of his collected plays in 1588, and secondly by the fact that, some twenty years later, he felt himself justified in writing a dramatic manifesto entitled *Ejemplar poético*. In this he explicitly enunciates the principle of *autre temps, autres mœurs* which he had applied with regard to the classics in the writing of his own plays:

> Introdujimos otras novedades,
> de los antiguos alterando el uso,
> conformes a este tiempo y calidades.

("We introduced other novelties, changing the customs of the ancients, to accord with the conditions of today.")

Thus boldly does he claim the right of Spanish drama to evolve for itself; and while his debt to the ancients is not negligible, his influence tended chiefly in the direction of a new, national and non-classical theatre.

The time had almost come for the emergence of this theatre. From among the different genres so far essayed, various strains had proved their ability to survive, and were awaiting the genius who would blend them into a satisfying whole: the popular devotion of the religious drama and the humour of the *commedia dell'arte*, the *pundonor* of the Italian tragicomedy and the Senecan mode of the later tragedians, the lyricism of Vicente and the national themes of Cueva. But before this fusion finally took place, there was one more dramatist whose work demands consideration, although he made his name in another sphere. He is Miguel de Cervantes. Cervantes seems to have been in everything an improviser and experimenter, moving forward by trial and error; always optimistically ready to try something new, despite repeated disillusionment, yet slow to acquire the self-knowledge which would have led him more directly to his goal. It was only after he had mistakenly sought literary fame through poetry and drama that he discovered his true métier of novelist; and his approach to drama, with the challenging problems which it was then presenting, was one of experiment rather than conviction.

Of all the great writers of Spain's Golden Age Cervantes is perhaps the most personal. In his literary works, and more especially in the prologues to them, he reveals himself in a most attractive way. The Prologue to his eight *Comedias y entremeses* (1615) recalls the impression the performances of Lope de Rueda had made on him as a child. This was the beginning of a lifelong interest in actors and acting, displayed later in two of his short novels, *El licenciado Vidriera* and *El coloquio de los perros* (*The Glass Scholar* and *The Dogs' Colloquy*), and one of his plays, *Pedro de Urdemalas*, where he expresses his high regard for the *farsante* and his calling, and his recognition of the difficulties an actor has to face; and even suggests that there should be a practical examination for entry into the profession.

With this love of the theatre it was natural that he should make an attempt at play-writing when, on returning in 1580 from five years' captivity in Algiers, he decided to enter the world of letters. He states, again in the 1615 Prologue, that about that time he wrote some thirty plays, all of which were put on the stage "without receiving the tribute of cucumbers or other missiles". He seems to have regarded this absence of disapproval as evidence of success, but it was not enough to earn him a living in the theatre. Later in life he tried again with a further eight plays, but this time "found no birds in the nests of yester-year"—no company would perform them. Reluctant to admit complete failure he publishes them, together with eight *entremeses*, but at the same time recognizes sadly that he has by now been eclipsed by the great Lope de Vega.

Cervantes begins as a supporter of the classical theatre. The two plays which survive from the earlier batch both portray heroic action with grandeur and pathos. *El trato de Argel* (*The Traffic of Algiers*) draws on its author's first-hand experience for a picture of the life of Spanish captives in Algiers. *La Numancia*, which dramatizes the noble but vain resistance of the Spanish township of Numantia when besieged by Scipio Africanus, is almost a pure classical tragedy. It has a story taken from antiquity, observance of the Unities, and a chorus provided by personifications of Spain and the river Duero. As often in classical drama the outcome is known in advance, and so no use can be made of dramatic suspense; the essence of the play resides not in the unfolding action itself, but in the depiction and contemplation of that action. But Cervantes has not the power of a Sophocles or a Racine to sustain emotional tension, and sinks back too often into rhetoric and sententiousness. Much of his play seems wordy and over-explicit. Even his very lines are often too long for what he has to say, and he packs his weary hendecasyllables with ugly repetitions. It is significantly in a scene of short lines and simple language, in which a starving child begs for bread, that the play first comes to life.

There are close parallels between the younger Cervantes and Juan de la Cueva. Both use national themes, both overcrowd their canvases with material which is epic rather than dramatic; Cervantes in particular, at this stage, fails to concentrate his action in a small representative group of characters, and tries to portray whole communities in a Brueghel-like manner unsuited to the stage. But both are also masters of the isolated dramatic situation, the poignant moment. Such are the sale and torture of Christian captives in *El trato de Argel*, and the suicide of the last surviving inhabitant of Numantia, a hitherto cowardly youth who throws himself from a high tower exclaiming:

> Yo heredé de Numancia todo el brío.
> ("I have inherited all the spirit of Numantia.")

The heroic strain in Spanish drama here briefly sounds some of its finest notes.

Among the later plays, where classical canons have been modified in accordance with the now prevailing practice, that most deserving of mention is probably *Pedro de Urdemalas*. Again construction is defective: we follow the career of the *pícaro* Pedro through a number of phases and occupations until he finally achieves success and fulfilment as an actor. The plot, in so far as there is one, is therefore episodic and unilinear. But the play is memorable both for its exaltation of the theatre, and for its natural dialogue and painting of customs in the various backgrounds against which Pedro is set: the primitive local government, for instance, and the village girls using traditional devices on Midsummer Eve to find out whom they are to marry. In forsaking the classical for the popular Cervantes has not found the way to great drama, but he has discovered a mode more suited to his own talents.

The eight *entremeses* in the collection are comparable: lively, humorous sketches from everyday life, with a strong hint of social satire, and usually a more interesting plot than the *pasos* of Lope de Rueda of which they are the direct descendants. All Cervantes' longer works, whether plays or novels, tend to be fragmentary and episodic, and it is in the single scene that he excels. His *entremeses* are probably the culminating point of the mime tradition in Spain.

So we see Cervantes achieving felicitous moments in both the heroic and the popular spheres, but failing to create a uniformly successful type of drama. That task, as he came to realize in his old age, had already been accomplished by another man.

Texts

CERVANTES, M. DE, *Comedias y entremeses*, 6 vols. in *Obras completas de Cervantes*, ed. R. Schevill and A. Bonilla (Madrid, 1915–20).

Entremeses, ed. M. Herrero García (Madrid, Clásicos castellanos, 1952).

CUEVA, JUAN DE LA, *El infamador, Los siete Infantes de Lara, Ejemplar poético*, ed. F. A. de Icaza (Madrid, Clásicos castellanos, 1941).

ENCINA, JUAN DEL, *eglogas*, ed. Humberto López Morales (Madrid, 1963).

RUEDA, LOPE DE, *Obras*, ed. E. Cotarelo, 2 vols. (Madrid, 1908).

Teatro, ed. J. Moreno Villa (Madrid, Clásicos castellanos, 1934).

Pasos completos, ed. F. García Pavón (Madrid, 1966).

RUEDA, LOPE DE, *Pasos*, and CERVANTES, *Entremeses*, ed. J. M. Blecua (Zaragoza 1945).

Teatro medieval, ed. F. Lázaro Carreter (Valencia, 1958).

Torres Naharro, B. de, *"Propalladia" and Other Works*, ed. J. E. Gillet, 4 vols. (Bryn Mawr, 1943–61).

Vicente, Gil, *Obras dramáticas castellanas*, ed. Thomas R. Hart (Madrid, Clásicos castellanos, 1962).

General Works

Bonilla y San Martín, A., *Las Bacantes, o del origen del teatro* (Madrid, 1921).

Casalduero, J., *Sentido y forma del teatro de Cervantes* (Madrid, 1951, reprinted 1966).

Donovan, R. B., *Liturgical Drama in Medieval Spain* (Toronto, 1958).

Keates, Laurence, *The Court Theatre of Gil Vicente* (Lisbon, 1962).

Shergold, N. D., *A History of the Spanish Stage* (Oxford, 1967).

Wardropper, Bruce W., *Introducción al teatro religioso del Siglo de Oro* (Madrid, 1953).

Wickersham Crawford, J. P., *Spanish Drama before Lope de Vega* (Philadelphia, 1937).

2

THE CONTROVERSY

THE hesitation shown by Cervantes typifies the general uncertainty around the turn of the century as to which direction the Spanish theatre would take. The struggle was between not merely two types, but two distinct concepts of drama. This had usually been understood in sixteenth-century Spain simply as the enactment of a story for the purpose of entertainment; but some attention was claimed by those classicists who saw it as the imitation, or representation, of a known action, submitted to the artistic discipline of a strict form, for the sake of a proper direction of the intellect and emotions. A long battle had still to be fought between the upholders of these two views.

The strength of feeling with which this battle was conducted arose partly from the fact that moral as well as æsthetic considerations were involved. The theatre has often been regarded as the home of vice. The strictures of Tertullian in his *De spectaculis*, of St. Cyprian, St. Augustine and others of the Fathers are well known, and attention was called to them by the moralists and theologians of Spain as soon as the theatre there began to be an important social institution. With the advent of Lope de Vega in the 1580's the attacks became more vehement. The censure accorded well with the austere attitude of Philip II, who on the death of his daughter in 1597 ordered the theatres to be closed during the period of national mourning. The stricter ecclesiastics at once took advantage of this suspension, and began to campaign against any eventual reopening. In the ensuing controversy the King invited the opinions of a number of people, and the memoranda then submitted to him contain some of the strongest attacks which the theatre had to face.

The criticisms of ancient writers are frequently reiterated. It is argued that playgoing has a softening effect on the populace, predisposing it to the pursuit of pleasure; that plays are "the corruption of the republic and the food of sin and vice" (García de Loaisa y Girón, 1598). Lupercio Leonardo de Argensola, author of the neo-classical *Isabela* and *Alejandra*, relates the argument more closely to prevailing conditions. He inveighs against the wickedness of actors who drink, swear and blaspheme in their dressing-rooms, even while garbed as characters in sacred plays, and who can commit murder with impunity, since their popularity with the public will always protect them from justice. He has even more to say about the immorality of actresses, whose husbands are usually *complaisants*, and who lead good men into unspeakable depravity. Their participation in religious drama was a disgrace: the part of the Virgin Mary was habitually played by women in no sense suitable to the role, with the result that any atmosphere of devotion was completely shattered. "So much so that when a certain play was being performed in this city on the life of Our Lady, the actor who took the part of St. Joseph was the lover of the woman playing Our Lady, and the affair was so public that the audience became quite uproarious on hearing the words that the most pure Virgin replied to the Angel: 'How shall this be, etc.?' "

Eleven years later the historian Mariana wrote a whole book attacking the theatre (although admitting he had never been to one in his life). Not only, he argued, were the lives of actors and actresses notoriously unchaste: the very opportunity which the stage provided for feminine display was highly insidious, particularly when the display went to the lengths of actresses appearing in doublet and hose, as many plots required them to do. Indeed, the baser feelings of the populace were deliberately exploited in this way for gain, and modesty was habitually

sacrificed to box-office appeal (*Tratado contra los juegos públicos,
Treatise against Public Entertainments*, 1609).[1]

Such criticisms of the theatre were not, of course, confined
to Spain. They were voiced also in France, and even more per-
sistently in England, where the opposition was on a broader
front, coming less from ecclesiastics and men of letters than from
the large Puritan citizen class. Here even the school drama of
Oxford and Cambridge, privately performed, came under
attack; and though in the public theatres women did not perform
—the appearance at court of some French actresses, invited over
in 1629 by Queen Henrietta Maria, provoked a public outcry—
nevertheless the wearing of women's clothes by the boys who
played female parts was felt to be just as grave a moral danger
as the opposite practice appeared to Mariana in Spain.[2]

There is no doubt that conditions in that country were very
much as critics of the theatre described them. Independent
literary works of the time, with no axe to grind, often give us
glimpses of the free-and-easy ways of travelling players.[3] Lope
de Vega himself, the irregularities of whose private life included
affairs with more than one actress, offered powerful ammunition
to the puritans.

Denunciations of the theatre in the name of respectability
continued well on into the seventeenth century; but there were
also strong forces on the opposing side. The arrangement whereby
the theatres provided a large source of income for the hospitals
was a weighty economic argument for their retention. The
hospitals themselves pleaded vigorously for the renewal of
theatrical performances after the death of Philip II in 1598,
and their plea was supported by the municipality of Madrid,
on whose funds they would otherwise have become a charge.
In fact, the voices of these two bodies, reinforcing the demands of

[1] For all these documents see E. Cotarelo, *Bibliografía de las controversias
sobre la licitud del teatro en España* (Madrid, 1904).

[2] See E. N. S. Thompson, *The Controversy between the Puritans and the Stage*
(New York, 1903).

[3] See Agustín de Rojas, *Viaje entretenido*, Libro primero; and Quevedo,
Vida del Buscón, Libro segundo, cap. IX.

a public by now wedded to the theatre, soon prevailed against the moralists, and from the year 1600 plays were again being performed. Further suspensions occurred during later periods of national mourning, the longest being from 1646 to 1649, but there was never any extended closure as in England under the Commonwealth.

Moreover, in Spain as elsewhere, there was a large body of humanists who remembered that, whatever the early Christian Fathers may have said, there was support for the stage in the works of other writers, yet more ancient and almost equally venerable. Taking as their masters Aristotle, Cicero and Horace, they saw drama as something essentially good, and only temporarily debased. What Aristotle had described in the *Poetics* had been a highly stylized artistic genre. If modern drama could be made to conform to his precepts, and be converted from a popular entertainment to a cultured and uplifting art form, its pernicious influence would be eliminated, and the reputation of Spanish letters enhanced. What was required was not suppression of the theatre, but its dedication to a different type of play.

Thus it was that æsthetic reform came to be seen as the corollary to moral reform. Indeed, the two were largely identified. The supporters of a classical theatre were by no means all familiar with Aristotle at first hand, and still less with Greek tragedy itself. They relied rather on the work of sixteenth-century commentators, such as the Italian Robortello, and later the Spaniard Alonso López, "el Pinciano", whose *Philosophia antigua poetica* appeared in 1596. Through this work, which was a thoughtful and critical exposition of Aristotle, the famous precepts came to be widely known: the theory of drama as imitation, the distinction between tragedy and comedy, the five-act structure, the Unities of Time, Place and Action. Even El Pinciano, however, seems slightly to have misunderstood his master, and to have confused Aristotle's teaching on catharsis with the Horatian principle that art should delight and edify at the same time. It seems doubtful whether he or any of his contemporaries, familiar as they were with the moral tragedies of Seneca but not with Greek classical drama, were able to distinguish clearly between Aristotle and Horace in this respect, or to grasp that the *Poetics* had an æsthetic rather than an ethical basis.

It was therefore a drama constructed along Aristotelian lines, but with a moral preoccupation deriving rather from Horace and Seneca, that the theorists who took El Pinciano as their mentor wished to see established in Spain; while against the theorists were ranged the practitioners of the theatre, headed by Lope himself, who had by now evolved the highly successful, if un-Aristotelian, dramatic genre known as the *comedia*. Between these two bands there developed a fierce Battle of Ancients and Moderns, which affected a great deal of the literary activity in Spain in the early seventeenth century.

In view of Cervantes' hesitation over the developing drama it is not surprising to find him involved in the debate. He is obviously familiar with El Pinciano. When in *Don Quixote*, Part I, Chapter 47, he voices his criticisms of the romances of chivalry through the mouth of the Canon of Toledo, it is partly on the grounds that they aim solely at pleasure and not at instruction, and that they shun verisimilitude. In the following chapter the same principles are applied to drama. The new *comedia* is criticized because in its infringement of the Unities it sins against imitation; and because, aiming simply at pleasing the largest possible audience, it abrogates any didactic value. Argensola's recent neo-classical tragedies are praised, and Lope is roundly condemned for the prostitution of his talent.

Don Quixote, Part I, was published in 1605. Ten years later, as is apparent in the Prologue to the *Eight Comedias*, Cervantes is beginning to realize that he has been on the losing side. In one of these plays, *El rufián dichoso* (*The Blessed Ruffian*), he openly admits as much. The first act of this work takes place in Seville, the second and third in Mexico; and this change of scene is the subject of a conversation between two personified figures, Comedia and Curiosidad. The latter objects that drama in the past had customarily observed the Unity of Place. Comedia replies, of the precepts in general:

> He dejado parte dellos,
> y he también guardado parte,
> porque así lo quiere el uso,
> que no se sujeta al arte.

("I have abandoned some of them, and I have retained others, for this is required by modern usage, which does not conform to the rules.")

The contrast pointed between "uso", the prevailing practice, and "arte", the Aristotelian precepts, reflects very neatly the struggle then being fought. Again Cervantes is forced into a rather unhappy compromise, and fails to achieve any real dramatic success.

What does Lope himself have to say? At first very little: he is far less concerned with dramatic theory than with attracting an audience and earning a living. In 1604 he makes the simple statement: "Let foreigners note that Spanish plays do not conform to the rules (*'arte'*), and that I went on writing them as I found them, without daring to observe the precepts, because with that strictness they would never be accepted by Spaniards" (Prologue to *El peregrino en su patria, The Pilgrim in his own Country*). In other words, there is for him no problem: he was not the first to disregard "arte", but he has no compunction in doing so, since that is what his countrymen want.

Five years later he is drawn out a little further by a request for a treatise on his own methods of play-writing, and produces his well-known *Arte nuevo de hacer comedias en este tiempo (New Art of Writing Plays in Modern Times)*.[4] This is a light-hearted piece in verse. It begins with references to Aristotle, to Plautus and Terence and their "arte", which he contrasts with his own lack of it. "It is true", he says, "that I have sometimes written in accordance with 'arte'; but when I see the monstrosities that ordinary folk and women will flock to, I go back to my barbarous ways, and when I write a play I lock up the precepts

---

[4] In *Obras sueltas de Lope de Vega, BAE*, Vol. 38, pp. 230–2, and also in H. J. Chaytor, *Dramatic Theory in Spain* (Cambridge, 1925), pp. 14–29.

with six keys, and banish Terence and Plautus from my study so that they won't cry out at me; and I write in accordance with the art of those who seek popular applause; for as it is the public who pay, it's only fair to write the kind of nonsense that they like."

There is certainly an ironical dig here at the *preceptistas* and the neo-classical plays, like those of Cervantes, which had *not* won popular applause, but it is a genial irony, which does not entirely travesty Lope's own attitude. He respected learning, as can be seen from much of his non-dramatic writing, but it was not relevant to his purpose in the theatre. He was writing a different kind of play. "If you wish for 'arte' ", he goes on, "there is Robortello there for you to read. If, on the other hand, you want the opinion of those who now fill the theatres, then I will give you mine." This he proceeds to do.

Lope's two cardinal principles are to give pleasure, and to be true to life; all his detailed injunctions are elaborations of one or other of these.

(1) Comedy may be mingled with tragedy, "for such variety gives great delight".

(2) Unity of Action must be observed, but the other two Unities yield to verisimilitude and to popular taste: "It seems to me that if the aim is to give pleasure, the method that will achieve this is the best one."

(3) A play should have three acts and be well constructed, with the dénouement kept for the last scene so as to maintain interest.

(4) Language should always be suited both to the subject-matter and to the status of the speaker, so that usually a simple and natural style will be most appropriate.

(5) On the appearance of actresses, "let ladies not belie their name, and if they appear in men's costume, let it be with due decorum, for male disguise usually gives great pleasure"—an attempt at a sop to the moralists, made meaningless by reversion to the main criterion of what will please.

(6) Different verse-forms should be used for different topics;

décimas are suitable for plaints, *sonnets* for characters left alone
on the stage, *romance* for narration, *tercets* for "grave matters",
and *redondillas* for love scenes.

(7) Affairs of honour make good subjects, since everyone
finds them moving. Over and over again the reaction of the
audience is offered as the main criterion.

The work ends with an apology in the same jocular tone as
the beginning:

> I am the most barbarous of all, since I dare to put forward precepts
> which go against "art", and I let myself be swept away by the popular
> current to the point where France and Italy call me ignorant. But what
> can I do, since I have, including one finished this week, 483 plays written,
> all but six of them sinning gravely against "art"? Anyhow, I stand by what
> I have written, well aware that in a different style they might have been
> better, but would not have pleased nearly so much; for sometimes what
> is contrary to the rules for that very reason gives the greatest pleasure.

It has been suggested that the *Arte nuevo* was in part an answer
to Cervantes' strictures in *Don Quixote*, and this may well be the
case. It was, of course, not a blueprint, a set of rules drawn up
beforehand for the cultivation of a genre, but an abstraction
from a genre already in existence. But in the self-confidence
of the final sentence, and in the claim, implicit in the title, to a
new "art" as reputable and valid as that of the ancients, Lope
is seen to be gradually moving forward to take up a more positive
attitude as leader of his band.

The fiercest controversy came during the next decade. The
Apologética de las comedias españolas (1616) of Ricardo de Turia
followed Lope in appealing to public taste, and also argued that
the precepts were inapplicable to the modern situation, since
they dealt with tragedy and comedy, and not with the tragicomedy now being written.

On the opposite side, the extreme conservative view was
expressed by Francisco Cascales in his *Tablas poéticas* (published
in 1617, but written some time earlier). The ancients must
perforce be followed, since "truth is one, and what has once been
true must always be so, and the passage of time cannot change

it". Moreover, art must follow nature as closely as possible, and nature always adheres to the same pattern; so that those hermaphrodite plays which fail to observe the classical distinction between tragedy and comedy should be shunned as freaks of nature are. Cascales does, it is true, tentatively propose some extension of the Unity of Time, and suggests ten days as suitable duration for the action of a play; but then goes on to add, with disarming modesty: "If anyone disapproves of this suggestion, let him hold fast to the rules; for it is better to be wrong with Aristotle than to be right with me."

In the same year as Cascales' urbane defence of the precepts, there appeared two other works tending in the same direction, but written in a very different tone. *El pasajero* (*The Traveller*) of Cristóbal Suárez de Figueroa (1617) is a miscellany in which he uses the conversation of four companions on a journey as a vehicle for the exposition of his own ideas on a variety of subjects. The section dealing with the *comedia* is less of a reasoned argument on æsthetic gounds than a personal attack upon Lope, who is criticized not only for the disorderliness and impropriety of many of his plays, but also for writing for a living, and for the immorality of his private life. It was probably also Suárez de Figueroa who persuaded another man, Pedro de Torres Rámila, to publish an even more outspoken attack. Torres Rámila was a young priest who held a minor teaching post at the University of Alcalá de Henares. His book, written in Latin, had the curious title of *Spongia*, the "sponge" which was to rub out and obliterate the writings of Lope de Vega.[5]

We have no means of knowing exactly what the *Spongia* said. It was apparently so scurrilous that Lope and his supporters at once destroyed all the copies they could find, and we can only deduce its contents from the replies it provoked. It seems to have been a wholesale and indiscriminate condemnation of Lope's works for their failure to adhere to classical forms and

[5] See J. de Entrambasaguas, "Una guerra literaria del Siglo de Oro. Lope de Vega y los preceptistas aristotélicos", in *Estudios sobre Lope de Vega*, Vols. I and II (Madrid 1946, 1947); originally published in *BRAE* 19–21 (1932–4).

precepts, but with the writings in the more cultured genres receiving even more attention than the *comedias*. This in particular must have incensed Lope, for, as he had hinted in the *Arte nuevo* and was to reiterate later, he had a high respect for learning and "art", and observed them wherever he thought appropriate. His pastoral novel *La Arcadia* and his epic poem *Jerusalén conquistada*, owing their inspiration as they did to Sannazaro, Tasso and the Italian Renaissance, both followed long-accepted literary traditions which were entirely learned and respectable, deriving ultimately from the classics, and it must have been galling to have them ridiculed as inartistic.

The first rejoinder came at once from Lope himself, in the form of two long and libellous satires in verse, which remained unpublished until 1932. They were followed in 1618 by a more formal reply, a compendium in Latin entitled *Expostulatio Spongiæ*. To this a number of Lope's supporters contributed, but the greater part is by his close friend Francisco López de Aguilar, who tries to refute in turn each of Torres Rámila's accusations, and thus gives us some idea of what the latter had said.

This phase of the dispute had consisted chiefly of personal vilification on both sides, with little concern for objective æsthetic criteria. But one contributor to the *Expostulatio Spongiæ* brought the controversy back to a higher level. He was Alfonso Sánchez de Moratalla, Professor of Greek and Hebrew at Alcalá; but his classical learning did not obscure for him the merits of Lope's theatre. His defence of it is an elaboration of the claim tentatively made by Lope himself in the *Arte nuevo*:

> It is only modesty which prevents Lope arrogating to himself the title of creator of a new art, although he is in a position to formulate precepts with the same authority as Horace. But I do not hesitate to grant him what nature has already accorded him. He excuses himself as having adhered to the manner of play-writing which he found accepted in his own country, disregarding the example of the classics. But what concern have you, great Lope, with classical drama, since you yourself have given to our age better comedies than all those of Menander and Aristophanes? You have done many things *outside* the laws of the ancient poets, but not *against* those laws. Antiquity deserves respect as the originator, and because

distance begets veneration. But let the ancients keep their own glory; yours will be proclaimed immortal by present and future ages alike.[6]

The rest of the essay is a paean of praise to the master.

Only one of the dramatists of the period, other than Lope himself, took any notable part in the controversy. This was Tirso de Molina, Lope's follower and disciple, who expresses views very similar to those of Alfonso Sánchez. In 1621 he wrote an interesting miscellany, somewhat like Suárez de Figueroa's *Pasajero*, but set within a more Boccaccian frame: a group of Toledan ladies and gentlemen leave the city during the hot weather and retire to their near-by estates—the "Cigarrales de Toledo" which give the work its title—where they take it in turn to entertain the company with stories, plays and other courtly diversions. The performance of one of the plays, Tirso's own *Vergonzoso en palacio* (*The Shy Man at Court*), provokes a general discussion on drama, and Tirso puts into the mouth of one of his speakers a long discourse which may almost rank as the manifesto of the Lopean school. He begins by defending his own disregard of the Unity of Time, on the grounds that twenty-four hours is not long enough for the action of a play to be presented with any verisimilitude; particularly when it concerns a love-affair. Imitation of life is always to be the yardstick. (Here at least the moderns coincide with Aristotle; but they derive different deductions from the same premise.) Then apparently answering the arguments of Francisco Cascales that what was once true must always be true, Tirso agrees that the ancients deserve respect for their pioneer work, but distinguishes between the "substance" of their achievement, which cannot change, and the "accidents", which can be improved upon in the light of experience. Nature, it is true, always follows the same pattern, so that the pear-tree can only produce pears, and the oak acorns; but art is not tied to this uniformity. "Why should not drama vary the laws of its antecedents, and subtly

[6] Originally in Latin, but here translated from the Spanish of Menéndez y Pelayo, *Historia de las ideas estéticas en España*, Vol. III (ed. of Madrid, 1920), p. 449.

interweave the tragic and the comic, creating a harmonious blend of these two contrasted genres which, partaking of both, will introduce now serious characters like the one, now humorous and laughable figures like the other?"

Lastly he echoes, in very similar terms, Alfonso Sánchez's eulogy of Lope as creator of a new art:

> Lope, having established the *comedia* in its present subtlety and perfection, is great enough to lead a school of his own; and those of us who claim to be his disciples should think ourselves fortunate to have such a master, and should constantly defend his teaching against those who heatedly impugn it. For if he declares in many of his writings that he ignores the art of the ancients just to satisfy the taste of the common people, who have never accepted the restriction of laws and precepts, he says it out of natural modesty, and so that ignorant malice shall not attribute to arrogance what is in fact consummate skill. But for our part it is right that we should esteem both him as reformer of the new *comedia*, and it as a fairer and more pleasure-giving creation, fondly entreating time not to efface their memory.

This panegyric is echoed more briefly in one or two of Tirso's plays from this same period; and Lope himself, his confidence strengthened by the support of his friends, now transcends his earlier spitefulness and answers Torres Rámila more effectively by means of a clever burlesque. Into his long poem *La filomena* he inserts a debate between the starling and the nightingale as to who can sing more sweetly. The starling, representing Torres Rámila, challenges the nightingale with a show of classical learning. The latter replies with a long account of Lope's career, and an exposition of the artistry and literary respectability of each of those works that the *Spongia* had attacked; then, with a reference to the fact that 900 of Lope's plays had already been performed in Spain and no small number in America, asks the jury for their verdict. It is given unhesitatingly in the nightingale's favour, and the starling is condemned to perpetual silence. So sure is Lope now of the support of public opinion. Whatever the views of the scholars, in the actual theatres the "new art" has unquestionably prevailed.

His achievement must not be minimized, nor the opposition to him necessarily seen as snobbish or ultra-conservative.

Three centuries of acceptance can easily dull our minds to the startling nature of Lope's victory. He lived in an age which took it for granted that there were rules for the writing of literature; and the audacity of a man who broke the precepts of legitimate drama and admitted, even proclaimed, that his only guiding principle was the vulgar taste of the common people, must have seemed shocking indeed. There is an analogy with the controversies over moral and æsthetic standards which have recently surrounded television in Britain. Lope's glory is that, while unashamedly providing popular entertainment for the masses, he had the genius to create out of it a new æsthetic, and masterly works of art.

Yet changing circumstances were to carry the drama on to a further stage of development. Declining moral standards in the 1620's caused concern; the theatre was again blamed; and as the Aristotelians were silenced, the moralists became more vocal. Liñán y Verdugo thought that too many plays were being written, and that they should be performed only on holidays; Ágreda y Vargas and others deplored the connection of churchmen with the theatre. Francisco de la Barreda, in an *Invective against the plays prohibited by Trajan and apology for our own* (1622), feels obliged to defend the moral, as well as the æsthetic, superiority of the modern theatre. In 1622 the authorities were driven to legislate for social reform, among other things by sumptuary decrees against extravagance in fashion; and they could hardly fail to take cognizance of the theatre too.

There certainly had been cause for complaint, not only in theatrical conditions but also in much of the dramatic fare provided, more particularly by his followers than by Lope himself. Tirso de Molina was censured for the bad examples set by his characters; and few readers in any age could fail to find distasteful such plays as Guillén de Castro's *Los mal casados de Valencia* (*Unhappy Marriages in Valencia*), in which four out of the five main characters are adulterous in fact or intent, and one woman behaves with such depravity that even a man who is himself keeping a mistress in his own home alongside his wife feels moved to rebuke her. Some raising of standards seemed necessary if the theatre was to survive.

The change was chiefly effected by Lope's great successor, Calderón. In his theatre the concern for decorum is such that even the touching of hands is thought compromising. Much more than this, he made it possible for both theorists and moralists finally to come to terms with the *comedia*. In form it remains Spanish and un-Aristotelian; his plays are all cast in the mould perfected by Lope. But in content and manner they show a subtle classicizing which enabled a theorist of the 1630's, González de Salas, at last to approach the modern theatre uncontroversially, praising it as a blend of what was best in old and new.[7] And at the same time Calderón converts the genre itself into an instrument of morality, choosing the actions of his more serious plays less as stories to entertain than as examples to warn or persuade.

The compromise achieved by Calderón is almost as great a phenomenon as Lope's original creation of the *comedia*. It was, of course, the policy of the Counter-Reformation to use the arts as vehicles for moral and religious propaganda; but it is still remarkable to see the once-despised *comedia* being accepted and ennobled in this way. A mere thirty years have brought a complete reversal, from the appeals to Philip II to close the theatres in the name of decency, to a drama almost wholly dedicated to the service of the Church and the promotion of Christian values.

General Works

CHAYTOR, H. J., *Dramatic Theory in Spain. Extracts from Literature before and during the Golden Age* (Cambridge, 1925).

COTARELO, E., *Bibliografía de las controversias sobre la licitud del teatro en España* (Madrid, 1904).

ENTRAMBASAGUAS, J. DE, "Una guerra literaria del Siglo de Oro. Lope de Vega y los preceptistas aristotélicos", in *Estudios sobre Lope de Vega*, Vols. I and II (Madrid, 1946 and 1947).

MENÉNDEZ Y PELAYO, M., *Historia de las ideas estéticas en España* (1st complete edition Madrid, 1890–1912), cap. X.

[7] See E. C. Riley, "The dramatic theories of D. Jusepe Antonio González de Salas", *HR* 19 (1951) 183–203.

MOIR, DUNCAN, "The classical tradition in Spanish dramatic theory and practice in the seventeenth century", in *Classical Drama and its Influence. Essays presented to H. D. F. Kitto* (London, 1965).

NEWELS, MARGARETE, *Die dramatischen Gattungen des Siglo de Oro* (Wiesbaden, 1959).

PÉREZ, LUIS C. and SÁNCHEZ ESCRIBANO, F., *Afirmaciones de Lope de Vega sobre preceptiva dramática* (Madrid, 1961).

SHEPARD, SANFORD, *El Pinciano y las teorías literarias del Siglo de Oro* (Madrid, 1962).

3

THE *COMEDIA*

"Nature's monster" is the name Cervantes gives to Lope de
Vega; and quite apart from the vastness of Lope's output,
there is something almost fabulous in the process by which he
instinctively gathered together all that was promising and good
in earlier drama, and by a miracle of synthesis and artistic
creation fashioned out of it the Spanish *comedia*. He followed
on a long period of experiment; yet when one compares his
work with that of Juan de la Cueva and remembers how close
they were in time, his achievement seems startlingly sudden.
Lope, born two years before Shakespeare, is in his different way
just as unexpected and unaccountable a genius.

Although each later dramatist introduced his own emphases
and modifications, the *comedia* created by Lope remained the
mould in which all subsequent plays of the period were cast.
The analysis of it which follows will attempt to take the whole
period into account, but will be based primarily on the theatre
of Lope de Vega himself.

Firstly the name: *comedia* is the Spanish for "play", without
any distinction between comedy and tragedy; so that all plays
are *comedias*. But "the *comedia*", as a genre, covers specifically the
type of play written by Lope and his followers between about
1580 and 1680, and constituting probably the largest distinctive
corpus of national drama in existence.

The *comedia* is always in three acts, and in verse; but the verse
bears no resemblance either to the Alexandrine of French drama
or to the Shakespearean iambic pentameter. For one thing
the rhythms vary; there will usually be about eight or nine

changes of metre in one act. For another, they are not metres which would seem to be particularly suitable for drama; they are, in fact, those of lyric poetry.[1] Among them we find the heptasyllable and hendecasyllable adopted from Italy at the Renaissance, but passages in these rhythms are rather infrequent, and are usually reserved for royal or noble speakers. The backbone of the *comedia* is the eight-syllable line indigenous to Spain. *Romance*, or ballad metre (a series of octosyllables with the same assonance in alternate lines throughout), is one of those most commonly found. Here is an example from Lope:

> ¿ Qué Faetonte se atrevió
> del sol al dorado carro,
> o aquél que juntó con cera
> débiles plumas infausto,
> que sembradas por los vientos,
> pájaros que van volando
> las creyó el mar, hasta verlas
> en sus cristales salados?
> ¿ Qué Belerofonte vio
> en el caballo Pegaso
> parecer el mundo un punto
> del círculo de los astros?
> ¿ Qué griego Sinón metió
> aquel caballo preñado
> de armados hombres en Troya,
> fatal de su incendio parto?
> ¿ Qué Jasón tentó primero
> pasar el mar temerario,
> poniendo yugo a su cuello
> los pinos y lienzos de Argos,
> que se iguale a mi locura?

(El castigo sin venganza, Act II)

("What Phaeton aspiring to the gilded chariot of the sun; what ill-fated youth joining feeble feathers with wax, only to have them scattered by the winds, so that the sea took them for birds on the wing, until they fell into its shimmering salt expanse; what Bellerophon mounted on Pegasus, seeing the world as a tiny point in the sphere of the stars; what Greek Sinon, bringing into Troy that horse pregnant with armed men, and delivered of its fatal burden in the flames; what Jason first venturing boldly to cross the sea, setting the timbers and canvas of Argos like a yoke around its neck; which of these is there whose mad daring can match mine?")

---

[1] See S. G. Morley, "The curious phenomenon of Spanish verse drama", *BH* 50 (1948) 445–62.

To understand the effect created by the use of this simple and traditional metre, we must try to imagine the plays of Shakespeare written in the rhythm of the Border Ballads or "Gather ye rose-buds while ye may". The other metre most frequently found, also an octosyllabic one, is the *redondilla* (four lines, rhyming a b b a):

> Aunque fuerza de obediencia
> te hiciese tomar estado,
> no he de estar desengañado
> hasta escuchar la sentencia.
> Bien el alma me decía
> (y a Tello lo contaba
> cuando el caballo sacaba,
> y el sol los que aguarda el día),
> que de alguna novedad
> procedía mi tristeza,
> viniendo a ver tu belleza;
> pues me dices que es verdad.
>
> (*El Caballero de Olmedo*, Act II)

("Even if force of obedience should make you marry, I will not give up hope until I hear my sentence. Well did I know in my heart (and so I told Tello while he was getting the horse out, and while the sun made ready those which bring in the day), that there must be some new happening to account for my feeling sad when I was coming to see you; now you tell me this is so.")

The preponderance of short lines helps, of course, to increase the pace of the play, and is perhaps not unfitting in what is primarily a theatre of action and movement. But it may possibly be argued that it also has the effect of inhibiting reflection and soliloquy.

There is no strict separation of comedy and tragedy. Probably the majority of plays are pure comedy, but all the remainder have some comic relief, and very few are real tragedies. The term "tragicomedy" has been applied to some, even by Lope himself, and is not inappropriate. There are a number of historical and religious dramas.

Very little classical material is used, at least before the time of Calderón. The most frequent sources of plot are Spanish history, legend and literature, and other modern literatures, particularly the Italian *novelle*. In other words, the range of substance used is analogous to that of Shakespeare, but with the addition of much religious material.

The three great motifs of Golden Age drama are undoubtedly religion, love and honour. Religion as a dramatic motif takes various forms which will later be examined in more detail; but love admits of easier generalization. There springs to mind only one play with virtually no love interest at all—Tirso de Molina's *La prudencia en la mujer* (*Prudence in Woman*)—and the great majority are based primarily upon it. Perhaps sex would be a better word, for it is a love which seldom looks beyond physical fulfilment. The *comedia* does not conceive of love platonically. The attraction between the sexes is mainly a physical one, very rarely one of personality. Characters normally fall in love at first sight; and thereafter their desire is their chief spur to action. Unlike some Italian plays such as Machiavelli's *Mandragola*, the *comedia* never adopts an amoral attitude to love, or treats adultery as a joke. Love is moral and respectable, and fulfilment in marriage is the rule. But because the lovers are striving so hard for that marriage that they have not time to savour and enjoy each other's company on the way, it seems to remain earthbound. With a few exceptions to be noted later, there is little idealism about it, little sense of its power to uplift or ennoble. A Spanish heroine would not be likely to exclaim, with Shakespeare's Julia:

> Oh, know'st thou not his looks are my soul's food?
> (*Two Gentlemen of Verona*, II. 7)

and when Lope tells the story of Romeo and Juliet, in his play *Castelvines y Monteses*, he gives it little of the idyllic quality which in Shakespeare constitutes all the magic. In Lope's equivalent of the balcony scene the lovers, when first alone together, scarcely bother to express their feelings, which are taken for granted; but get down at once to the practical problem of how to marry in the face of the family feud.

Feminine beauty is usually described in extremely conventional metaphors—the lady's cheeks are roses, her eyes suns, she has lips of coral and pearls for teeth—but there is never any doubt that it *is* beauty in women, and the corresponding physical qualities in men, which inspire love. More marked even than the contrast with Shakespeare is that with French classical drama, in which personal appearance is never mentioned, and the characters seem to be thought of simply as personalities, with no bodies at all.

The almost inevitable concomitant of love, at any rate in the comedies, is jealousy. It is thought of as adding piquancy to love and allowing for the trial of constancy; and it fulfils a useful practical purpose in providing material for the plot. Jealousy between rivals, or the confusions arising between two or more pairs of lovers, are frequent sources of intrigue.

The third great motif in Golden Age drama is the one which was first used by Torres Naharro and which must now be examined in greater detail: the code of honour. This unwritten but fetish-like code regulated all social relationships: those between king and subject, between superior and inferior, between friend and friend, and between members of the same family. Its basis is the paramount importance of the right ordering of social relationships. The wholeness, or integrity, of society comes before personal integrity; in fact the latter can scarcely be thought of apart from the former. The criterion of behaviour is thus always a social one: not so much to be, as to be seen to be. Honour resides not in the ordering of one's own life, but in the esteem in which one is held by others.

Any action on the part of others which might be thought to impair that esteem dishonoured the individual. Such would be the effect of a blow, a verbal insult, or accusation of lying. However unjustified the affront, the recipient was dishonoured until he had expunged the insult in a duel. In addition to his own honour, the head of a family was responsible for that of his female dependants, which was forfeited by any suspicion of an illicit relationship with another man. Only two solutions were here available for the offended father, brother or husband: he must see that the guilty couple marry, or, if this is impossible—

if it is his wife who is involved, or if the man refuses marriage—
he must kill them. If the woman is guiltless and has been an
unwilling victim of rape, then her life may be spared, but she
will have to spend the rest of it in a convent, since no other man
can be expected to marry her.

The code of honour is intimately related with class structure.
The king, as the head of society, is the embodiment and fount
of honour. No vengeance can ever be taken on him, or upon
others in his presence, or even in his palace. Any courtier found
using violence in the palace might suffer dire penalties, including
banishment. Generally speaking honour is the prerogative of
noblemen, acquired by virtue of their birth:

> Honor
> tengo y las palabras cumplo,
> porque caballero soy;
> (Tirso de Molina, *El Burlador de Sevilla*, Act III)
> ("I have honour and I keep my word, because I am a gentleman;")

and the preservation of it affects only their dealings with their
equals. The squire in Lope's *Fuenteovejuna* asks incredulously of
his villeins: "Have *you* honour?", and when challenged to fight
by one of them refuses to defend himself, since that would be
to acknowledge equality with him and thus to demean his own
status. (The use of the phrase "to have honour" in the last two
examples, as though honour were a possession with an objective
existence, is significant; it was indeed thought of like this.)

But the peasant usually conceives of honour rather differently,
as a matter not of blue blood, but of the essential human dignity
of the individual; and on this basis he claims it for himself:

> CAPTAIN: ¿ Qué opinión tiene un villano?
> JUAN: Aquella misma que vos.
> (Calderón, *El alcalde de Zalamea*, Act I)
> ("What repute can a villein claim?" "The same as you.")

In so far as the *comedia* sustains this view, as it often does, it
is adopting a more human and universal scheme of values, and
departing from the rigid canons of *pundonor*.

Because of the social basis of the code, the fact that a man was known to have lost his honour was worse than the loss itself. The enormity of an affront actually increased in proportion with the number of people who knew about it; appearances were what mattered most. Hence the principle "a secreto agravio secreta venganza" ("secret dishonour demands secret vengeance"): when the insult was not public the revenge should also be kept secret, so as not to proclaim the original loss of honour.

It is easy to see the dramatic possibilities of such a rigorous and awe-inspiring code of behaviour, and particularly of those provisions which concerned women; these are understandably the aspects of *pundonor* which furnished most material for drama. Perhaps because of the insistence on those infringements of the code which carried the harshest penalty, it has seemed something unnatural which demanded an explanation, and there has been much speculation about its origins. Some have seen them as purely literary, in Italian drama (which, however, as we have seen, does not antedate Torres Naharro), or the novels of chivalry. Others, looking back into the actual life of the Middle Ages, have related them to the Arabic custom of keeping women closely guarded, or to the idealization of women presupposed in the conventions of courtly love. The problem is perhaps not as great as it appears. In many communities adultery has been considered a crime punishable by death. The Puritans made it a capital offence in England for a time. The woman taken in adultery was stoned by the Jews. Two medieval Spanish codes of laws, the *Fuero Juzgo* of the Visigoths and the later *Fuero real*, specifically gave a husband power to kill an unfaithful wife and her lover, so long as he killed both. This provision, along with many others of the *fueros*, was incorporated into the *Nueva recopilación de las leyes de España* (*New Compendium of the Laws of Spain*) compiled in 1567, and was thus part of the law of the land during the lifetime of the *comedia*. Even in modern times the Spanish Penal Code of 1870 only imposes deportation on the husband who kills his wife or her lover on surprising them in adultery and not the long period of imprisonment which is the normal penalty for homicide; while the following extract describes the situation existing in another Latin country in 1966:

> "Murder for honour" flourishes mainly in Italy's hot-blooded South where the family is still of paramount importance and a man's good name his most cherished possession. . . . Every month one or more of these crimes are reported in the national dailies. The most usual is the murder of the adulterous wife by the husband (the wife who kills her husband is rare); more unusual is the murder of the daughter by the father, or of the sister by the brother or brothers. Article 587 of the Italian Penal Code, which is now being widely discussed, quotes these three types as "homicides with honour as the motive", and it prescribes a penalty of from three to seven years' imprisonment, in sharp contrast to the normal 21 to 30 years (or life).
>
> (Francesca Campbell, "Homicide with Honour", *Guardian*, 30th June 1966.[2])

That many seventeenth-century husbands exercised their right to defend their honour by such extreme methods is evident from the records of the time. It has been argued that the known cases of wife murder were recorded precisely because they were unusual;[3] but attention has been drawn to the diary kept by a parish priest in Valencia from 1589 to 1629, which records the astonishing number of violent acts committed in the city. From this it appears that wife murder was quite frequent (though in the same period only two wives murdered their husbands, and they were both hanged for it). Comparable documents from other parts of Spain tell the same story.[4] It is not surprising that the *comedia*, maturing in such an atmosphere, should make dramatic capital out of a situation which was familiar in real

[2] See also Julian Pitt-Rivers, "Honour and Social Status", in *Honour and Shame. The Values of Mediterranean Society*, ed. J. G. Peristiany (London, 1965). Pitt-Rivers describes attitudes very similar to those of Golden Age drama still held in an Andalusian village today. He even argues that the device, common in the *comedia*, whereby a dishonoured girl adopts male disguise to go out and pursue her lover, may be not merely a stage convention but a parable: feminine dress is the sign of feminine modesty; a woman who has lost her modesty has lost her peculiar feminine quality, and become no different from a man; when her honour is restored she dresses as a woman again.

[3] See C. A. Jones, "*Honor* in Spanish Golden Age drama: its relation to real life and to morals", *BHS* 35 (1958) 199–210.

[4] See A. Mas, *La caricature de la femme, du mariage et de l'amour dans l'œuvre de Quevedo* (Paris, 1957), pp. 348–51.

life. The extension of the idea to premarital relationships involving family dishonour seems to need no profound explanation.

As for the code as a whole in its application to the nobility, the notion of a class of gentlefolk with its own privileges of access to the king and the bearing of arms, and its own status to be jealously defended, was of course a commonplace of European social thinking until very recent times. In nineteenth-century England,

> a man's reputation as a gentleman was looked on as his most valuable possession. Any action, or even association, incompatible with it was regarded as a stain which must be immediately expunged. This accounted for the extreme sensitivity with which public men reacted to any slight on their honour, vindicating it, if necessary, in some dawn encounter with pistols on suburban common or foreign beach. Pitt, Castlereagh, Canning, Wellington and Peel all risked their lives in this way while holding high office.
>
> (Arthur Bryant, *The Age of Elegance*, London, 1950, p. 290).

A comparable punctilio in the nobly-born heroes of Spanish drama is therefore not specially remarkable.

The concern of humbler people for their honour surely originates in the basic need of every individual for integration into society. Self-respect is born above all of acceptance and respect by others. Most communities, again, will permit a man to defend his reputation; Spanish moralists had recently ruled, taking Aquinas as their guide, that the same means were licit for guarding honour as for guarding life. As Américo Castro has pointed out, the only real problem presented by *pundonor* in the *comedia* is one of degree: why should this particular dramatic motif have been so frequently used?[5]

The answer is perhaps partly that we are dealing with a dramatic convention. Once its possibilities had been realized the code soon fossilized into a hard-and-fast pattern, which has justly been compared to the modern conventions of English drawing-room comedy or Western films.[6] But again there were ideas

---

[5] A. Castro, "Algunas observaciones acerca del concepto del honor en los siglos XVI y XVII", *RFE* 3 (1916), reprinted in *Semblanzas y estudios españoles* (Princeton, 1956), pp. 319–82.

[6] C. A. Jones, *loc. cit.*

current in Spain at the time which encouraged a rigid adherence to the code, against the advice of those few moralists who condemned it as barbarous. They concerned the view of society then being generally taught and held, a view which has been very well expounded by Castro. He draws attention to the remarkable degree of social cohesion which prevailed in seventeenth-century Spain. Among other factors, the presence of many former Jews and Moslems, superficially at least converted to Christianity but potentially a subversive force, made it essential for society to demand complete conformity from its members. For the individual to be out of step with the community on any matter of importance was a disgrace; only within the framework of the traditional principles on which society rested could he attain the full realization of his personality. Since his reputation in the eyes of others was the guarantee of his adhesion to those principles, it was not surprising that reputation became a matter of such grave importance, both in the life of the time and in the literature which reflected it.[7]

The *comedia*, and this is perhaps the outstanding thing about it, is social through and through. It is always written from the viewpoint of society. It supports the accepted social institutions: marriage and the family, the Church, the monarchy and the hierarchy of class structure. It has sometimes been called "romantic" because of its love of violence and sensation, its rejection of the Aristotelian precepts, and the contrast it offers to French classical drama; but nothing could be less "romantic" than its attitude to the rebel or individualist, for whom it shows not the slightest sympathy. Ultimately he always submits to the established principles, or is damned.

Lope de Vega's *Fuenteovejuna* tells how a whole village rises in revolt against its overlord because of his licentious treatment of their women; and some readers have hailed this as a drama of revolution. They are quite wrong. The villagers do not revolt against the social order; on the contrary, they act in support of

[7] A. Castro, "El drama de la honra en España y en su literatura", *Cuadernos* 38 (3–15) and 39 (16–28) (1959).

it. As long as the nobleman behaves well they gladly accept his tutelage, and offer him homage and affection. Only when he himself disrupts the pattern of society by trying to appropriate other men's wives and daughters, and ceasing to fulfil the obligations of his status, do they defend themselves and finally revolt. And their act is never completely vindicated. At the end the King, who has ordered an investigation, still refers to it as a crime; but he does pardon it. Thus it is the head of the body politic, the very incarnation of social order, who has the last word in the matter.

This play illustrates almost better than any other the seventeenth-century moral teaching on man and society. Society represents the pattern of existence laid down for man by God, and is essentially good; but it can be corrupted by the sinfulness of individual men. When this happens it is society, not man, which finds itself in a truly dramatic situation. Society is the helpless victim of sin; whereas for man, endowed with moral sense and free-will, the course is always clear. Here we see why the Spanish dramatists did not produce much great tragedy: unquestioningly accepting as they did the moral and theological teaching of their age, they found it difficult to imagine their heroes faced with a really tragic conflict. Dilemmas there might be, but none to which the established values did not provide an answer. *Sub specie æternitatis*, all was well. (This is, of course, like much in this chapter, the broadest of generalizations, which is all that is possible at this stage. When the field has been surveyed in greater detail it will be possible to analyse the question of tragedy more profoundly.)

The social approach of the *comedia* naturally has a bearing on the presentation of character. Its lack of profound character portrayal has caused it to be criticized as superficial; and some scholars in recent years, attempting to rebut this criticism, have read into it subtleties of characterization and of meaning which it will hardly bear. But it is a mistake to judge the *comedia* by the standards of the nineteenth-century novel. Its own standards in this respect are those of most pre-Romantic literature. It subordinates personality to plot, and individualism to the tradition of the age. Lope de Vega and Calderón were very little concerned with the portrayal of character. Of the three great dramatists of the period only Tirso de Molina shows any real interest in it, and even he is chary of carrying it too far.

Characters in the *comedia* tend to be seen primarily in their relationships with other people; that is, from the viewpoint of society. We know them as we know other people in real life, from the outside; not from within, as we know ourselves. Elizabethan drama at its greatest, as its titles show, is often that of the individual soul: *Hamlet, King Lear, Volpone, Dr. Faustus*. In the titles of Spanish plays, instead of single names of individuals, we have *Fuenteovejuna*, the name of a whole village; *Peribáñez y el Comendador de Ocaña*, two names indicating a social relationship; *El alcalde de Zalamea* (*The Mayor of Zalamea*), a title indicating position in society; *El príncipe constante* (*The Constant Prince*) and *El Burlador de Sevilla* (*The Trickster of Seville*), attributes of behaviour; or, as in numerous cases such as *Las paredes oyen* (*Walls have Ears*), *El perro del hortelano* (*The Dog in the Manger*) and *El vergonzoso en palacio* (*The Shy Man at Court*), a reference to a proverb or saying, recommending or dissuading from some manner of behaviour. The viewpoint is always that of society.

The media of character portrayal are dialogue and action more often than soliloquy. Not only is there little philosophizing or reflection (at least before the time of Calderón), but even character itself yields in importance to action. What men are is of less interest than what they do. The swift dialogue, helped by the brisk octosyllabic metre, reflects the swiftly moving action. This is often of a sensational type: passion, duels, murder and revenge, plots and counter-plots form the substance of many plays. *Comedias de capa y espada*, cloak-and-sword dramas, constitute much of the theatrical output of the age. Even when there is no physical violence the romantic element persists in concealments, deceptions, mistaken identity, disguises (usually of women as men) and supernatural occurrences.

Although when contrasted with the rigid classical framework

and diction of French drama the *comedia* impresses by its naturalism, nevertheless there is in it a very strong element of convention,
of which the cloak-and-sword plot is but one aspect. Others are
a stereotyped nomenclature; the constitution of the family,
which as in Elizabethan drama consists usually of an unnaturally
aged father and either one or two children, but no mother; and
the stock types around whom most plots are constructed. These
are the gallant and the lady (who are often duplicated), the
comic servant or *gracioso*, who may be matched by the witty
maidservant, and the father.

Similar figures are, of course, part of the usual structure of
Shakespearean comedy, and any flourishing theatre will evolve
its own stock types once the regular acting companies are there
to serve it. It becomes customary for plays to include a part
for a comic actor; so companies regularly employ such an
actor; and thereafter a play without a role for him is unthinkable.
It must never be forgotten that *comedias* were written for performance, in certain specific conditions; and what may seem
defects from a literary point of view are often found to arise from
the exigencies of the stage.

Of the stock types, the only one to merit special consideration
is the *gracioso*. He is usually, according to the type of play, either
the hero's lackey, in which case he is a man of the world, slick,
quick-witted, and ready to abet his master in all his adventures;
or a village bumpkin, who gives rise to humour by his *naïveté*.
In either case he will be a complete materialist, very much
concerned with food, drink, financial reward and the safety
of his own skin. His humour is broad, sometimes even obscene.
He is usually paired off at the end with the maidservant or village
girl who has been parrying his advances throughout the play.

As many works of the period show, it was common for youths
at school and at the university to be provided with a servant who
shared in his master's studies as part of his remuneration. This
custom perhaps lent colour to the literary convention of the
gracioso, since such men had a close companionship with their
masters and were also in a position to acquire the learning

which the more sophisticated type of *gracioso* often displays. But like his Shakespearean counterparts—the Gratianos and Stephanos, not the jesters, for they never figure in the *comedia*— the *gracioso* is primarily a literary creation. The lackey derives, via Torres Naharro and Italian comedy, from the quick-witted slaves of Plautus and Terence. For the ancestors of the comic rustic we can look back to the Nativity plays and the early shepherds' farces, and beyond them to the mime tradition; then forward again along a different line of development to the *zanni* of the *commedia dell'arte*.

The comparative naturalism of the diction of Spanish drama has been mentioned. It is true that, in keeping with Calderón's elevation of the genre into something more acceptable to men of letters, in the later period a more lofty and artificial manner of speech is to be found, full of metaphors, subtleties, plays upon words, mythological allusions and stereotyped phraseology. It is known as the *estilo culto*, and was used more strikingly by the lyric poets of the time, particularly Góngora. The *comedia*, although written in verse, is seldom poetic, and its language, whether in the naturalistic or the elevated style, is not easily memorable. Virtually only in the plays of Calderón is the *estilo culto* ever used with true poetic effect. It is employed increasingly as time goes on, and in Calderón has almost ousted naturalism; but it is by no means absent from the works of Lope de Vega.

Yet over the whole period it is the more naturalistic manner of speech which predominates, and which helps to give the *comedia* its strong flavour of realism, despite the sensational action. Language on the whole, although versified, tends towards that of everyday speech. Examples of the two styles can be seen in the passages quoted on pp. 40 and 41. The only hints of an elevated manner in the second are the phrase "tomar estado" for "to marry", and the reference to the horses of Phœbus's chariot; the rest, and in particular the last line, is of extreme simplicity. The first passage, on the other hand, uses rhetorical questions, inversions, euphemisms like "pinos" for "timber" and "cristales salados" for "sea water", and a whole series of classical

allusions. The effect is certainly to convey something excessive
and extreme, but hardly to create great poetry. For the most
part we look in vain in the *comedia* for arresting verbal miracles
like Shakespeare's

> Look how the floor of heaven
> is thick inlaid with patens of bright gold!
>
> (*Merchant of Venice*, V. 1)

or Marlowe's

> See, see where Christ's blood streams in the firmament!
>
> (*Doctor Faustus*, Scene XVI)

Beside these, Spanish drama is apt to appear either pedestrian
or cliché-ridden and bombastic. Yet at its best it attains an
eloquent simplicity which is of great dramatic effect. Let Calderón
this time provide an example: the poignant words in which
Mencía, of *El médico de su honra* (*The Doctor of his Own Honour*),
rejects the thought of her former lover because she is now
married:

> Tuve amor y tengo honor;
> esto es cuanto sé de mí.   (Act I)
> ("I had love once, now I have honour; that is all I know of myself.")

And just as Lope can make great drama out of the lives of simple
people, so too their everyday speech, captured and conveyed
without any suggestion of patronizing—the jokes of friends at
a wedding, for instance, or the talk of girls discussing what to
wear for an outing to Toledo—can in his plays acquire a positive
aesthetic value.

There are also, particularly in the plays of Lope, interludes
in which the dramatist suspends the action to allow for the
recitation of a sonnet or gloss which falls appositely, or to let
his characters join in a popular song. Lope's songs, like those
of Gil Vicente or of Shakespeare, are sometimes traditional,
sometimes written or modified by the author himself. They occur
most naturally in the plays of country life, they are often closely
related to the action, and at times, as when the harvesters in
Peribáñez sing themselves to sleep with

Trébole ¡ay Jesús, cómo huele!
Trébole ¡ay Jesús, qué olor!
Trébole de la casada,
que a su esposo quiere bien;
de la doncella también,
entre paredes guardada . . .   (Act II)

("The clover, how it smells! The clover, Lord, what a scent! Clover for the
wife, who loves her husband well; and for the maiden too, kept under close
guard . . .")

they produce scenes of pure lyricism.

A skilful playwright will always vary the pace of his action by the inclusion of such pause scenes, in which atmosphere is created or character and background sketched in. It is in this background material that Spanish drama is perhaps truest to life. There is on the whole little attempt to re-create other ages or atmospheres. However remote in space or time the ostensible setting of a play, its background is virtually always that of contemporary Spain; or rather, of a somewhat rose-coloured version of it, in which signs of economic decline are barely apparent. The pictures of rural life are particularly happy: the men cultivating the land, the wives spinning, the young men and women chatting in the square, the village worthies discussing local affairs, and above all the popular festivities with which the story is so often linked and in which the trace of medieval rituals can be seen. Weddings, religious festivities, bull fights, homecomings all offer occasions for an outburst of song and dance. Music was performed before and in the intervals of all *comedias*, and it has a small part to play in the action of many of them.

The urban type of play has its painting of customs too. There is a clear picture, particularly in the comedies, of the fashionable life of Madrid: the ladies going out early to Mass or to take the waters, the surreptitious encounters at church, the promenade of coaches along the Paseo del Prado. It is possible for the glamour of the foreground action to blind the reader to the astonishing number of references to mundane realities. One can perhaps single out food, clothing and money as things which play an important part in everyone's daily life, and which the *comedia* by no means overlooks. Refreshments are provided for visitors; men and women consider what clothes to wear for special occasions; servants mention their wages, and ladies are interested in the size of their suitors' incomes. The peasant plays similarly often refer to animals.

This, in broad outline, is the *comedia* created by Lope. It has few outstanding features; it is memorable for the whole rather than for any of its parts. It is many-faceted; but it is the overall impression rather than the details which persists in the mind. The few masterpieces of each author apart, memory does not always easily distinguish one play from another. But this overall impression is of a strongly individual art form.

General Works

AUBRUN, C. V., *La comédie espagnole* (*1600–1680*) (Paris, 1966).

PARKER, A. A., *The Approach to the Spanish Drama of the Golden Age* (No. VI in the *Diamante* series of the Hispanic and Luso-Brazilian Councils, London, 1957).

PRING-MILL, R. D. F., Introduction to *Lope de Vega* (*Five Plays*), translated by JILL BOOTY (New York, 1961).

REICHENBERGER, ARNOLD G., "The uniqueness of the *comedia*" in *HR* 27 (1959) 303–16.

SALOMON, N., *Recherches sur le thème paysan dans la "comedia" au temps de Lope de Vega* (Bordeaux, 1965).

4

LOPE DE VEGA

THE attempt to give any real account of Lope's works in the restricted scope offered by a book of this kind is almost foolhardy. It is impossible to do him justice.

The difficulties are of two kinds, the first and more obvious one being that of quantity. Three years before he died Lope claimed in the *Égloga a Claudio* to have written 1500 plays. His friend Montalbán, in the *Fama póstuma* which he brought out in homage on Lope's death, raised this figure to 1800 plays and 400 *autos*. It is now generally recognized that these claims are exaggerated, and it has been shown that "mil y quinientos", 1500, was a phrase commonly used to mean simply a large number, in the same way as we say "a thousand and one".[1] S. G. Morley and Courtney Bruerton, who have done work of inestimable value in establishing the canon and chronology of Lope's theatre, declare that "800 plays would be a generous allowance for Lope's total dramatic production".[2] Of these possible 800, only about half survive. In their *Chronology of Lope de Vega's Comedias* (New York, 1940), Morley and Bruerton examine the texts of 314 authentic plays, a further 26 probably by Lope, 72 doubtful ones, and 86 which have been attributed to him, but which their researches lead them to discard. This makes a total of 498, of which some 350-400 may reasonably be assumed to be Lope's. The original figure of 1500 has been considerably

[1] C. P. Wagner, "Lope de Vega's 1500 comedias and the date of *La moza de cántaro*", *HR* 9 (1941) 91–102.

[2] S. G. Morley and C. Bruerton, "How many comedias did Lope de Vega write?", *Hispania* 19 (1936) 217–34.

whittled down; yet the student of his work who wishes to say anything valid about Lope is still left with a dauntingly large corpus of writing to take into account. It becomes hard even to acquire an overall view, let alone to present one; and it will be possible to find exceptions to almost any generalization that is made.

The second difficulty arises from the nature of the plays themselves. Although Lope created a new genre with its set forms and characteristics, there is in his work no sense of rigidity, and he is less amenable than any other Spanish writer of his day to analysis along the conventional lines of literary criticism. His plays do not easily submit to classification, and their essential quality remains somehow elusive to the critic who would try to capture it and set it down.

For these reasons all that will be attempted here is an exposition of the more obvious features of Lope's art and the best-known aspects of his dramatic output; and while the resulting picture will be little more than a sketch, I hope it will offer a recognizable likeness.

Lope wrote many other works besides plays, works in which, notwithstanding the criticisms of Torres Rámila, he usually followed the accepted literary patterns of his day. As well as epic, novel of adventures and pastoral romance, they include hundreds of lyric poems, whose merit alone would have won him fame quite apart from his theatre. It is, paradoxically, in these more "cultured" works that he tells us most about himself. The drama, for all its "natural" style, remains almost entirely impersonal; occasionally Lope appears in his own plays under the name Belardo, but it is nearly always in a minor role and with very little self-revelation. It is in his odes, epistles, ballads and sonnets that he recounts his life and pours out his heart. From these more personal writings, therefore, we can build up a fairly clear picture of Lope's career. True, he is not always accurate. In the late *Égloga a Claudio*, for instance, after telling of his service with the Armada he asks: "Who would have imagined that on returning from the war I should find a sweet wife?" Yet poems from the actual period make it plain that he was married before the Armada sailed. A study of contemporary documents, and of his many letters, has therefore been necessary to correct and fill in details; but thanks to the researches of a number of scholars we now have reliable information about the main events of Lope's life.

Lope de Vega was born in 1562 (seventeen months before Shakespeare), the son of a craftsman from the Cantabrian mountains who had recently settled in Madrid. He was a child prodigy, read both Spanish and Latin by the age of 5 and composed verses even before he knew how to write them down. He studied at a Jesuit school and then, it is believed, at the University of Alcalá de Henares, though it is not known what form his studies took; his work reveals no trace of any particular academic discipline. He himself in his polemic verse often opposes his own natural talent to the learning of his detractors. From his early twenties he was famous as a writer, though at this stage of poetry rather than plays. The first well-documented event of his adult life is his love affair with the actress Elena Osorio. This affair lasted five years, and was of such importance to Lope that he left many literary testimonies to it. Even three years before his death he published a work, the *Dorotea*, which retold the story in fictional form, and from which it is apparent that he had never quite ceased to smart from Elena's treatment of him. She was a woman who bore out the moralists' allegations about actresses, for she was already married when she met Lope, and deserted him in turn for a richer lover. Lope replied with some bitter and libellous verses on her and her family, which led to litigation and the imposition of a harsh sentence: banishment from Madrid for eight years, and from the whole kingdom of Castile for two.

The exile from Castile was spent in Valencia, with an interruption from May to December 1588, when Lope sailed with the Armada. (This brief episode provided the initial impulse for one of his non-dramatic works, the epic poem *Dragontea*, which is a sustained attack on Sir Francis Drake.) By this time

Lope was married, to Isabel de Urbina, and was also becoming well known as a dramatist. From Valencia when the exile had expired he moved to Toledo, and then to Alba de Tormes, near Salamanca, where he was secretary to the Duke of Alba from 1590 to 1595; a hundred years exactly after Juan del Encina's employment by an earlier duke of the same house. This apparently idyllic period came to an end with the death of Isabel in 1594, closely preceded or followed by that of the two daughters she had borne him.

Lope then returned to Madrid, the longer exile now being over, and found employment as secretary to the Duke of Sessa. His relations with this nobleman were much closer than with his previous patrons. He became his friend and confidant, and it is to the intimate correspondence between them that we owe much of our knowledge of the events of Lope's later years. Sessa remained his patron, and one of the chief sources of his income, for the rest of his life.

Before long Lope was involved in a love-affair with another actress, Micaela de Luján. This affair was probably of some ten years' duration, and several children were born of it; but it did not stop Lope contracting a second marriage, to Juana de Guardo, in 1598. In the succeeding years he seems to have maintained two homes, always in different towns; and it was ironically the illicit family which was more favoured as regards health and survival. Juana's son, Carlos Félix, died in 1612 at the age of 7, and she herself only lived for another year. Her other child, Feliciana, was the only one of Lope's legitimate offspring to reach maturity.

This double bereavement brought much sadness to the father and was the chief factor in causing him to take, in 1614, a step apparently quite incongruous with his earlier career: that of being ordained priest. One is tempted to accuse him of disingenuousness and to look for questionable motives for the act; yet the tone of the religious poems dating from this period leaves no doubt as to the strength and sincerity of Lope's devotion. There were clearly two conflicting strains in his personality, and the disintegration of his family life allowed his religious fervour to assert itself more strongly for a time.

It must also be remembered that the morals of ecclesiastics were often lax. The Valencian diary referred to in Chapter 3 mentions a large number of scandals involving priests; and Lope seems quite genuinely to have seen no necessary connection between priesthood and private morality. It was a shock to him when his confessor forbade him to go on composing love-letters for the Duke of Sessa to send to his mistresses, as he had done for some years, and he declares:

> They assured me that I was in mortal sin, and this has filled me with such regret that I believe I would not have had myself ordained had I believed that I should have had to cease serving Your Excellency in anything, and especially in those matters in which you take so much pleasure. (Letter of June 1614, quoted by H. A. Rennert, *Life of Lope de Vega*, (Glasgow, 1904, pp. 217, 218.)

An even more flagrant profanation of his priesthood was soon to follow. In 1616 the 54-year-old Lope fell in love with a young married woman, Marta de Nevares, with a passion which he told Sessa was as strong as any he had ever known. The affair became notorious, and provoked satirical references in the literature of the time. After the birth of a daughter, Antonia Clara, and the death of Marta's elderly husband, Lope continued to live near her, together with four of his children, only one legitimate, born of three different mothers. (The house where they lived in Madrid has been very pleasantly arranged as a museum.) Scandalous though this way of life was for a priest, it can be said in Lope's favour that he recognized and brought up his children, often wrote of them with great affection, and was deeply moved by their loss; and that some of his amours were of very long duration. He was clearly, if immoral, also warm-hearted, and capable of both giving and inspiring great love.

The personal happiness of this period was not prolonged into his old age. Marta contracted some disease of the brain which caused blindness and insanity, and predeceased him in 1632. Of Micaela de Luján's surviving children, the son, Lope, was lost at sea, and the daughter, Marcela (the only one of Lope's offspring who is known to have inherited any of his poetic talent), entered a convent. Antonia Clara eloped at the age of 17 with a young nobleman who failed to marry her. These misfortunes were probably necessary to bring to full ripeness a man of supreme talent, but for whom perhaps in his earlier years too much had gone too well. The *Égloga a Claudio* expresses very well the wisdom and detachment to which he attained in his final years:

> No es ciencia la que vive de opiniones
> y consta por ajenas amistades,
> ni han de arrastrar verdades
> violencias y pasiones;
> que, puesto que le admiten y le aclaman,
> aquel es sabio que los sabios aman.
>
> El mundo ha sido siempre de una suerte;
> ni mejora de seso ni de estado;
> quien mira lo pasado
> lo porvenir advierte.
> Fuera esperanzas, si he tenido alguna;
> que ya no he menester a la fortuna.

("True knowledge is not dependent on opinion, nor attested by friendship; nor is truth to be brought low by violence and passion; for however accepted and acclaimed a man may be, he only is truly wise whom wise men love.

The world has always been the same; it gets neither wiser nor better; to observe the past is to take warning for the future. Away with hopes, if I have harboured any; I have no need of fortune now.")

Lope died on 27th August 1635. His patron the Duke of Sessa arranged an elaborate funeral for him, and he was mourned by the whole populace of Madrid. His cortège made a detour at one point to pass in front of Marcela's convent so that she might pay her last respects to her father.

Lope's greatness was clearly recognized in his lifetime. He had even given his name to a popular saying: "es de Lope", "it's real Lope", was a phrase commonly applied to any object to indicate its excellence. Although he had made some enemies in literary circles, he had won a general affection and regard which his personal immorality did little to counteract, and the tributes paid to him on his death were in keeping with his great achievement.

Lope's full and intensely lived life, together with his knowledge of literature, offered plenty of material for drama; but this would have been no good without the ability to arrange that material suitably for stage presentation. Lope possessed this ability in supreme degree. The necessity to submit his inventive facility to the discipline of a fixed form seems to have been even more beneficial to him than to most writers. He was so prolific and natural a versifier that in his longer compositions he often got carried away by the torrent of his own verbosity; but when the flood was channelled into the fourteen lines of a sonnet or the three acts of a *comedia*, his artistry was able to take control.

Lope excelled in dramatic technique, which with him was apparently instinctive and unlearned. He knew exactly how much material was needed for a good play. Unlike Juan de la Cueva or Cervantes, or his successor Tirso de Molina, he never overloaded his structure with superabundant action. Very occasionally there is too little action; as, for instance, in *Porfiar hasta morir* (*Persistence until Death*), which tells the story of the hopeless love of the medieval poet Macías, and is almost more of an elegy than a play. The reverse, however, is scarcely ever true. Nor does he often sin against the cardinal principle of unity of action, upheld in the *Arte nuevo*. His sub-plots serve the main action, and never swamp it.[3] He knows too how much material to put into each act—measured not merely by the four sheets of paper which he suggests in the *Arte nuevo* as the right allowance, but also by the amount by which the action is advanced—and how much into each speech. His speeches, unlike those of later dramatists, are seldom too long for either the actors' convenience or the audience's concentration.

[3] See D. Marín Molina, *La intriga secundaria en el teatro de Lope de Vega* (Mexico, 1958).

One of the severest tests for a dramatist is his handling of the initial exposition, by means of which the audience is put into the picture. It is a test in which both Tirso and Calderón often fail, the first resorting to clumsy and implausible monologues, the second even on occasion to such a threadbare expedient as to make a character say:

> Ya sabes, pero es forzoso
> repetirlo, aunque lo sepas . . .
> > (*La cisma de Ingalaterra*, Act I)

("You already know, but I must needs repeat it, even though you do know . . .")

Lope usually contrives his expositions so naturally and unobtrusively in the dialogue of his opening scenes that one does not notice it happening. Thereafter he skilfully varies the pace of the action by the introduction of pause scenes, in which background is sketched in, atmosphere created, or relationships clarified or deepened in conversation. Such a pause scene frequently occurs near the end of a first or second act; but it will then be followed by a new spurt of action which leads to an unresolved climax, and leaves the audience in an expectant mood until the next act begins. Such variation of pace is very marked, for instance, in *El Caballero de Olmedo* (*The Knight of Olmedo*).[4] Act I moves briskly: the hero meets the heroine and falls in love, finds he has a rival, and employs an old crone who is both go-between and witch, and who works on the heroine's feelings by means of a spell. The whole of Act II is virtually a pause act, given over to the depiction of the change in Inés's character and the deepening love between her and Alonso, and to a large amount of comic relief provided by the crone and the *gracioso*. It ends, however, in a mood of excitement with preparations for the forthcoming May-day festivities. In the course of these celebrations in Act III the hostility between Alonso and his rival comes to a head; the latter plans Alonso's murder, and the action hurtles along to its tragic end.

Metre is varied as skilfully as pace. Lope, who always had

[4] Edited by I. I. Macdonald (Cambridge, 1934).

his audience in mind, was conscious of the effect of spoken verse; and though the Spanish octosyllable is a flexible metre, with none of the almost benumbing, hammer-blow regularity which the French Alexandrine acquires in performance, he takes care to intersperse long stretches in *romance* or *redondillas* with shorter sections in the heptasyllabic and hendecasyllabic metres which Spain had imported from Italy. However, these changes of metre are not haphazard: they very often mark a change of atmosphere or of scene; and Italian metres are usually reserved, in the *comedia* as a whole, for speakers of noble birth.

The excellence of Lope's dramatic technique easily escapes the attention. He has the unobtrusive skill of the expert, which makes it all look easy. Only in the comparison with the works of his fellow dramatists does Lope's superb craftsmanship become fully apparent.

For the substance of his plays he could draw, when he wished, on his knowledge of town and country, the nobility, the bourgoisie and the peasants, the armed forces and the Church. Yet little of his own experience went to the making of his actual plots. These he took, like Shakespeare and the other dramatists of his day, from literary, legendary and historical sources; in his case the literature of Italy and the history and balladry of Spain were probably the most fertile fields. He sometimes needed to eke out the substance of a *novella* with material of his own invention, or to utilize more than one source for the same play. One of his striking qualities is his skill in synthesizing unrelated antecedents to form a homogeneous whole. *El Caballero de Olmedo*, for instance, is built round an anonymous medieval ballad which states:

> Que de noche le mataron
> al Caballero,
> la gala de Medina,
> la flor de Olmedo.

("For by night they slew him, the Knight, the pride of Medina, the flower of Olmedo.")

This ballad provides Lope with the character of his hero and the manner of his death, and is sung with great dramatic effect at the climax of the play. But the mention of the town of Medina calls to mind another ballad, this time a contemporary one:

> Por la tarde salió Inés
> a la feria de Medina,
> tan hermosa que la gente
> pensaba que amanecía.

("In the afternoon Inés went out to the fair of Medina, so beautiful that people thought the sun was rising.")

In this way the heroine of the play comes into being. The machinations of the go-between are taken over directly from those of Celestina, the bawd-witch of the great dialogue novel of 1499 which bears her name. And so the outline of the plot is drawn, and certain other ready-made literary elements are introduced to fill it out: a couple of glosses on well-known refrains, one of them suggested by the name Inés; and a mock lesson, one of the commonplaces of Italianate drama, such as occurs in *The Taming of the Shrew*. It sounds a hotch-potch, and yet the result is a perfectly integrated drama, and an undeniable masterpiece. The French scholar Marcel Bataillon has shown how another play, *El villano en su rincón* (*The Peasant in his Corner*), is an even more remarkable synthesis of a number of elements: a Spanish short story which derives from an earlier French one, *Le charbonnier et le roi;* a Spanish legend, found recorded in a number of epitaphs, concerning one Juan Labrador who made a boast of never having seen the king; and topical allusions to the royal marriages of 1615 which linked the reigning houses of France and Spain.[5] In a recent edition of the play (Madrid, 1961), Professor Alonso Zamora Vicente indicates still more elements that went to its making: the popular philosophy of the well-known proverb, "Este es rey que nunca vio al rey" ("He is king who has never seen the king"); the cultured theme of Horace's *Beatus ille;* and Lope's own knowledge and love of the countryside. This blending of literary topics with reflections of his personal experience is typical of much of Lope's writing.

[5] Marcel Bataillon, "*El villano en su rincón*", *BH* 51 (1949) 5–38 and 52 (1950) 397.

This same play illustrates very well the common tendency to hispanify the setting, whatever the origin of the source material. The "corner" where the peasant hero lives is near Paris, and it is the King of France whom he has no desire to see. Yet on his farm he cultivates vines and olives, and there is nothing to differentiate his background or his way of life from those depicted in such plays as *Fuenteovejuna*, which deal with rural life in Spain.

Lope does go to rather more trouble to establish epoch, by reference to historical events. *Fuenteovejuna* is set in the year 1477, when Queen Isabella is still fighting against a rival claimant for the throne of Castile. The action of *Peribáñez*,[6] another play which tells essentially the same story of a vassal defending his honour against his overlord, takes place in the reign of Enrique III, 1390–1406. In any play concerned with honour the figure of the monarch is important, as he is the final arbiter who must appear at the end to establish that justice has been done; and Lope takes care to avoid a too mechanical appearance by integrating the national events in which the monarch is involved into the main action. Enrique III is setting out on a campaign against the Moors, and this provides the opportunity for the peasant Peribáñez to be called up, leaving his wife unprotected against the advances of Don Fadrique. The Comendador of *Fuenteovejuna* is fighting in the war over the Castilian succession, but on the wrong side; this serves to deflect the audience's sympathy from him from the beginning, and to make his murder still more defensible, since his rebellious vassals are at the same time vindicating their own personal rights and rising against an enemy of the Catholic Sovereigns.

Even so the history remains very much in second place, and it is the human story of ordinary people which is Lope's chief concern. He did also write plays in which the main action is historical, but these have made much less impression than those works in which humble figures are portrayed with humanity and dignity, and made the protagonists of serious drama. Américo Castro has pointed out that in the period under review

[6] Edited by C. V. Aubrun and J. F. Montesinos (Paris, 1943).

this happens only in Spain;[7] and in the Spanish theatre it happens virtually only in the plays of Lope de Vega. Even Tirso de Molina finds it difficult to depict common people without either deriving humour from them, or raising them to the nobility at the end. Lope does not need to do this. Accepting the rigid distinctions of the social structure he can still find nobility in ordinary people; and one of his greatest achievements is to have created men like Peribáñez.

It is partly because of this sympathetic portrayal of the whole community that Lope has so often been called Spain's national dramatist and the mouthpiece of his age. Patriotic critics have perhaps exaggerated this role: on the one hand the human quality of his work carries it beyond barriers of place or time, and on the other it is being increasingly realized how much of literature as well as of life his theatre contains. Yet it is right to distinguish between the didactic Calderón who regularly gives his audiences examples of what they should or should not be, and Lope, who very seldom preaches, and is usually content to show men as they are.

It is chiefly in the rich background material supporting the action, the songs and ballads, the popular celebrations, the details of domestic or of country life, that Lope seems to convey the reality of the Spain he knew. He depicts both the everyday and the seasonal: the ladies of the capital going out early to take the waters in *El acero de Madrid* (*Madrid Spa*), or the bustle of a great port in *El Arenal de Sevilla* (*Seville's Riverside*); May-day and Midsummer holidays in *Santiago el verde* (*St. James the Less*) and *La noche de San Juan* (*Midsummer Night*), harvest on a Castilian farm in *Peribáñez*. It is surprising how often we are aware in Lope of what time of day or what month of the year it is, and how much this helps to make the fiction seem real. Regional differences, too, make the picture more complete and more convincing: *Peribáñez* refers to the costumes and the local festivities of the province of Toledo, *El Caballero de Olmedo* to those of Medina del Campo in Old Castile. And as with the historical background,

[7] A. Castro, *De la edad conflictiva* (Madrid, 1961), Vol. 14, pp. 49–50.

this local material is made integral to the action of the play, for it was at Medina Fair that Alonso first met Inés, and because of the events at the May-day bullfight that Rodrigo decided to kill him; while Peribáñez became aware of the threat to his honour through both the evidence of the harvesters, and the portrait of his wife sketched, unknown to her, as she was watching the annual Procession of the Virgin in Toledo. By being related in this way to what is known and familiar, the sensational aspects of the plot are made more readily acceptable.

Violent action must not be allowed to obscure the ordinariness of Lope's characters. Despite the abnormal things which happen to them, they are for the most part very normal people, with no outstanding endowments of personality, without inner conflicts or philosophical doubts. (The occasional exception may be noted. *El divino africano* portrays, with some success, the mental torments which preceded the conversion of St. Augustine, torments with which Lope himself must have felt some sympathy. *La fianza satisfecha*, which was staged in London in 1966 in a version by John Osborne entitled *A Bond Honoured*, presents a type which other dramatists were beginning to make popular, the unbridled sinner who glories in his wickedness; but recent textual studies have cast considerable doubt on Lope's authorship of this play.)[8] It has already been stated that the earlier Golden Age drama in general seldom concerns itself, as do Shakespeare's greatest tragedies, with the individual soul. Least of all in Lope must one look for the mind at war with itself, the misfit in society, the accursed of the gods, the accomplice of the devil. There are no great archetypes in his work; there are not even many memorable characters. What is memorable is the picture of a whole society, instinctively apprehended and delightfully portrayed.

Lope's plays have much in common with the paintings of Velázquez. Both artists have a gift, almost unequalled in their

[8] W. L. Fichter, "Orthoepy as an aid for establishing a canon of Lope de Vega's authentic plays", in *Estudios hispánicos. Homenaje a Archer M. Huntington* (Wellesley, Mass., 1952), p. 150, and J. H. Arjona, "Improper use of consonantal rhyme in Lope de Vega, and its significance concerning the authorship of doubtful plays", *Hispanófila* 16 (1962) 32.

respective spheres, for conveying warm, genial humanity. Velázquez portrays no anguished or ecstatic states of mind; for them one must look to El Greco or Ribera. Even when he paints an ostensibly superhuman figure like the god Vulcan, the result is very much a creature of flesh and blood. His large groups such as the Maids of Honour, the Tapestry Weavers, the Drinkers, or the Forge of Vulcan, are not much concerned with penetration into character. Each portrays some four to eight figures observed from the outside, in activity, and in relationship with each other; and this is exactly what is found in Lope's theatre.

For Velázquez as for Lope life went well on the whole, and in both cases this freedom from great trouble reinforced a naturally sanguine temperament. Velázquez's period as court painter to Philip IV saw Spain's power and vitality ebb even lower than during the lifetime of Lope de Vega; but this decline is not to be suspected from the canvases of the one any more than from the plays of the other. In a few of the later portraits of Philip—such as the smaller of the two in the London National Gallery—there emerges something of the tragedy of that unfortunate king, conscious of his country's plight but also of his own inadequacy to remedy it. But this is an infrequent strain in Velázquez's work. His court portraits in general, though sympathetic to their sitters and fully aware of them as human beings, accept the pomp of royalty at its face value and give no hint of the hollowness underneath.

So too with Lope there is little probing into the depths. He has not much of the tragedian in him. He clearly preferred happy endings, and sometimes even altered his source material in order to achieve them. His treatment of the Romeo and Juliet story, for instance, in *Castelvines y Monteses*, ends with the marriage of the lovers and the healing of the feud; while from the story of the overthrow of Boris Godunov he creates, not a tragedy like Pushkin's, but a tragicomedy, *El Gran Duque de Moscovia*, in which the main character is the ultimately triumphant Demetrio. His natural optimism is reflected in a general impression of harmony and serenity, a sense of the rightness of life. He is a complete stranger to the spirit of disillusion which was to colour so strongly the works of his followers—men who felt all earthly certainties slipping from beneath their feet, and came to mistrust appearances and the natural life. For Lope there was no such dichotomy; life for him was still integrated, and nature good.

5

LOPE DE VEGA *(continued)*

LOPE DE VEGA's best-known plays, and those in which his
temperament and his view of life find their clearest expression,
are probably the ones depicting country life. His peasants are
always sane and healthy in their outlook and their social morality,
and happy until some discordant element, such as a licentious
nobleman or the insidious attraction of the court, comes to
disturb their peace. The superiority of rural to urban life was,
of course, a well-worn topic of the Renaissance. In 1539 the
Bishop Antonio de Guevara had written a whole book on it,
the *Menosprecio de corte y alabanza de aldea* (translated into English
in 1548 with the title *A Dispraise of the Life of a Courtier*). But
this is a mere rhetorical exercise, and Guevara himself, like
most of those who have treated the theme, never put his ideas into
practice by actually living in the country.

Lope too was primarily a town-dweller; but his presentation
of the same idea, for example in *Los Tellos de Meneses*, is not
just empty convention. He puts into the mouth of an old farmer
one of the versions of Horace's *Beatus ille* at which virtually
every poet of the period tried his hand; but after the obligatory
denunciation of court life, the old man goes on to give a much
livelier picture of himself, going out early to break the ice on his
streams, busying himself in the morning with his livestock, all
branded with their owner's initial, and in the afternoon with
his crops and orchards. Here and elsewhere Lope writes as one
who had lived and been happy in the country, but who also
knew from close observation that rural felicity was dependent

upon constant hard work. He does not idealize the natural way of life beyond all recognition, as does the pastoral novel; his countryside is not Arcadia.[1] It is, admittedly, more fertile and productive than was the reality towards the end of his life, when agriculture was in sad decline, and even the simple supper of stew and olives which Casilda prepares for her husband Peribáñez would be beyond the means of many. Yet it remains recognizably Spanish.

Fuenteovejuna is full of references to farm produce and to animals. Not merely do the peasants pay their overlord rich homage in the form of geese and capons, sausages, cheeses and wine; even the imagery of the play is drawn from the land. Laurencia is for the Comendador a doe, or a hare, to be pursued; her friend fears that she will prove to have a heart as soft as butter; but she promises, though she may be but a chicken in years, to resist as firmly as any oak. Peribáñez, in the play which bears his name, expresses his feelings for his bride in rustic terms: she is more beautiful than spring meadows, than trees laden with olives, or the golden oil in its vat. Indeed, his love for his wife and his joy in his land are part of the same thing for him, and when his marriage is threatened the sight of his fields gives him pain.

Peribáñez is another play like *El Caballero de Olmedo* in which Lope has evolved a complete and consummate work of art out of the merest snatch of an old ballad:

> Más quiero yo a Peribáñez
> con su capa la pardilla,
> que no a vos, Comendador,
> con la vuestra guarnecida.

("I love Peribáñez with his old brown cloak, more than you, Comendador, with your embroidered cape.")

These words are put into Casilda's mouth at the climax of Act II, when she rejects her would-be seducer. They are over-

---

[1] He did include poems on the *Beatus ille* theme in his own pastoral novel *La Arcadia*, and in *Los pastores de Belén* (Lope de Vega, *Poesías líricas*, ed. J. F. Montesinos, Madrid, Clásicos castellanos, 1952, Vol. II, pp. 18–21 and 69–72). Even these have a stronger flavour of realism than is usual in such poems during the Renaissance.

heard by the reapers who turn them into a song; and it is when Peribáñez hears this sung that he knows his honour is at stake. They are therefore the very core of the play. And their significance is not confined to the plot: out of their hint of characterization through dress, Lope builds an important motif in the play. Clothing becomes, as well as an indication of class, a topic of conversation, an agent of realism, even an augury; and it has its part to play at the dénouement. When the King confirms that Peribáñez's murder of his wife's assailant was just, and grants him a nobleman's right to bear arms, the Queen makes Casilda a present of four of her dresses; thus symbolically raising her too to the level of the Comendador with the embroidered cape.

In the domestic happiness of the newly-married Peribáñez and Casilda there is a striking instance of the harmony and serenity which Lope so often conveys in his drama. It has been stated earlier that love in the *comedia* can usually be equated with desire, and has seldom anything of romantic idealism about it. But Lope does at times contrive to paint it in a different way: he seems to be almost alone among the dramatists of his age in knowing how to express tenderness. Casilda gives a simple and perfect description of her evenings with her husband: how they feed the animals together, punctuating the task with kisses; then eat their frugal meal, say their prayer of thanks, and go to bed,

> donde le pesa a la aurora
> cuando se llega la hora
> de venirnos a llamar.
> ("where the dawn is sorry when it is time to come and wake us.")

Her friend's comment is appropriate:

> ¡ Dichosa tú, casadilla,
> que en tan buen estado estás!
> ("How lucky you are, little wife, to be in such a happy state!")

But it would be difficult to find in any later dramatist of the period a similar picture of the rightness and goodness of natural human values. By the time of Calderón supernatural values predominate, and earthly love is often a wile of the devil. Lope knew it too well to dismiss it in this way.

As with love, so too with honour, Lope's treatment of the conventions is sometimes coloured by his warm humanity. It has become almost a commonplace to contrast the apparently harsh Calderonian handling of the theme, applied chiefly to marital relationships, with the more positive, vital concept of *Peribáñez* and *Fuenteovejuna*, where honour concerns nobleman and vassal, and is thought of as a natural human dignity to which all men have a right, irrespective of birth. This is an exaggerated distinction. Firstly, in both instances honour is a matter of the right ordering of a social relationship, which, once it has gone irremediably wrong, must be dissolved by the shedding of blood. Secondly, Lope can, when he chooses, outdo Calderón in horror, as in *Los Comendadores de Córdoba* (*The Knights-Commander of Córdoba*), where the outraged husband slaughters not only his adulterous wife, but all the servants and even the domestic animals, obliterating the whole household which has witnessed his shame. Lastly, and this is what has been least realized, Lope does not state that the peasant has an equal right to honour with the nobleman; on the contrary, he seems to take pains to avoid this suggestion. When the Comendador wishes to remove Peribáñez so as to have free access to Casilda, he appoints him a captain in his private army and gives him a sword, thus conferring rank upon him; and Peribáñez makes much of the fact that then, and only then, is he the Comendador's equal in honour. Sancho, of *El mejor alcalde el rey* (*The King's Justice is Best*), who has to defend his honour in similar circumstances, is not a simple peasant but of impoverished *hidalgo* stock. The villagers of Fuenteovejuna cannot claim any such justification for their attack on their overlord; and it is significant that the Catholic Sovereigns at the end of the play do not condone their act, but merely state that it cannot be punished since the precise culprit remains unknown.

Nevertheless it is true that there can be sensed in these plays a notion of honour more ample and more human than the rigid concept of the code. The truth is probably that it never occurred to Lope to think the matter out. He was not a moral philosopher, nor a didactic dramatist like Calderón, and he doubtless saw no need for consistency. He was primarily a popular entertainer, who made use of the conventions that his audience knew and looked for, but could not help modifying them in accordance with his own personality.[2]

There is at least one play that treats honour in a thoroughly light-hearted manner, and uses it as the basis for broad humour. This is *El castigo del discreto* (*A Shrewd Punishment*), a work of complicated intrigue, in the course of which a wife writes to her intended lover, offering him a nocturnal assignation. The husband intercepts the letter, goes himself to the rendezvous, and in the dark, without revealing his identity, gives his wife a thrashing. Here we see the Lope whose own conduct flouted the code of honour too often for him to regard infidelity as invariably a matter of life and death. We are given, moreover, a good reason for not doing so in one of the very rare references found in the *comedia* to the actual law of the time:

> que no permiten las leyes
> su muerte por un papel,
> que por dolor más cruel
> dieron licencia los reyes.   (Act II)

("for the law does not authorize her death merely for having sent a letter; only in the case of graver misconduct do our rulers countenance it.")

El castigo del discreto is an excellent and clever comedy, in which Madrid comes wonderfully to life. We are told the names of streets and buildings; we learn how a rich young man consults his Genoese bankers, goes gambling, gets involved in brawls, and neglects his wife to pay not very serious court to a pretty neighbour; we are given a list of the servants in his household,

---

[2] On *Fuenteovejuna* see G. W. Ribbans, "The meaning and structure of Lope's *Fuenteovejuna*", *BHS* 31 (1954) 150–70; and Leo Spitzer, "A central theme and its structural equivalent in Lope's *Fuenteovejuna*", *HR* 23 (1955) 274–92.

On *Peribáñez* see E. M. Wilson, "Images et structures dans *Peribáñez*", *BH* 51 (1949) 125–59; and Victor Dixon, "The symbolism of *Peribáñez*", *BHS* 43 (1966) 11–24.

and their probable occupations at a certain hour; we see the welcome given to a relative from the provinces (a welcome that includes the gift of a dozen hand-embroidered shirts). And as always in Lope, within the improbable convolutions of the plot there are the recurrent sharp little strokes which keep his work human: the lesson that a man will usually take a woman at her own estimate of herself; the admission of a wife that she would rather know her husband was unfaithful than suffer the torment of suspicion; and the same wife's most vocal insistence on her honour at the very moment when she is beginning to think of losing it. Above all this is a very funny play, with the humour of the situations fully matched by the witty repartee.

As could be expected from a man of Lope's sanguine temperament, there is a great deal of humour in his theatre, at a number of different levels. There is straightforward amusement in the situation of Teodoro, secretary to the Countess Diana in *El perro del hortelano*. He is loved by his employer, but she can bring herself neither to lose status by marrying him, nor to give him up to his former betrothed. So he alternates helplessly between the two, both of them convincing witnesses to Lope's familiarity with jealous women, until his servant devises a stratagem by which he can appear to be of noble birth, and so marry Diana. Again one is struck by the flippancy with which Lope can, on occasion, treat a fetish of the *comedia*. Last-scene revelations of identity are common, but here none of the main characters really believes in Teodoro's noble birth; and though appearances are saved, Diana does in fact commit the social sin of marrying beneath her. Lope is clearly laughing at a convention of his own *comedia*, and a new note of satire accompanies the more obvious humour of the plot.

He could also use humour more subtly still, and combined with an essential seriousness of purpose, as *La dama boba* (*The Half-wit*) will illustrate. The heroine of this play is Finea, a mentally retarded girl whose father has settled a large dowry on her as his only hope of getting her off his hands. A suitor is duly enticed, but takes fright at the girl's inane conversation and the stupidity she shows in her reading and dancing lessons. To win laughs from oafishness is, of course, an easy and well-worn stage device; the comedy here is not of a very high order. Yet Lope achieves his effect quite as successfully as Moliére was to do when he showed Monsieur Jourdain learning to fence and to speak prose.

Meanwhile Finea's sister Nise troubles their father on a different score, for she is a *femme savante;* and here the humour takes the form of literary satire. Through Nise Lope pokes fun at the cultured writings of the day, his own included; for the books she reads, to her father's despair, are:

> *Historia de dos amantes,*
> sacada de lengua griega,
> *Rimas* de Lope de Vega,
> *Galatea* de Cervantes . . .

("*The Story of Two Lovers*, translated from the Greek, *Rhymes* of Lope de Vega, *Galatea* by Cervantes . . .")

He goes further, and puts into the mouth of one of her *cénacle*, clearly intending it to be laughed at, a highly involved cosmological sonnet. Yet this very sonnet also appears twice in his non-dramatic works, and each time in a perfectly serious context. In his long poem *La Circe* it is even given an explanatory commentary.[3] It thus presents an instance of that dual standard which Lope applied to his writings: on the one hand "arte", with its rules and its classical ancestry, for the cultured few; and on the other "natural" drama for the common people, for which "arte" may even provide an object of satire and a source of humour.

But there remains the main point of *La dama boba*, which is the fact that Finea eventually finds a suitor who makes her love him, and that love speeds up her mental development to the point where she is no longer witless, but able to bring to marriage both charm and resourcefulness, in addition to wealth. Lope is here dramatizing one element of the popular philosophy of the sixteenth century .The neoplatonic view of love penetrated the Peninsula chiefly by means of the *Dialogues of Love* of Leone

[3] See Dámaso Alonso, "Lope en vena de filósofo", *Clavileño* 1 (1950) 10–15.

Ebreo, a work which, while probably not widely known in detail, must have had sufficient vogue for quotations from it to be acceptable in the theatre; for they are found even in such a "popular" play as *Fuenteovejuna*. *La dama boba*, demonstrating the power of love over the intellect, derives from this same source. Attention has already been drawn to Lope's skill in creating drama out of a wide range of material; here he builds a play out of a serious philosophical idea. But it is characteristic of his customary gaiety that the play should nevertheless be a comedy, with its main theme reinforced by humour.

This does not mean that he was incapable of writing tragedy. It is true that he sometimes preferred to avoid it, changing his source material in order to do so. But when that source material was too familiar to allow of alteration, or simply when he chose to, he created tragedies which are among the finest and the most moving in the Spanish theatre. Two such works, very different from each other, may be instanced.

El Caballero de Olmedo has already been referred to, and its story outlined. In both atmosphere and setting it is completely Spanish: its title places it firmly in Old Castile, the historical figures of Juan II (1406–54) and Álvaro de Luna appear, and regional festivities like Medina Fair and the local May-day celebrations have an important part to play. Although it derives from a number of literary sources, its general effect is not of anything contrived or artificial, but of a simple charm and poignancy. It opens ebulliently, with Alonso's account of his first glimpse of Inés at the fair, and for much of its duration the mood is light-hearted. The servant-*gracioso* provides plenty of conventional humour, and even the go-between Fabia, who is in league with the Devil, is primarily a comic character. There are, too, touches of background realism, unthinkable in a more sophisticated kind of tragedy, as when Alonso announces that he is going to get changed before appearing outside Inés's window, or when Fabia comes to the house selling cosmetics, and then astutely passes off as a laundry-list the love-letter which Inés has entrusted to her.

But while to a modern audience the play may seem to be developing as a typical comedy, a seventeenth-century Spaniard would have known better. The very title would have told him otherwise, for he knew the famous ballad,

> que de noche le mataron,
> al Caballero,
> la gala de Medina,
> la flor de Olmedo,

and was thus prepared for a tragic outcome. He would be alert, as we perhaps are not, to the hints of future catastrophe which occur from the earliest scenes. When Alonso, trying to make contact with Inés, follows her into church, he declares:

> Vime sentenciado a muerte,
> porque el amor me decía:
> 'Mañana mueres, pues hoy
> te meten en la capilla'.

("I saw myself sentenced to death, for love said to me: 'Tomorrow you die, since today you are being taken into chapel'.")

(The Spanish prisoner under sentence of death spent his last night in a chapel, which was thus the equivalent of the condemned cell.) Here what seems merely a pleasing conceit is, in the light of the ballad, a significant foreshadowing of disaster, used with great dramatic effect. As the action of the play progresses such foreshadowings become more frequent, preparing us for the reversal of fortune in Act III. Once we know what the outcome is to be, the earlier light-heartedness is revealed as a superb piece of sustained dramatic irony. Similarly, Lope's public would see no incongruity between the prevailing realism of Acts I and II, and the supernatural elements of the dénouement, for again the ballad had prepared them for the latter:

> Sombras le avisaron
> que no saliese,
> y le aconsejaron
> que no se fuese . . .

("Ghosts warned him not to set out, and advised him not to go . . .").

and so for them the realism would simply heighten the tension:

how pathetically irrelevant for Alonso to be thinking about looking smart, when ghostly visitations and death are just round the corner! Thus Lope is able, by means of the audience's foreknowledge, to build up a tragic atmosphere out of the most unlikely elements.

The counterpoint of gay confidence and premonition is resolved at last in the simple statement of the tragic theme. Alonso, setting out at night on the road to Olmedo, is confronted by his own ghost; but refuses to be deterred. Then he hears a peasant singing the ballad which has been in everyone's mind, but which we now hear for the first time, the ballad which tells of his coming murder; and the eeriness grows when the rustic tells him that he learned the song in Medina from one Fabia. This scene leading up to the murder is of great lyrical beauty. The combination of music, darkness and supernatural warning builds up suspense and creates a powerful atmosphere, shattered by the shot that leaves Alonso mortally wounded.

Perhaps what is remarkable above all in *El Caballero de Olmedo* is Lope's ability to take over much that is derived, much that is literary or purely conventional, and out of it all to create something individual and fresh, and valid in its relevance to life.[4]

If *El Caballero de Olmedo* has the grace of a Mozart, *El castigo sin venganza (Punishment Without Vengeance)*[5] has the power of a Verdi. It is sombre and highly charged throughout; the tragic implications of its dramatic situation are obvious from the beginning. Its Italian setting keeps it remote from everyday realism. The *estilo culto* predominates in the language, and the characters habitually address each other in conceits. In these respects it shows how Lope as an old man—the autograph manuscript of this play is dated 1631—was being influenced

[4] The tragic irony of this play is examined (and the same metaphor of counterpoint used) by William C. McCrary in *The Goldfinch and the Hawk: a Study of Lope de Vega's Tragedy "El Caballero de Olmedo"* (Chapel Hill, University of North Carolina Press, 1966). Also on this play see C. Alan Soons, "Towards an interpretation of *El Caballero de Olmedo*", *RF* 73 (1961) 160–8.

[5] Edited by C. F. Adolfo Van Dam (Groningen, 1928), and by C. A. Jones (Oxford, Pergamon, 1966).

by the more cultured type of drama then being written by Calderón.

The story is taken from a *novella* of Bandello, which Lope probably read in a Spanish version. The Duke of Ferrara has lived a debauched life and has an illegitimate son, Federico, to whom he had planned to leave his dukedom; but his people demand an undisputed heir, and so he agrees to marry, although well advanced in middle age. His bride, Casandra, is of Federico's generation, and it is not surprising that these two fall in love. For a time they repress their feelings, though Casandra deeply resents the fact that while she is required to be faithful, the Duke pays her no attention and continues in his former way of life. So oblivious is he of the danger that he even throws Federico and Casandra together and goes off to the wars, leaving them alone. On his return an anonymous letter informs him that they are lovers. He thereupon devises a horrible way of expunging his dishonour. He has Casandra gagged, bound and covered with a sheet, and tells Federico that this is a person who has offended against his honour, and whom it is therefore his son's duty to kill. Only when the deed is done does Federico discover the victim's identity. The Duke then summons his household and tells them that Federico has killed his stepmother because she was going to bear a legitimate heir. They respond violently and Federico dies at their hands.

The dishonour has been kept secret, as the code demanded, and the Duke can casuistically claim to be a minister of justice punishing two wrongdoers, rather than an individual taking personal vengeance; hence the apparently inapt title. Yet *El castigo sin venganza* is much more than a straightforward drama of honour, like *Los Comendadores de Córdoba*, concerning simply a husband and an adulterous wife. Lope is here at pains to create out of this basic and conventional dramatic situation a human tragedy. He makes two significant changes in his source material.[6] The wife was originally a wanton, who deserved

[6] See Amado Alonso, "Lope de Vega y sus fuentes", *Thesaurus* 8 (1952) 1–24.

punishment; whereas Casandra, although strongly attracted to Federico, is prepared to be honourable and dutiful, even in the face of her husband's adulteries, until her will is weakened by jealousy. She is thus involved in a tragic conflict which the wife in the Bandello story never knew. The Duke, for his part, is made to undergo a change of character in the course of the play. While away at the wars he experiences a moral conversion and comes home determined to be a good husband at last; but it is too late. By this means Lope balances more evenly the elements of good and evil in the tragic situation, giving it greater poignancy and power.

His whole handling of the story underlines the fact that, though the laws of honour must be obeyed, this is not a clear case of right and wrong. Federico and Casandra are suited to each other by age, and there is a natural inevitability and a rightness about their love which is lacking in the marital relationship between Casandra and the Duke. The necessary laws of society are in conflict with a force which is natural and vital, and therefore also in some measure good. Even though he is writing for a theatre now largely given over to moral drama, Lope prefers to the clarity of an exemplum the complexity of a human tragedy.

Another work of his last years, *La Dorotea*, will provide a brief *envoi* to this study of Lope.[7] It does not properly come within the scope of this survey, since it is not a play. It is a novel in dialogue form, modelled on the *Celestina*, to which it owes much. Yet its characters and situations are dramatically conceived, and it has something of the same tragic sense of life as *El castigo*. The story is that of Lope's own unhappy love-affair with Elena Osorio. It seems probable that an earlier version of it was written soon after the event; but when Lope returns to it in his old age, he is able to give it a more polished treatment.[8] Although based on his own experience, *La Dorotea* is full of literary reminiscences,

[7] Edited by José M. Blecua (Madrid, 1955), and by Edwin S. Morby (Berkeley–Los Angeles, 1958).

[8] See Alan S. Trueblood, "The case for an early *Dorotea*: a re-examination", *PMLA* 71 (1956) 755–98.

and so typifies that fusion of literature and life which characterizes so much of Lope's writing; and it also reveals its author more fully than do any of his plays. Its hero depicts the young Lope in all the impetuosity of his passion; while the mature reflections which the episode provokes are evidence of the ripeness to which he ultimately attained.

Texts

Comedias escogidas, ed. J. E. Hartzenbusch, in *BAE*, Vols. 24, 34, 41, 52.
Obras, ed. M. Menéndez y Pelayo, 15 vols. (Madrid, 1890–1913).
Obras, ed. E. Cotarelo and others, 13 vols. (Madrid, 1926–30).
Obras escogidas, ed. F. C. Sainz de Robles, Tomos I y III: *Teatro* (Madrid, Aguilar, 1946 and 1955).

Biographies and General Introductions

ENTRAMBASAGUAS, J. DE, *Vida de Lope de Vega* (Barcelona, 1936).
ENTRAMBASAGUAS, J. DE, *Vivir y crear de Lope de Vega*, Vol. I (Madrid, 1946).
HAYES, FRANCIS C., *Lope de Vega* (New York, Twayne's World Authors Series, 1967).
LÁZARO, F., *Lope de Vega. Introducción a su vida y obra* (Madrid, 1966).
RENNERT, H. A., *Life of Lope de Vega* (Glasgow, 1904; reprinted New York, 1937).
ZAMORA VICENTE, A., *Lope de Vega, su vida y su obra* (Madrid, 1961).

Critical Works

MONTESINOS, J. F., *Estudios sobre Lope de Vega* (Mexico, 1951).
SCHEVILL, R., *The Dramatic Art of Lope de Vega, together with "La dama boba"* (Berkeley, 1918, reissued New York, 1964).
VOSSLER, K., *Lope de Vega und sein Zeitalter* (Munich, 1932); translated into Spanish, *Lope de Vega y su tiempo* (Madrid, 1933).
El teatro de Lope de Vega. Artículos y estudios, ed. J. F. Gatti (Buenos Aires, 1962). (A useful collection of recent important articles: the studies of Amado Alonso, Aubrun and Montesinos, Bataillon, Ribbans, Spitzer and Wilson referred to in the notes to Chapters 4 and 5; all here given in Spanish versions.)

6

A NOTE ON PUBLICATION

ALTHOUGH Lope wrote his plays to be performed, and initially
with very little thought of their survival, long before the end
of his life their printing and publication had become a flourishing
business; and it is perhaps relevant to enquire at this stage into
the processes by which the surviving texts have come to be preserved, and into the problems which these processes present to
the modern scholar.

The system was as follows. Having written his play, the author
(usually referred to in Spanish as the *poeta*), sold it outright to
the manager of an acting company (the *autor*), whose property
it then became. At this stage there was a single manuscript
copy in the author's own handwriting. The *autor* would then
prepare the text for rehearsal, by making excisions and alterations
where he thought fit; and actors' copies would be made on the
basis of his revised version, every process of copying probably
producing its own small crop of inaccuracies. The play as
produced, therefore, was almost certain to be a modification
in some degree of the author's original text, which by now
might well have been discarded and lost. After its short run it
was of no further interest and virtually ceased to exist, except
for such producers' and actors' copies as survived, all in some
measure unfaithful to their original. It was of course in these
circumstances that the great majority of the plays written and
performed were irretrievably lost. We have already seen that
only some 400 by Lope survive out of a probable 800. Tirso
seems to have been proportionately even more unfortunate,

if we are to believe his figure of 300 plays written by 1621, and compare it with the eighty extant today.

This was the situation in the early years, when the drama was still thought of solely as popular entertainment. But its increasing success, and the growth of a public for light literature, led booksellers to realize that there was money to be made from the diffusion of plays in print; so they began to gather in all the copies they could find, and to print them, either singly as *sueltas* (loose copies), or in collections of some dozen or so works by various authors. Later in the seventeenth century *sueltas* were also sometimes bound together to give the appearance of a newly published volume. The act of printing naturally gave a further opportunity for inaccuracies to creep in; and where, as often happened, an actor's copy was incomplete, the bookseller would have no scruples about filling in the gaps with passages of his own. There was a further practice which similarly resulted in the mangling of texts: publishers would sometimes employ men with phenomenal memories to attend performances and then write down as much of a play as they could recall. But however outstanding their ability, these men were not infallible, and so again the printed version often differed considerably from that which had been staged. Thus it is that, with the exception of those few works which survive in a manuscript in the author's own hand, the texts of all Golden Age plays must unfortunately be regarded as to a greater or lesser extent corrupt.

Problems concerning correct attribution arise somewhat similarly, as the result of both accidental and deliberate falsification. As the text of a play became another's property almost as soon as written, the concept of a dramatist's claim to his own work was somewhat vaguer than in our day; and when a manuscript several years old was being prepared for the press, there may well have been genuine uncertainty about its true author. In a few cases the uncertainty was there from the beginning, as a number of plays were written in collaboration between two or three men, and a dramatist might also avail himself of sections of another's work. A well-known instance of this is Act III of Tirso's *La venganza de Tamar* (*Tamar's Vengeance*), which was taken over bodily by Calderón as the second act of *Los cabellos de Absalón* (*Absalom's Hair*). In time, and particularly when Lope's name and fame had become marketable, false attributions were sometimes made deliberately in the attempt to increase sales. Lope himself complains in the *Égloga a Claudio* of two parallel practices: the misappropriation of his name to boost the works of poetasters, and the publication of plays genuinely by him under the names of other dramatists. Not only the texts, therefore, but also many of the attributions of authorship which have come down to us must be regarded as suspect.

Once the spurious attributions showed signs of becoming a real abuse, the authors themselves began to take steps to counter it. In 1604 Lope prefaced his novel *El peregrino en su patria* with a list of the titles of his plays up to that date, and a greatly extended list accompanied the second edition of the same work in 1618; both lists are invaluable in establishing the *terminus ad quem* as well as the authorship of each of the plays they include. A much more substantial task was the collection and publication of their own works, which first Lope and then Tirso undertook. Lope (or his close associates) supervised the issue of no fewer than twenty volumes, or *partes*, in the years 1604–35, Tirso brought out five. The playwrights naturally suffered from the same handicap as the booksellers in so far as the original texts were usually long since lost. They, however, were in a better position than anyone else to produce an approximate and acceptable version; and at least, with one notable exception to be referred to later, the appearance of a play in one of the *partes* of these two men usually settles the question of its authorship.

Dating raises still further problems for the modern scholar. It is usually very difficult to determine with certainty the year of composition of any play. The safest guides, where they exist, are records of the sale of a manuscript to an *autor*, or independent references to first performances.[1] General indications of period may be deduced from the name of the *autor* who first presented the play, when sufficient details of his career are known; or from the proportions in which different metres are employed, when an adequate number of autograph manuscripts exists to establish a dramatist's changing norms in this respect. (This is the method used in Morley and Bruerton's invaluable *Chronology of Lope de Vega's "Comedias"*, New York, 1940.) Plays have often been dated on the basis of topical references in the text; but such references to current events or debates were sometimes inserted when a play was revived, perhaps for provincial presentation, and may therefore be an uncertain guide.

In short, the student of the Spanish *comedia* is in no better case than the modern reader of Shakespeare, or than any scholar who attempts to bring literary criticism to bear on what, at the time of its production, was considered mere ephemeral entertainment. It is probably in connection with the plays of Tirso de Molina that the problems he faces are the most tantalizing.

[1] Among the many joint publications of N. D. Shergold and J. E. Varey which are the fruits of their researches into Spanish archives, some of the most interesting are those which have a bearing on the dating of plays and *autos*, e.g. "Some early Calderón dates", in *BHS* 38 (1961) 274–86, and "Some palace performances of seventeenth-century plays", in *BHS* 40 (1963) 212–44.

7

TIRSO DE MOLINA

The fame and popularity which Lope de Vega achieved in his lifetime, and enjoys today, have not remained constant through the intervening centuries. The whole Golden Age drama declined in esteem in the eighteenth century, when with Bourbon kings on the throne French influences came to predominate; and it was only after its rediscovery by German writers in the Romantic period that it won renewed appreciation in the theatres, and became for the first time the object of literary study.

Tirso de Molina may be said to have emerged from eclipse in the year 1848, 200 years after his death, when a collection of his plays was published as volume V of *Biblioteca de autores españoles*. A number of nineteenth-century scholars contributed introductory remarks to this volume. One states that Tirso became a monk in 1620 being then about 50 years of age (which dates his birth round about 1570), another that he was born about 1585; a third surmises that "Tirso probably never experienced love, which is why he misrepresents it so frequently"; while in the opinion of a fourth, "his youth must have been very turbulent, and he must have felt in no small degree the influence of the passions".

These contradictory statements appearing on almost consecutive pages indicate how little was then actually known about Tirso's life. Unlike Lope, he committed few biographical facts to paper. Recent researches have discovered some but many still remain inaccessible, so that our picture of the man is tantalizingly indistinct. We know that "Tirso de Molina" was the literary pseudonym of the monk Fray Gabriel Téllez; and this surname "Téllez" occasioned one intriguing theory which attracted attention over a number of years, but is now generally dismissed. Early this century a young Spanish woman, Blanca de los Ríos, discovered in one of the parish registers of Madrid what she became convinced was the entry for "Tirso's" baptism. The date was 9th March 1584, and the child was described as Gabriel, son of Gracia Juliana and of an unknown father. A few words had been added in the margin and then struck out; but it was on this marginal entry that Doña Blanca's exciting theory was founded, for she claimed to decipher under the heavy obliteration the words "Tz. Girón, hijo del Dq. Osuna", that is, Téllez Girón, son of the Duke of Osuna. If she was right, and if the entry did indeed refer to the Gabriel Téllez who became Tirso de Molina, then the latter was the illegitimate son of one of the great noblemen and statesmen of his day.[1]

The evidence for this theory was at once seen to be somewhat flimsy, but it appealed by the element of romance which almost likened it to one of Tirso's own plots, and by the fact that it offered a plausible explanation, both for the general silence about Tirso's origins, and for the evident sympathy shown in his plays for bastards, younger sons, and others deprived for various reasons of the advantages of their birth. Within the last twenty years, however, it has been questioned on a number of grounds; and the strongest argument against it is offered by more recently discovered documents which show that Tirso cannot have been born as late as 1584. One gives his age in the year 1616 as 33, and in another, doubtless the more trustworthy, he himself declares in January 1638 that he is 57 years old.[2]

But even if her theory of Tirso's noble but illegitimate birth falls to the ground, Blanca de los Ríos' subsequent documentary researches into the annals of the Mercedarian Order and other archives produced useful discoveries about events in Tirso's life and the dates of some of his plays. Now, after a number of years in which others have continued and built upon her work,

---

[1] Blanca de los Ríos, *El enigma biográfico de Tirso de Molina* (Madrid, 1928).
[2] G. E. Wade, "The year of Tirso's birth", *Hispanófila* 19 (1963) 1–9.

what can be stated with certainty about the life of Tirso de Molina? He was born in Madrid, probably in 1580. Nothing has been established about his parentage, though he himself claims Catalan ancestry, and retains connections fairly late in his life with the cities of Barcelona and Tortosa. He became a novice in the Mercedarian Order in Guadalajara in 1600, and professed a year later. It is likely that he then followed a long course of study in Arts and Theology, in accordance with the normal pattern of education in this Order, but no documents confirm this. In so far as his works show any evidence of learning, it is of a superficial acquaintance with Aristotle, St. Thomas Aquinas and some modern theologians and hagiographers. In 1606, 1607 and again from 1612-15 he is in the house of his Order at Toledo. It was probably in Toledo that he first met Lope de Vega, who was making his home there at that time; and it was certainly during this period, and one may assume under Lope's stimulus, that he began to write for the theatre. A document proves the sale of three of his plays to an actor-manager in Toledo in 1612; and a number of his best plays appear to date from the years immediately following.

In 1616 Tirso sailed to the West Indian island of Santo Domingo or Hispaniola, as one of the seven monks accompanying the newly appointed Vicar-General of that province. He stayed there two years, teaching theology; but returned to Spain in time to attend the general chapter of his Order at Guadalajara in 1618. This expedition to the Caribbean was presumably the occasion of his getting to know the ports of Seville and Lisbon. After his return his presence is recorded in Toledo again, until in 1621 he begins a period of residence in Madrid which may be seen as the climax of his literary career. During the four years which follow he is in contact with many contemporary men of letters, attends literary academies, participates in poetical competitions, and adds more plays, including some of his finest, to the 300 he claimed to have written by 1621.

Suddenly this heyday comes to an end. The precise circumstances in which this happened constitute as yet another of the mysteries of Tirso's life. The agitators for moral reform were still active, and there existed an official body, the *Junta de reformación*, appointed by the Council of Castile to watch over public morality. On 6th March 1625 this *Junta* issued the following edict:

> Maestro Téllez, otherwise known as Tirso, who writes plays.—The meeting considered the scandal caused by a Mercedarian friar named Maestro Téllez, otherwise known as Tirso, by his writing of profane plays which set a bad example. And since the affair is notorious, it was agreed to petition His Majesty that the confessor should tell the nuncio to expel him hence to one of the more remote monasteries of his Order, and forbid him on pain of excommunication to write plays or any other kind of profane verse. This to be done immediately.

This edict gives incidentally a measure of Tirso's popularity in the theatres of Madrid, but it does not offer such an easy explanation of his sudden silencing as at first appears to be the case.

It is true that after 1625 Tirso seems to have resided very little in Madrid and to have written few plays. But when he was sent in 1626 to Trujillo, certainly "one of the more remote monasteries of his Order", it was perhaps with some thought of expediency but hardly of reproof or exile, since he went as *comendador*, that is, in a position of honour and responsibility. Moreover a handful of comedies do seem to date from his later years; and he went on to collect and publish many of his earlier plays, thus presumably extending their pernicious influence much further— and this with censor's approval and royal licence.[3]

It seems that the moral considerations of the edict cannot be taken altogether *au pied de la lettre* as the reason for Tirso's virtual withdrawal from the theatre. Another possible cause suggests itself. In more than one play of the 1620's he expresses, usually by means of an historical analogy, his opposition to the government of the day and his disappointment at the increasing domination of the young Philip IV by the unpopular Count-Duke of Olivares. This political outspokenness may well have

[3] A. Cioranescu, "La biographie de Tirso de Molina. Points de repère et points de vue", *BH* 64 (1962) 157–92.

been the chief reason for the edict. There is certainly a suggestion of intervention by authority in the fate of Tirso's first volume of collected plays. Dr. A. K. G. Paterson has shown that Tirso was planning such a volume as early as 1624; that it was probably printed in 1626 but never published; and that the *Primera parte* which appeared in 1627, without any censor's approval, was a pirated edition.[4] This first volume included one play, *Tanto es lo de más como lo de menos* (*Too Much is as Bad as Too Little*), which could easily be construed as being offensive to Olivares.

Even this may not have been all, for the sparse innuendoes Tirso himself makes in his later writings all contain a note of personal bitterness which suggests more than a reproof from an official body. He uses such words as trickery, fraud and envy. In addition he lets it be seen that a breach had occurred in his friendship with Lope de Vega. A number of passages show resentment against his master for some unspecified ill-treatment, and it has long been observed that Tirso, almost alone among the writers of the day, did not contribute to the *Fama póstuma* compiled in honour of Lope at his death. These facts lead one to speculate whether Lope could possibly have had any connection with the edict. If so, he may perhaps have been prompted by some professional jealousy, or by resentment of the jibes at his private life in which Tirso, like most of his literary contemporaries, certainly indulged. And it is perhaps relevant that during the early 1620's Lope was working hard to ingratiate himself with the new régime, and was probably dismayed by utterances which risked bringing the whole theatre into disfavour.[5]

However this may be, the fact is that after 1625 Tirso wrote very little more for the theatre; and that this was not a drifting away but a deliberate break. It is with a note of stubborn pride that he declares himself in a preface of 1634 to have been asleep

[4] A. K. G. Paterson, "Tirso de Molina: two biographical studies", *HR* 35 (1967) 43–68.

[5] Ruth Lee Kennedy, "A reappraisal of Tirso's relations to Lope and his theatre", *BC* 17 (1965) 23–34 and 18 (1966) 1–13.

for ten years, and heedless of all efforts to woo him back to the writing of comedies. Instead he worked on the collection and publication of a number of his plays, five volumes of which— known as the five *partes*—appeared during the period 1627–35. At the same time he rose to positions of eminence in the Mercedarian Order, including that of official historian; and in this capacity wrote an *Historia general de la Merced*, still unpublished, in which, incidentally, the political attacks are renewed. Further dissensions, this time within the Order, seem to have arisen in his later years, but they did not prevent his re-election as *Definidor provincial* of the Mercedarians of Castile, a position which he still held at the time of his death in Almazán in 1648.

While Tirso certainly experienced a change of course in the mid-1620's, thereafter devoting himself more fully to his religious profession, one cannot but be aware of a doubtless uncomfortable dichotomy throughout his active life. On the one hand is the writer of plays, a number of them serious dramas, but the majority high-spirited comedies, and very far from prudish; on the other the exemplary monk. He spent a lifetime in the cloister, where he appears to have risen steadily in importance and esteem. He did not take his priesthood frivolously or need recall to his ecclesiastical duties, as did later writers such as Mira de Amescua and Góngora. Even the *Junta de reformación* does not impugn his private life, and the critic who credited him with a turbulent and passionate youth was probably quite wrong. (One may perhaps justifiably discern in occasional plays, and in one of his later prose tales, reminiscences of a youthful unhappy love, but if so, it was one which ended in renunciation, and preceded, perhaps even precipitated, his religious profession.) There is no particular problem here for the understanding of either Tirso's personality or his plays. It was not unnatural for a dedicated monk to seek some escape in the fantasy-life of the *comedia*; his wide travels in Spain offered scope for the observation of contemporary life; and his characterization, as will be shown, is not so convincingly natural as to presuppose an intimate acquaintance with women—or even such knowledge of feminine psychology as, it was once suggested, he may have acquired in the confessional. The point is rather that Tirso appears as a very different figure from Lope de Vega, who was always deeply involved in life, and whose plays, for all their quota of literary convention, have a vital warmth making them seem all of a piece with their poet. In Tirso there is a greater divorce between literature and life. In particular, he must have lacked Lope's close contact with the theatrical world, and his plays must on occasion have suffered from this, in performance if not in composition. He himself speaks with feeling of the initial débâcle of his excellent comedy *Don Gil de las calzas verdes*, because the role of the heroine was unsuitably allotted to a fat and ageing actress.

If Tirso did in some of his serious drama reach the heights, with most of his many comedies he careers across plains of wearisome drabness. Few of them lack verve, and taken singly they probably all fulfil their function of light entertainment; but when read or seen in quick succession their sameness becomes boring, and their dramatic resources appear increasingly banal.

Their main *raison d'être* is the plot, which almost invariably turns on rivalries in love. Jealousy is the natural concomitant of love, and seems to be thought of as necessary for the testing and refinement of true feeling:

> No hay criatura sin amor
> ni amor sin celos perfeto.
> (*La gallega Mari-Hernández*, Act II)

("There is no creature without love, nor perfect love without jealousy.")

Indeed the main argument against the Unity of Time put forward in Tirso's enthusiastic defence of Lope's *comedia*, is that one day is not long enough for all the obligatory vicissitudes of a love-affair:

"What chance has a gallant to conceive jealousy, proclaim despair, console himself with hope, and display the other emotions and fluctuations without which love is of no esteem?"

(*Cigarrales de Toledo*)

Of the various emotions portrayed by Tirso jealousy is perhaps the one which rings truest, and a fine passage in his late prose work *Deleytar aprovechando* (*Pleasure with Profit*), beginning: "No one who has not experienced it can understand the rabid frenzy of this diabolical passion", leads one to imagine that he was not a stranger to it himself.

For the most part in his comedies, however, it remains a dramatic device, an element in a formula. This commonly presents a group of lovers, most of whom have become infatuated at first sight, and amongst whom a tangle of attractions and pursuits—one cannot call them relationships—develops. A plot based upon two pairs of lovers is of course a commonplace, but in Tirso the number is more frequently five, usually three men and two women. This gives greater scope for rivalry, but also results in endings which deny the satisfaction of a neat dénouement. One lover is left alone at the end or is married off, with every appearance of content, to a lay-figure introduced simply for that purpose; or a woman will sweetly accept the hand of a suitor to whom she has shown antipathy throughout the play. An outcome of this kind is no real dénouement, but a mere cutting of the knot when the appropriate number of pages has been filled; and the author clearly has no real interest in his characters as people outside the limits of his play, or he would not condemn them to marriages which in human terms have not the slightest hope of success.

The complications of such intrigues with their two or more separate strands need skilful handling. Tirso sometimes contrives them very well, as in *Don Gil de las calzas verdes* (*Don Gil of the Green Breeches*), which builds up to an hilarious climax in which there are four characters on the stage at once all wearing green breeches and all pretending to be Don Gil, a figure who in fact does not exist. At other times the intricacies of pretence, impersonation, disguise and switched affection become too much to follow; and the plot leans too heavily on flimsy pretexts and downright lies for which there is no proper motivation. The characters exasperate us with their deceits, and we almost want to shout at them to tell each other the truth; but then of course there would be no play.

On first reading Tirso one is impressed by his use of certain dramatic devices which undoubtedly constitute good theatre; but when they are pressed into service in play after play and harden into clichés, they become tedious. For instance, in the early *Cómo han de ser los amigos* (*True Friendship*) the hero is temporarily driven mad by the conflict between love and loyalty to a friend, and his madness is convincingly and movingly portrayed; but when in a second, a third and yet a fourth play one meets characters suffering, or feigning, madness for love, appreciation is more grudging. Analogous resources are the simulated love scene, in which a gallant gets the unsuspecting object of his affections to play at love-making with him; the dream in which a woman reveals her feelings while talking in her sleep (or, of course, pretending to be asleep); the disguise which deceives even a close relative; and conversely, the mysterious affinity felt between characters who are closely related although they do not know it—an affinity sometimes mistaken for love by a couple who are in fact brother and sister. Among such characters whose true identity is only revealed in the final scenes are many bastards and unacknowledged heirs, who feel a similarly mysterious urge to improve their social status. They are the "nameless sons" as Blanca de los Ríos calls them, whose recurrence led her to believe that Tirso's own family background was mirrored in theirs. As he is so content to repeat other devices and situations, however, it is perhaps unwise to attach much special significance to this one. Other stock figures are the handsome and upright Spaniard who stands out among the men of a foreign country; the Portuguese so quick to lose his heart that *seboso*, "tallow-like" or "easily melted", comes to be a synonym for "Portuguese"; and the near-idiot rustic *gracioso*, an innocent in love but devoted to his donkey, who uses the conventional *sayagués* dialect and whose humour is often outspokenly scatological.

To complete the case against Tirso's comedies, it must be

acknowledged that he is inferior to his master Lope in dramatic technique. Where he has no precise source material to limit his inventiveness his plays are overburdened with material; and he lacks Lope's skill in deft, unobtrusive exposition. The result is too many long, undramatic narrative speeches, in one or two of which he even draws attention, like Calderón, to his own clumsiness:

> La historia del malogrado
> Duque vienes a contarme,
> como si yo la ignorara.
>
> (*La gallega Mari-Hernández*, Act I)

("Here you come telling me the story of the unhappy Duke as if I didn't know it".)

> ¿ Qué me dais cuenta tan larga
> si estuve presente a todo?
>
> (*Marta la piadosa*, Act III)

("Why do you give me such a long account, when I was there all the time?")

It may well be asked at this point if Tirso's comedies merit any consideration at all. In many of these plays there is no trace of inspiration, of any inner force or inevitability compelling them into existence. Their author remains firmly outside, devising his plots cerebrally, dipping into his bag of tricks for characters and intrigues, and manipulating the whole like a puppet-master. To a much greater extent than Lope, Tirso uses proverbs or common sayings for his titles; and so often one feels that this mere external form of words, rather than an inherently dramatic situation, still less any profound apprehension of human nature, has been the starting-point of the play. When Shakespeare takes a similar plot, as in *Twelfth Night* or *Two Gentlemen of Verona*, he cannot help, for all its conventions and improbabilities, giving it something of the feel of real life, by showing the pathos of Viola, bereaved of a brother and emotionally frustrated by her disguise; or of Julia, compelled to overhear the declarations which her unfaithful Proteus makes to another woman. Tirso seldom believes in his situations sufficiently to see pathos in them; and he lacked that experience of the maturing of love-affairs which enabled Lope to be such an exquisite poet of tenderness.

What he does give to the best of his comedies—and it is now high time to credit him with the very real contribution which he did make to the development of this genre—is a new vitality and heightening of interest in the female characters. In the early *El vergonzoso en palacio*,[6] the two women among the five lovers are sisters. This is a pattern which is repeated fairly often; and it is in such pairs of sisters, clearly differentiated and frequently acting as foils for each other, that we first become conscious of characters who are more than mere counters in a game. The shy man who gives its title to this play is one of the "nameless sons", finally revealed to be of royal birth, who meanwhile takes the post of secretary to a duke's daughter, Magdalena. It is difficult to believe in Mireno, whose aspirations to what he senses to be his true social status hardly accord with his bashfulness in making advances to a lady of supposedly superior rank. But Magdalena's repeated attempts to get him to do so, in which she never exceeds the limits of feminine charm, make delightful theatre. She contrasts effectively with her younger sister Serafina, who is averse to men and marriage and whose only love is the stage, until she loses her heart to a portrait of herself, painted unbeknown to her when she was acting in male costume. Lucía of *Marta la piadosa* (*Pious Martha*) is little more than a cipher, but thereby throws into greater relief her resourceful sister, who feigns a religious vocation in order to get rid of two unwanted suitors. (This was an expedient adopted also by Inés of *El Caballero de Olmedo*, and it is enlightening to contrast the behaviour of these two heroines: Inés, stimulated by love and Fabia's spell into an excitement and daring in which her sister scarcely recognizes her, and yet sweetly feminine, a still largely passive focus for the emotions which provoke the action; and Marta, scheming, comic, a "character" in every sense, and completely dominant. In other words, the very titles of these two plays indicate where the main interest lies in each case, and underline the importance of the Tirsian heroine.)

---

[6] Edited by Américo Castro (Madrid, Clásicos castellanos, 1910, revised 1922 and 1958).

It is perhaps *Por el sótano y el torno* (*Throug h Basement and Hatch*),[7] a delightful play on every count, that presents the most fascinating pair of sisters. Bernarda, a young widow, is left with the responsibility which usually devolves on the male head of the family for guarding the honour of her flighty sister Jusepa. She takes it very seriously; and there is a lively tension between her exasperated insistence on decorum and Jusepa's brazenness, resolved only by one of the usual mystification scenes and the appearance of a suitor for Bernarda herself.

It was brazenness and sexual licence that the nineteenth-century critics remarked chiefly in Tirso's female protagonists. In view of the importance of honour for the society which the *comedia* portrays, it is surprising how many Tirsian heroines admit without shame to having surrendered their virtue on a mere promise of marriage, and disguise themselves as men to go out in search of a now reluctant lover. It might perhaps be pointed out in mitigation of their conduct that the clandestine marriage, which recognized the validity of vows exchanged in secret, had only relatively recently been forbidden by the Council of Trent. In any case, the situation is almost invariably regularized at the end of the play. A modern reader will doubtless see greater immorality in the outrageous predatoriness of these women, the lies and deceits they employ, the loveless and unpromising marriages they strive for, and in the romantic veneer which turns into heroes and heroines men and women of equal moral mediocrity. But all this is to take these *divertimenti* far too seriously. Tirso is seldom deeply concerned with honour as a dramatic motive, and in perhaps only one play, *El celoso prudente* (*Jealous but Wise*), where the hero narrowly escapes killing his wife on unfounded suspicions, can the action be said to arise directly out of the code of *pundonor*. For the comedies it still remains true that the plot is the main thing, and where this is skilfully and entertainingly contrived, as for example in *Don Gil de las calzas verdes*, it scarcely matters that the heroine is a hussy.

What chiefly remains in the memory about these girls is not

[7] Edited by A. Zamora Vicente (Buenos Aires, 1949).

their immodesty but their charm. They are dazzling, vivacious, irrepressible. One of the most outrageous of all is the Galician peasant Mari-Hernández, who comes upon a handsome young nobleman asleep under a tree. From that moment he has no chance against her. It makes no difference that he is already betrothed to a lady at the Portuguese court. Before ever he awakes she is determined to win him, and win him she does, partly through her own attractions, but also by following him to court and declaring to the King, untruthfully, that he has seduced her. Her behaviour is monstrous, and all our sympathy should by rights be with the discarded Portuguese lady, casually paired off at the end with someone she does not love. And yet Mari-Hernández is likeable, partly for her very lack of inhibition, and shares with many another of Tirso's heroines a sparkle and a vitality which it was one of his greatest merits to convey.

Mari-Hernández is ennobled by the King to make her a more acceptable wife for Don Álvaro; and so, technically at least, the social conventions are not violated by a marriage cutting across class distinctions. But Tirso does not always bother about this safeguard, and the unions between noblemen and peasant girls which take place in his theatre do not conform with the general acceptance in the Golden Age of the existing class structure. It is very rare in any play by Lope for a man of rank to marry an inferior, unless he has raped her and is being forced by the king to restore her honour before paying for his crime on the scaffold; while in the romantic fiction of the period, which is quite syco-phantic in its esteem for blue blood, neither parent of an illegiti-mate child suffers very much opprobrium, but a landed gentleman who marries beneath him brings disgrace on his whole domain. Tirso, however, so frequently writes of the power of love to unite "seda con sayal" (silk with sackcloth) and "cayados con cetros" (crooks with sceptres), that this very departure from convention hardens into a personal cliché (it does not seem to be put forward with any ring of conviction which would make it more than this); and the occurrence of these phrases in any play of doubtful authorship is a strong argument for ascribing it to Tirso.

There are very occasional hints of departure from conventional values—hints which suggest that Tirso had it in him to create real character in the modern sense, had he possessed the courage to stand out against the conformist tendencies of his age, or even the vision to see that such a thing was possible. Doña Jerónima of *El amor médico* (*Love the Doctor*),[8] for instance, astonishes her maid by not sharing in the universal homage to Eros, and replies that she would find it irksome to be restricted to the narrow world of the needle and the embroidery frame:

> El matrimonio es Argel,
> la mujer cautiva en él;
> las artes son liberales
> porque hacen que libre viva
> a quien en ellas se emplea.
> ¿ Cómo querrás tú que sea
> a un tiempo libre y cautiva?   (Act I)

("Marriage is an Algiers in which woman is held prisoner; the arts are called liberal, because they enable those who practise them to live in freedom. How do you expect me to be free and captive at the same time?")

If Queen Isabella could learn Latin, why can't she? But it is really medicine which she wants to study; and as she extols the merits of the able and dedicated doctor, surprised as we are by this outburst of feminism two and a half centuries before its time, we feel that she has a sincere vocation. Tirso seems to have glimpsed a higher motive than the sex and social endeavour which prompt so much *comedia* action, and to be on the point of creating a real character, the intellectual woman, out of whose inevitable tensions fully satisfying drama might have been made. But of course we are disappointed; it is no good looking for Ibsen in Tirso. Jerónima soon experiences the usual infatuation, and is then all too ready for the slavery of marriage. Even after this débâcle she remains an individual. When the time comes, as it inevitably does, for her to don male disguise and follow the

[8] Edited by A. Zamora Vicente and María Josefa Canellada de Zamora (Madrid, Clásicos castellanos, 1947).

elusive object of her desires to Portugal, she is able to play a welcome variation on the commonplace theme by pretending to be a doctor, and much of the humour of the play derives from the smattering of medical knowledge which she brings out, with all the usual Tirsian wit and attractiveness. But her full potential remains unrealized.

She can be paralleled by a male protagonist, Rogerio of *El melancólico*. The title here leads us to expect a character of depth, possibly a pre-romantic, certainly an outsider from the run of extrovert and materialist gallants. At first we think we have found him. Rogerio, brought up in the country, is revealed unusually early in the play as the illegitimate son of the Duke of Brittany, now summoned to court to assume his position as his father's heir. He protests that he values more the *aurea mediocritas* of his own studious and solitary life, and prides himself on his own achievements:

> Yo con la industria mía,
> lo que no a la fortuna, le debía
> a la naturaleza,
> ambicioso de fama y de grandeza
> no heredada, adquirida
> con noble ingenio y estudiosa vida,
> que ilustra más la personal nobleza.   (Act II)

("I, by my industry, could compensate with my own nature for what fortune had denied me; ambitious for fame and for greatness not inherited, but acquired through a noble intellect and studious life which enhances personal nobility.")

Here again is something to make us sit up. Intellectual eminence is not a quality usually exalted by the *comedia*. This passage has a forcefulness which almost seems to lift it into the realm of conviction: is Tirso perhaps dramatizing something of his own story here? Then the bubble is pricked. Rogerio explains in a soliloquy that his reluctance in fact springs only from his love for a village girl, whom he cannot bear to leave. Otherwise power and riches would have been his heart's desire! Thereafter the plot follows a tediously familiar course, with an intrigue involving five lovers leading to a *deus ex machina* solution in which his beloved too is revealed to be of noble birth. One cannot help thinking how much finer this play could have been, if Tirso had allowed a real conflict of values to develop; but at least he did show that he had the power to portray abnormal but credible characters of a kind new to the *comedia*.

The views of critics on characterization in Tirso's theatre have fluctuated during the last hundred years. The nineteenth century limited its attention mainly to the heroines of the comedies, and saw them as too bad to be true. A later generation, with Doña Blanca as its chief representative, admired their quicksilver vivacity, and praised Tirso as a great creator of lifelike figures. Today, few people would see much verisimilitude —or even look for it. His comedies are for the most part unashamedly escapist, and his figures, when they are not mere pawns in the plot, are drawn considerably larger than life. An illusion of life is given, as in the *comedia* as a whole, by much of the background material and the dialogue. The language, particularly that of aristocratic characters, is often conventionally *culto*, unredeemed by very much telling imagery or poetic intensity. But in the livelier scenes it is excellent: colloquial, racy and pointed. Much of *Marta* and almost the whole of *Por el sótano*, for instance (both of them plays in which the action seldom becomes too extravagant), are written in short, fast-moving speeches, and in the authentic tones of Tirso's Madrid. Above all when one of the dynamic heroines is on stage—Tomasa of *La huerta de Juan Fernández* (*The Orchard of Juan Fernández*), for example, as she conducts a flirtation with the *gracioso*— there is electricity in the air, and the dialogue crackles and sparkles.

There is unevenness too in the use of background realism, between the tiresome reiteration of conventional satire on, for example, the proliferation of coaches or of *chapines*, the thick-soled shoes worn by smart women to add to their height—often dragged with wild inappropriateness into non-Spanish and non-contemporary settings, like the topical references of a pantomime, for the sake of a cheap laugh; and other, genuinely evocative scenes, in which the seventeenth century really comes alive.

Such are the numerous episodes of arrival at an inn, with discussion of its amenities and its menu—scenes Tirso must have often witnessed in his travels through Spain; or the settling-in of Bernarda and Jusepa at their new house in Madrid. Homely practical touches often help to secure acceptance of the improbable plots: the impish Sancha of *Averígüelo Vargas* (*Let Vargas Ascertain*) excuses her tears of jealous rage by saying that she has been peeling onions; Mari-Ramírez, the landlady and go-between of *Por el sótano*, comes to Bernarda's house ostensibly to sell wimples, and assures her that although the linen has gone a little yellow it will come white in the wash.

Tirso, like Lope, can convey the flavour of both town and country life. One is largely reconciled to the enormities of Mari-Hernández by the realistic picture of life in her Galician village, with a bear hunt and a birthday party, charcoal-burning and sausage-making, and a discussion of the wage which the Portuguese nobleman is to receive when for the peasant girl's sake he agrees to become a day-labourer; and there is probably no play of the whole period which re-creates Madrid better than *Por el sótano y el torno*. It is not just a question of the architectural details of the houses in the Calle de Carretas; the itinerant vendors; the rich sons of the landed gentry returning to their favourite lodgings in town. It is the whole slightly febrile, slightly unhealthy atmosphere of an exciting capital, where morals are slacker than in Bernarda's native Guadalajara, and where it seems almost a matter of chance whether one loses one's reputation or wins a husband with 6000 ducats a year. Bernarda is quickly aware of the mood of the town and its influence:

> ¡ Qué presto a mi hermana influye
> Madrid su sacudimiento!
> Es contagioso hasta el viento
> aquí: todo lo destruye.   (Act III)

("How quickly Madrid has infected my sister with its waywardness! Even the wind is contagious here; it destroys everything.")

If after this long survey the attempt is made to single out what is most significant in Tirso's comedies, leaving on one side so much that is mere hack entertainment, their essence will probably be found in this hint of the hectic, of the overcharged; whether this manifests itself in mercurial heroines, in effervescent dialogue, or in the heady atmosphere of a licentious city. The keynote of Lope's most typical plays is one of "rightness", of harmony temporarily disturbed, but restored in the final scenes. With Tirso it is usually inappropriate to look past the end of the play at all, and there is seldom any prospect of a lasting serenity born of well-blended elements. The day of harmony and rightness seems to be over, and the move has begun towards a theatre of imbalance.

8

TIRSO DE MOLINA (*continued*)

IT WAS stated in an earlier chapter that the plays of Lope do not submit easily to classification. Those of Tirso fall much more readily into different categories, and all that has been said so far concerns no more than one facet of his work, albeit the most extensive. Nevertheless there are similarities between the comedies on the one hand and the more serious historical and religious dramas on the other, over and above those essential features which all *comedias* share. Especially is this true in the case of the *comedias de santos*. These plays seem very often to have been prompted by provincial celebrations in honour of some local saint, or the canonization or beatification of more widely known figures; and they can often be dated accordingly. In many cases, however, the information furnished by legend and history about the saintly hero or heroine was either not sufficiently dramatic in nature, or else quite inadequate to fill three acts. Tirso would then eke it out with a second plot using the familiar conventional material, and the result is often something very close to a typical comedy: an entertainment for a holiday rather than a holy day. In default of truly dramatic action the *comedias de santos* lean heavily on the miraculous. In so far as they are religious plays at all, it is the religion of popular devotion.

Tirso was criticized during his lifetime for his cavalier treatment of historical fact. He gives the incident a fictional setting in the first *Cigarral*, stating that after the performance of *El vergonzoso en palacio* in the Toledan country house, an "historical pedant" among the company objected to the linking of imaginary adventures with the names of actual members of the Portuguese royal family; in answer to which Tirso indignantly claims "the licence of Apollo . . . to construct on foundations of real people, edifices of the imagination". It is true that *El vergonzoso en palacio*, *Averígüelo Vargas* and other comedies do make use of historical figures in this way (and it may be noted here how very often Tirso turns to Portugal for both characters and settings). Among the more serious dramas too are some which, like the *comedias de santos*, start from a briefly recorded historical incident, but expand it into a play which is almost entirely fictional. Such is *Escarmientos para el cuerdo* (*Warnings for the Wise*), which ekes out with love intrigues and heavy moralizing the tale of a shipwrecked family taken from Camoen's *Lusiads*.

But it is only with plays of which the main substance is recorded fact that one can fairly assess Tirso as an historical dramatist. Here, as in the comedies, he is uneven. Some years after the edict of 1625 he wrote a trilogy[1] about the Pizarro family of *conquistadores*, apparently in support of the claim to a title which a later Pizarro was making round about 1626–9. Whether he felt himself inhibited by the need to present his heroes in the best light, and cover up their more doubtful exploits in the New World, it is difficult to say, but he certainly fails to draw very much drama out of this exciting chapter of Spanish history. His treatment of it is more epic than dramatic, with an unusual number of long and boring narrative speeches, which are often mere versified chunks of his source material. There can be here no question of hispanifying the setting, yet despite his own two-year sojourn in the West Indies he makes no serious attempt to re-create the exotic atmosphere of Panama or Peru. His idea of doing so is to call in a tribe of Amazons to supplement the meagre action of the second play with prophecies and some typical feminine jealousy.

There is something of the Amazon too about Antona García, the eponymous heroine of another largely historical play set in

[1] *Todo es dar en una cosa, Amazonas en las Indias* and *La lealtad contra la envidia*.

the same period, the late fifteenth century, but this time firmly rooted in Spanish soil. Like Lope's *Fuenteovejuna*, *Antona García*[2] deals with events in a small community during the War of La Beltraneja, by means of which Queen Isabella established herself on the Castilian throne. But whereas in Lope's play the war is there as a background, mainly to turn sympathy away from the lecherous overlord who was fighting against the Catholic Sovereigns, here the exploits of Antona in the town of Toro constitute an episode in the war itself. She it is who leads the townspeople in revolt against their overlord, who is supporting Isabella's rival; and so there occurs an instance of that typical social pattern of Golden Age drama, of monarchy and people versus the nobility, which reflects the actual decline in the power of the nobles during the reign of the Catholic Monarchs. Here, significantly since the author is Tirso, each of the three main characters representing the three estates is a woman: the Queen, Antona, and María Sarmiento, the wife of the local lord, who dominates her husband and all the men in her faction. The historical Antona has of course been subjected to a distortion which turns her into a figure very much larger than life, a prodigy both of beauty and of strength, who carries on a typically spirited and class-disregarding flirtation with a Portuguese count. But the admixture of conventional material is here much less than is often the case, and any tastelessness is amply redeemed by the tremendous mob scene in which Antona confronts María and wins over her timid fellow peasants to the Castilian cause. Here Tirso *has* discerned a truly dramatic conflict in the pages of the history book, and brought it to life.

His best-known historical play also concerns the exploits of a woman; indeed, the fact is underlined in its title, *La prudencia en la mujer* (*Prudence in Woman*).[3] This is one of the plays which conforms least to the typical *comedia* pattern, and also which shows fewest of those characteristics which we have seen to be common in Tirso's drama. One would be tempted to question

[2] Edited by Margaret Wilson (Manchester, 1957).
[3] Edited by Alice H. Bushee and Lorna L. Stafford (Mexico, 1948).

his authorship of it, had he himself not published it in his *Tercera parte*. He adheres very closely to his source material in a medieval chronicle and Mariana's *History of Spain*, and does not avail himself of "the licence of Apollo" even to introduce a love interest. Nor is there any true *gracioso*; two slightly comic servants fade out at the end of Act I, and these actors would doubtless double the parts of the slightly comic rustics of Act III. There is, for Tirso, a remarkable paucity of material. The sub-plot is resolved by the end of Act I, and thereafter the action is unilinear. It is none the worse for this, but it can also be criticized for its excessively episodic nature, consisting as it does of the repeated contests of wit and will between the young widowed queen, María de Molina, and the princes who are trying to usurp the throne from Fernando, her small son. María herself really *is* the play. Whether she can justly be seen as an example of prudence is questionable. Her repeated forgiveness of Don Juan's successive disloyalties might be thought the reverse of prudent, and she usually seems to get the better of him as much by a knack of popping up unexpectedly at the critical moment as by any shrewdness of judgement. It is something on a grander scale which stands out: she is a noble and heroic character, partly because of the very *im*prudence with which she forgives her enemies and continues to expect the best of them. She shares with Antona García and Queen Isabella the warlike courage which wins for all three the appellation of Semiramis, but she is no freak of nature: her maternal love and her devotion to her husband's memory keep her truly a woman.

In language as in sentiment this is an heroic play, with many classical allusions, and much imagery and resounding rhetoric. This intensity of expression and a concentration upon a single theme were not fortuitous, for it has been amply shown that Tirso wrote *La prudencia* with the contemporary political situation in mind, and that his play is perhaps above all a tract for the times.[4] In 1621 Philip IV succeeded to the Spanish throne at the

[4] See Ruth Lee Kennedy, "*La prudencia en la mujer* and the ambient that brought it forth", *PMLA* 63 (1948) 1131–90.

age of 16, and it was not difficult for the Count-Duke of Olivares to dominate him and gather power into his own hands. More particularly in Act III of the play, where María's son, now a young man, comes under the sway of the wicked prince, is the contemporary relevance apparent. There are long passages of advice to a young monarch; insistent warnings against favourites, and the references to Fernando as the fourth of that name, point the analogy with the fourth Philip. For the first time in the *comedia* there appears an awareness of the plight of Spain, and a seriousness of purpose which far transcends the mainly idle social satire of the comedies.

Among Tirso's serious dramas are a handful based on Bible stories.[5] These exemplify not only something of that same quality of political parable found in *La prudencia*, but also the power revealed in the best of the histories to discern the potential drama in a given source. For three of them that source is the Old Testament; and they capture much of its characteristic flavour. They are not works of piety, but records of human conflict occurring at critical moments in the development of a race; and as such are far closer in temper, as also in achievement, to the better historical plays than to the insipid *comedias de santos*. These three are *La mejor espigadera* (*The Best Gleaner*), *La mujer que manda en casa* (*The Wife who Rules the Roost*), and *La venganza de Tamar* (*Tamar's Vengeance*).

The mannerisms of the comedies are still present; yet in these plays, with the biblical text to control and guide him, Tirso achieves some of his finest characterization. Women play the dominant roles in two of them. Ruth's metamorphosis from *comedia* princess to humble gleaner is unconvincing, but Naomi is the stable pivot of the play, unshakeably upright and constant, the incarnation of righteous and suffering Judah. Jezabel, on the other hand, dominating her husband, killing Naboth

---

[5] See J. C. J. Metford, "Tirso de Molina's Old Testament plays", *BHS* 27 (1950) 149–63.

whom she has failed to seduce, and fostering the lascivious worship of Baal, is the embodiment both of feminine wickedness and of false religion. In *La mujer que manda en casa* Tirso has tightened up the biblical story to good dramatic effect, by linking Naboth more closely with Jezabel than with the unimposing Ahab, whose coveting of the vineyard becomes merely a faint parallel to Jezabel's coveting of Naboth's body; and by giving Naboth a wife, Rachel, who in her sensitive, submissive womanhood serves as a foil to the unnatural queen—until the murder of her husband turns her into a very tigress, and makes her the chief instigator of Jezabel's death.

Tamar in the tragedy which bears her name is necessarily a passive figure, both as the victim of Amnon's incest and the cause of Absalom's revenge. Yet even she is well rounded out from the flat biblical sketch. In II Samuel 13 she disappears after the outrage; in Act III of Tirso's play she is present at the sheepshearing, all her former warmth and gaiety turned into cynicism and sour wit. But it is in Amnon that the most masterly characterization is seen. Behind the incestuous desire Tirso divines a tortured, neurotic temperament. Unlike his brothers and companions, the Amnon of the opening scenes takes no pleasure either in women or in war; when they go off to make love, or to gamble, he reads poetry. This absence of natural inclinations leaves him dangerously open to the unnatural passion which comes to possess him. "I am altogether strange", he declares of himself. Amnon is the supreme example of the misfit, the outsider, of whom we saw the germ in *El melancólico*; and here, with scriptural authority behind him, Tirso is bold enough to develop the character through to its full tragic fruition. The biblical plays as a whole prove what in the case of the comedies was only adumbrated: Tirso's power to write great drama when he chooses to portray humanity, rather than to contrive situations.

Their psychological realism is matched by a far greater concern for atmosphere and setting than is usual in the *comedia*. These are hispanified only in the case of isolated scenes of rural activity;

for example, the reaping in *La mejor espigadera* and the sheep-shearing in *La venganza de Tamar*, with their Castilian popular songs. Otherwise background is integrated to a remarkable degree with character and action. Famine-stricken Israel contrasts starkly with the lushness of Moab, where Ruth is first seen

> en el teatro verde
> desta alameda umbrosa,
> y al nacimiento desta fuente fría   (Act I)

"in the green theatre of this shady poplar grove, and at the source of this cool stream"),

and where Timbreo woos her in a speech suggestively full of the sensuous languor of nature. This hint of decadence contrasts in turn with the healthier Israel of Act III, where the land bears corn, and Ruth and Boaz pledge their love against a background of honest toil. A garden with birds, fountains and the clinging jasmine and briony is similarly the setting for Jezabel's lascivious desires, while Elijah is seen in the desert; and we are almost able to sense the hot, heady atmosphere of a summer night in the palace grounds which stimulates the perverted passion of Amnon.

In both *La mejor espigadera* and *La mujer que manda en casa* drought and famine bring hunger to the poor, while the rich still feast; and it has been plausibly suggested by Professor J. C. J. Metford[6] that this is an intentional reference to contemporary mismanagement and neglect of the public good by those in power, that is to say Philip IV and Olivares. The note of bitter criticism sounds clearest of all in the only play to be based squarely on New Testament material, *Tanto es lo de más como lo de menos*; and here Metford makes a good case for identifying the loathsome Nineucio, who attracts most of that criticism, with Olivares. The play is a curiosity. Rather than events recorded in the Scriptures, it takes its material from two parables, those of Dives and Lazarus, and the Prodigal Son. Apart from the fact that both

---

[6] J. C. J. Metford, "Tirso de Molina and the Conde-Duque de Olivares", *BHS* 36 (1959) 15–27.

Lazarus and the Prodigal, here called Liberio, are required to be reduced to poverty, with some consequent repetition, the parables are cleverly interwoven to give a cohesive plot. But the use of this particular moralizing material results in a much stronger didactic note than has hitherto been heard in Tirso's theatre. Liberio, the libertine, is significantly named; so is the heroine Felicia. She is sought after by all the main characters in the play; but Nineucio (Dives) finds that his wealth cannot retain her, and Liberio only wins her as an additional reward, after his repentance, when he has ceased to pursue her. In other words this is partially at least allegorical drama. Some forceful natural dialogue and a lively gambling scene also contribute a quota of realism; but the play must be seen as belonging to another tradition as well as that of the *comedia:* namely that of the allegorical *auto*, whose beginnings were sketched in Chapter 1, and the full development of which I shall attempt to survey at a later stage.

Tirso's biblical plays are less well known, even by students of Spanish literature, than they deserve to be. His firm reputation as a writer of comedies has tended to obscure more serious achievements; and he is everywhere given to lengthy lapses into the banal. But the author of *La mujer que manda en casa* and *La venganza de Tamar* certainly deserves a place among the great dramatists of Europe. That place is even more assured if he is credited with *El condenado por desconfiado* (*The Man Damned for Lack of Faith*) and *El Burlador de Sevilla* (*The Trickster of Seville*). Unfortunately the authorship of both these towering works has been, and to some slight extent still is, in doubt.

Our text of *El Burlador* dates from 1630 when it was published under Tirso's name in a volume of plays by various authors. But there is also an early version of the play with the title *¡ Tan largo me lo fiáis!* (*What Long Credit You Give Me!*); and both texts seem to be imperfect versions of a single original play, now presumably lost. Whether Tirso was the author of this original or merely of the reworking which we know as *El Burlador de*

Sevilla, it is impossible to tell.[7] *El condenado* was first published by Tirso in the *Segunda parte* of his collected works in 1635, and this ought to be sufficient proof of its authorship. But that volume carries with it a most tantalizing problem. In the preliminaries, after a jibe at men of letters who do not acknowledge the help they receive, he declares that he does not wish to be classed among them, and so dedicates his volume to the Guild of Booksellers of Madrid, in return for their kindness in rescuing his works from oblivion, and their generosity in bearing the printing costs; and he continues enigmatically: "Of these twelve plays I dedicate four, which are mine, in my own name, and in that of the owners of the other eight (which being children of such illustrious fathers, by I know not what misfortune of theirs have come to be laid at my doors) those which remain."

The cryptic nature of this statement seems almost perverse. It would surely have been so easy for Tirso to name the other "illustrious fathers" and their plays, or at the very least to declare which four were his own; and the fact that he does not do so suggests once again innuendoes and wounded pride. However, recent researches have established that three of the plays are indeed by other dramatists, and the authorship of the remaining nine, including *El condenado*, must therefore remain in doubt. The cause of the uncertainty probably lies somewhere in the muddled procedure of play writing and publication which has been described. Wrong attributions, by accident or design, corrupt texts, collaboration, reworkings—any or all of these may have had their part to play.

Even so the balance of critical opinion has always favoured Tirso's authorship of *El condenado*, and Dr. A. K. G. Paterson has recently discovered a piece of evidence which reinforces this view. This is a seventeenth-century jotting of the titles of twelve plays, headed "Primera de Tirso". It does not correspond

[7] On the chronological relationship of the two texts see Albert E. Sloman, "The two versions of *El Burlador de Sevilla*", *BHS* 42 (1965) 18–33. On the superiority of *El Burlador* to *Tan largo* see Daniel Rogers, "Fearful symmetry: the ending of *El Burlador de Sevilla* ", *BHS* 41 (1964) 141–59.

exactly with the contents of the *Primera parte* published in 1627, and probably represents those of the suppressed volume of 1626. The last title in the list is *El condenado por desconfiado*.[8]

The strong probability is that Tirso wrote both *El condenado* and *El Burlador*. Both plays were published under his name and no other convincing claim to the authorship of either has yet been made. Moreover, they certainly have enough in common, and are sufficiently unlike any other plays examined so far, to suggest that they are from the same pen.

El Burlador de Sevilla[9] is the work in which Don Juan makes his first appearance in European literature. All subsequent versions of the myth are indebted to this play, the original story of the libertine who seduces a number of women and kills the father of one of them; then, passing by the statue set up in honour of the dead man, tauntingly invites it to dinner; and finally accepts a return invitation and is carried off in the statue's grasp to hell. The main character of *El condenado* also goes to hell. He is the hermit Paulo, who for ten years has lived a life of austerity and religious devotion in the countryside outside Naples. He wants to be reassured that his mortifications have earned him a place in heaven, and prays to God for a sign that this is so. But in so doing he forgets that man can never be saved by his own works, but only by the mercy of God. To think otherwise is to commit the grave sin of spiritual pride. This lapse provides an opportunity for the Devil, who obliges with the revelation that Paulo had sought, a revelation whose authenticity he never doubts since he believes it to be from God. The Devil tells him that his end is to be the same as that of one Enrico, a Neapolitan whom he will find if he goes down into the city. Enrico proves to be a bragging villain, guilty of innumerable crimes of violence. Paulo, still convinced that salvation must depend upon good works, can only conclude that both of them

[8] A. K. G. Paterson, "Tirso de Molina: two bibliographical studies", *HR* 35 (1967) 43–68.

[9] Edited by Américo Castro (Madrid, Clásicos castellanos, 1910, revised 1922 and 1958).

are to be damned, and in despair abandons his holy life and himself becomes a murderous brigand. But he can find no pleasure in crime, or share any of Enrico's bravado. He is still tortured by the fear of damnation; and when his men succeed in capturing Enrico, he implores him to confess before being put to death, so that in going to heaven he will safeguard the way there for Paulo. Enrico refuses, though he assures the anguished and uncomprehending Paulo that he confidently expects to be saved, since despite his wickedness he has never lost his belief in the redeeming mercy of God. But Paulo never learns the lesson; and when Enrico finally dies shriven and is borne aloft by angels, Paulo also dies, with pathetic words of hope on his lips for the first time. But it is a false hope, still resting as it does on a diabolical prophecy and not on faith in the only power which could have saved him. A final vision of Paulo lapped by tongues of flame reiterates the lesson of the play.

This is the most straightforward didacticism so far encountered; and what the play teaches is not morals but dogma. Its essence is the question of St. Paul's jailer, "What must I do to be saved?"; its starting-point the whole Reformation and Counter-Reformation inquiry into the basis of salvation, the roles of faith and works, of predestination and grace. The answer given by this play is that of St. Paul to the jailer. Faith is what matters. Enrico, despite a life of wickedness, can be saved, but Paulo is damned because he does not trust in God.

But has Don Juan's disappearance in flames anything to do with eschatological dogma? Whatever later authors may have made of the story, there is no doubt at all that *El Burlador de Sevilla* is primarily a theological drama. The title of the earlier version, *¡ Tan largo me lo fiáis!*, underlines this fact. These words are Don Juan's repeated rejoinder to every warning that he will one day be called to account. He is not an unbeliever, like Molière's Don Juan. He has every intention of seeking the mercy of God when the time comes. But that time is still such a long way off; there is no need to think about it yet. As one critic succinctly puts it, Don Juan, in contrast to Paulo, is "el condenado por demasiado confiado"—the man damned for too much faith. As regards its doctrinal teaching, *El Burlador* has every appearance of being a companion piece to *El condenado*, but one which presents the other side of the coin, and restores the importance of good works. It is dangerous to rely on an eleventh-hour repentance: one's faith must all along be matched by one's way of life.

It would not be surprising to find the same author presenting two apparently conflicting doctrines, for both have their place within official Catholic teaching. St. Paul had preached faith, but had also taught that faith without works is dead; and according to a modern exposition, "it is only through, and in the measure of, our co-operation that we appropriate to ourselves the satisfactions and merits of Christ". (*Catholic Encyclopedia*, Universe Edition, 1913, under *Redemption*.) Justification by faith alone was a Protestant tenet, and the balance needed to be redressed. Even *El condenado* had not entirely minimized good works, for in the midst of all his wickedness Enrico had consistently retained one virtue: love and support for Anareto, his aged father. It is through this love, and in answer to his father's pleas, that he is finally prevailed upon to confess before his execution, and thus faith and works are seen to have a mutual interaction, both playing their part in opening the way to heaven.

An examination of their theological content, therefore, suggests the probability that *El condenado* and *El Burlador* are by the same author. Moreover, since in addition to this and to the bibliographical evidence the latter work displays such Tirsian traits as an intrigue involving five lovers, a statement of the power of love to unite "seda con sayal", and a character (Tisbea) who, like Jerónima, Serafina and Amnon, boasts of her immunity to love only to fall more dangerously later on, there would seem to be ample grounds for including these two outstanding works in a consideration of Tirso's theatre.

El condenado has been shown to derive from a widely diffused oriental legend which tells of a saint being equated in merit with a man who to all appearances is a great sinner. In most versions the result of the comparison with another man is to bring the saint to a clearer realization of what constitutes true goodness, and the ending is a happy one; but on to this legend Tirso grafts another, that of the hermit who apostatized on seeing a robber saved. In this way the holy man, his pride once having led to a fall, goes quickly further downhill, and a tragic ending is logically prepared for. For the final inexorable tragedy itself Tirso alone, as far as can be seen, is responsible.

El Burlador de Sevilla more obviously employs two sources: the myth of the young libertine, for whom real-life originals may not have been hard to find, perhaps even in Seville itself; and the grim fantasy of the stone guest. This is naturally the element which has been more fully investigated, and possible antecedents have been found for it in a number of tales of taunts, challenges and mocking invitations to the dead—perhaps most strikingly in a ballad from Castile, in which it is actually a statue which is invited to supper, and which returns the invitation.[10] Here again, however, the episode simply serves as a warning to the brash young man; its carrying through to a fatal conclusion appears to be Tirso's own contribution. We find, therefore, that the two works concur not merely in their dramatization of theology, but also in the treatment of their sources. Both effect a linking of two previously unconnected elements in order to point a doctrinal truth, and both exceed the warrant of all earlier legends in their relentless imposition of the ultimate penalty.[11]

It is in the very nature of the stories and of the truths they teach that both plays should present characters of extreme wickedness. But in this they belong very much to their period. Enrico, who among the crimes of which he boasts can list theft,

[10] See R. Menéndez Pidal, *Estudios literarios* (Buenos Aires, 1938), for essays dating originally from 1902 to 1906 on the sources of the two plays.

[11] I know of only one other Golden Age play which explicitly states that a character goes to hell, and that, interestingly enough, is also by Tirso: *El mayor desengaño*. The man in question here is only a minor figure in the play, but his sin is essentially the same as Paulo's. He has lived a holy life, and as he dies he prays not for mercy, but to be judged according to his deserts. His damnation is the result.

housebreaking, face-slashing, rape, arson, sacrilege and innumerable murders, is one of the many examples to be found in the later drama of the sinner on a grand scale. Often, like Paulo, the wicked man is a bandit, who has either undergone a sudden transition from holiness, or turns equally brusquely to repentance and religious zeal at the end. There is a clear conviction that the great sinner and the great saint are not very far apart.[12] Such characters seem to have held a fascination for seventeenth-century Spain, as it felt its vital energies frustrated, and came to a realization of its national impotence and decline. A French critic has spoken of them providing "la vaste catharsis dont l'Espagne a eu besoin pour vivre".[13] Certainly Tirso's genius seems to have been well fitted to create them. That hint of the hectic and the exaggerated observed in the comedies, and which sounded more stridently in the morbid sexuality of Jezabel and Amnon, has here become the dominant note. Lope, by his prodigious output, won for himself the title of "Nature's monster", but his plays seldom depart far from the normal and natural. It is in Tirso's theatre that we become familiar with the monstrous; and nowhere more than in the characters of Enrico and Don Juan.

It remains to substantiate the claim that both these plays are masterpieces. The fact that *El condenado por desconfiado* is, from its title onwards, avowedly thesis drama, might be expected to

[12] See A. A. Parker, "Santos y bandoleros en el teatro español del Siglo de Oro", *Arbor* 13 (1949) 395–416.

[13] C. V. Aubrun, "La comédie doctrinale et ses histoires de brigands: *El condenado por desconfiado*", *BH* 59 (1957) 137–51. But similar characters occur in Elizabethan drama. Cf. Leslie Stephen writing on Massinger in *Hours in a Library*, Vol. II (London, 1892), pp. 159, 160: "The world is for the daring; and though daring may be pushed to excess, weakness is the one unpardonable offence. A thoroughgoing villain is better than a trembling saint. . . . Pure, undiluted energy, stern force of will, delight in danger for its own sake, contempt for all laws but the self-imposed, those are the cardinal virtues, and challenge our sympathy even when they lead their possessor to destruction."

lessen its impact. Is it the prime function of drama to present ideas? And can a dramatist who starts from a concept ever speak so compellingly, even to his contemporaries living within the same ideological framework, as one who starts from a human situation?

Some bending of reality to the purpose of the thesis seems inevitable, and here more than in the comedies it would be futile to expect lifelike characterization. Of the main elements in the play, the character of Enrico is the one which seems most contrived. He is too bad to be true; and although there is certainly something of the *enfant terrible* about him which inclines us to dismiss some of his boasts as swashbuckling exaggeration, we do actually see him commit a murder on stage, and he clearly leads a criminal and brutal existence which it is difficult to reconcile with his mistress's affection for him, and still more with his own devotion to his father. This latter relationship must be interpreted almost entirely in terms of the lesson of the play. In realistic terms it is clearly ridiculous that Enrico should be dissuaded from his habitual thoughts of evil by his father's presence; and then, by simply drawing a curtain in front of the old man's sleeping figure, free himself to contemplate murder again. But his filial piety is vitally instrumental in his salvation, for even in the condemned cell Enrico arrogantly refuses to confess, until his father pleads with him to do so, and melts his resistance.[14] Enrico's love for Anareto, which is of course taken over from one version of the source legend, serves primarily in this play to show the vital link between faith and works.

But if verisimilitude in Enrico is largely sacrificed to the thesis of the play, this is not so much so with Paulo. The title requires him to be "desconfiado", mistrustful, lacking in faith. Yet the fact is that through much of the play he shows a capacity for

---

[14] Cf. Parker, *loc. cit.*, where it is shown that the father is the representative and the symbol of social authority, and that through his filial love Enrico has been kept in a fundamentally right relationship with society, enabling him to submit at the end to its discipline.

belief, and for total commitment to that belief, which is almost heroic. The trouble is that it is always belief in the wrong thing; first in the merit of his own ascetic life, and then in the reliability of the Devil's prophecy. It seems almost to be pig-headed credulity, rather than lack of faith, which damns him. But there is certainly something fine in the intensity and single-mindedness of his commitment. The Devil himself vouches for his steadfastness during ten years as a hermit:

> Siempre le he hallado firme,
> como un gran peñasco opuesto. (Act I)
> ("I have always found him firm, resisting like a great crag.")

He is probably at his finest, humanly speaking, in the moment of his rebellion. Facing for the first time the possibility that God may reward the good man and the evil man alike, his sense of fairness is revolted and he stands up to God, teaching him a lesson in justice:

> Perdone Dios si le ofendo,
> que si uno el fin ha de ser,
> esto es justo, y yo me entiendo. (Act II)
> ("God forgive me if I offend him, but if our ends are to be the same, then this is right, and I know what I am doing.")

If he is going to hell with Enrico in any case, then he will sin with Enrico first, and so *force* God to be just:

> Pues cuando Dios, juez eterno,
> nos condenare al infierno,
> ya habremos hecho por qué. (Act II)
> ("For if God, the eternal judge, condemns us to hell, at least we shall have done something to deserve it.")

This is a protest which must provoke some sympathy. Though his rebellion takes monstrous forms, it springs from the disgust felt by good men throughout the ages at the unfairness of life. It is the demand of the labourers in the vineyard for a just reward.

Paulo's indignation is not maintained. It soon gives way to renewed anguish, and as he falls further from grace he sinks deeper into mistrust and despair. Yet he dies professing faith in what he still believes to be a divine revelation. Has he really deserved hell? His fate reminds one of what Unamuno has to say in *The Tragic Sense of Life*, about "the sense of not deserving death, of wanting to ensure that our annihilation, if that is what awaits us, is an injustice". Paulo's damnation is, in human terms, an injustice; and in this presentation of the downfall of a man, blind and misguided but essentially good, we have, I believe, a superb dramatic statement of the "tragic sense of life". Its eschatological context, while compelling to a seventeenth-century Spaniard, is not universally meaningful today. But I think it is still possible to see Paulo himself as a character of universal validity, demanding justice in life (and after it), willing to be judged on his merits, and unable to accept the altogether different terms he is offered.

Even within its own sphere of thesis drama *El condenado por desconfiado* is a great æsthetic achievement. There is very little straightforward preaching; the dogma is conveyed almost entirely through character, setting and action. Enrico is responsible for plenty of turbulent action on stage, contrasting with those more static scenes where the violence is all in Paulo's tortured mind; and there are moments of relief from both, the reposeful pause scenes in which Enrico tends his old father, and the shepherd-lad, searching the hills for his lost sheep, gently tries to show Paulo his mistake. It was inevitable that some recourse should be had to supernatural mouthpieces—the Devil, the shepherd-boy, and an invisible choir—but all the substance of the drama lies in the opposition between Paulo and Enrico. They are contrasted in almost every possible way. Paulo is a neurotic, intro-spective thinker, Enrico a man of action, an extrovert, an exhibitionist even. He needs to be among people, to stand in some relationship to them: he has friends, enemies, a mistress, a father; Paulo is by nature a solitary. (His servant-*gracioso* does little more than provide opportunities for dialogue and humour.) Enrico's natural setting is the town, and his crimes are urban crimes; Paulo belongs in the country. Both as hermit and as brigand, nature is the background he chooses; and his contact with the things of nature, the only other created beings truly real for him, it would seem, is almost a *leitmotif*. He is apostrophizing them when the play opens; he proclaims to the birds and the trees his intention to be wicked; and at the end, when pursued and nearly broken, he pathetically begs the stream and the birds to give him solace. Paulo and Enrico both receive two supernatural visitations: Paulo mistakes the Devil for God and heeds him almost obstinately, but cannot believe the Good Shepherd; Enrico is able to distinguish and choose aright.

The work is given great beauty of structure by the opposition between these two men. Its shape is that of an X. At the beginning of the play the two are unknown to each other, physically apart and spiritually remote. The Devil's prophecy establishes a connection between them, and their trajectories start to move together. By the end of Act I, though they have not spoken, they have been in each other's presence, and Paulo has reacted to what he has seen with the resolve to become a bandit, thus bringing himself closer to Enrico. The revelation of Enrico's filial devotion early in Act II conversely raises the latter in the moral scale; and the point of intersection is reached at the end of the Act in the magnificent scene of confrontation, perhaps the most poignant dramatic encounter in the Golden Age theatre. Paulo and Enrico, on this one occasion only, meet face to face. Paulo has Enrico tied to a tree, and can kill him if he wishes. He holds Enrico in his power. Yet he is desperately dependent on him too. With Enrico's refusal to confess the tables are turned; and it is the helpless captive who with his calm, confident profession of trust in God shows himself to be the stronger of the two. This is the crux of the drama. Thereafter they separate and continue on their upward or downward courses, to those destinations where they will remain eternally apart.

El condenado succeeds, then, on more than one level: as a formal, intellectual construction; as the translation of an abstract concept into valid theatre; and as a cry of unavailing protest and despair at the unfairness of the human condition.[15]

---

[15] T. E. May gives an interesting study of the play in "*El condenado por desconfiado:* 1. The Enigmas. 2. Anareto", *BHS* 35 (1958) 138–56, though not all his interpretations would find universal acceptance.

It is on the second of these counts that *El Burlador de Sevilla* has most in common with *El condenado*. It too starts from a theological concept which it renders in wholly convincing dramatic terms. There is the same variety in the settings, and similarly sensational and rapid action. This time the play dispenses with all exposition and starts in the very middle of an episode, as Don Juan makes his escape in the dark after an amorous adventure.

A momentum is thus established which is maintained almost consistently throughout the play, by the pace of the action and the often staccato dialogue. There are elements of pure theatricality: a funeral procession with torches winding its way through the dark streets of Seville; the stone statue knocking on the door; the sinister chapel ablaze with the flames of hell. *El Burlador de Sevilla* offers plenty of scope to an imaginative producer.

Its construction, however, is less organized and impressive than that of *El condenado*. It shares with *La prudencia en la mujer* the defect of a largely episodic structure, one seduction following disconnectedly on another, until the tale is rounded off by Don Juan's punishment at the hands of the statue. The fact that there are clearly two distinct sources—the myth of Don Juan and the legend of the stone guest—has led some critics to see them as merely juxtaposed and not organically related, and to complain of a sudden change of mood.[16] Here, however, the criticism goes too far, and what may be true of *Don Giovanni* cannot justly be said of *El Burlador*. There are plenty of forewarnings of tragedy in the early scenes, with repeated references to God, to death and to hell, and the figure of Don Gonzalo is there to provide an effective link between the two parts. He is the father of Doña Ana, one of Don Juan's intended victims. He challenges the assailant of his honour, but is himself killed in the fight. A statue is erected on his tomb, and this same statue becomes the means of Don Juan's destruction; thus providing

[16] e.g. C. V. Aubrun in "Le *Don Juan* de Tirso de Molina. Essai d'interprétation", *BH* 59 (1957) 26–61.

a connecting element in an otherwise loosely constructed play.[17]

More than this, Don Gonzalo is supremely fitted to be the instrument of retribution. By his crimes and his light-hearted delaying of repentance, Don Juan has wronged both man and God. Don Gonzalo is one of his human victims, but in the shape of the statue he is also a supernatural figure, endowed with heavenly powers of punishment; so that through him both man and God can be avenged. For whatever we may think of *El condenado*, *El Burlador* is a play which leaves no room for any lingering sense of unfairness. Its emphatic message is that justice will be done; and in the burning grasp of the stone hand we see it done. "Quien tal hace, que tal pague" ("Who acts thus must pay for it"): this decree, which to judge from its threefold repetition in the closing scenes may perhaps have been the earliest title of all, proclaims an unbreakable link of cause and effect between man's actions and his fate.

Don Gonzalo, however, whether in human or supernatural form, remains a mere instrument. He has no individuality. There is in this play no opposing or matching of personalities, everything is overshadowed by the gigantic personality of Don Juan. Variety is given to the seduction episodes by the fact that in the list of victims a fisher-girl follows a duchess, to be followed in turn by another noble lady and then a peasant; but three of these four are little more than ciphers. Tisbea, the fisher-girl, is the only one to be individualized, and the only character of much interest apart from Don Juan. She displays a familiar Tirsian trait: she introduces herself with a boast that she alone from all the girls of that part of the coast is immune to love; only moments later she has cradled the shipwrecked and unconscious Don Juan in her arms, and encourages his advances as soon as his eyes are open. She knows that men are not to be trusted, and her words are full of apprehension and warning:

---

[17] The unity of the work is also seen in the strands of imagery which run right through it. These have been well studied by C. B. Morris in "Metaphor in *El Burlador de Sevilla*", *RR* 55 (1964) 248–55.

Advierte,
mi bien, que hay Dios y que hay muerte.   (Act I)
("Remember, my love, that you must one day face God and death");

but her deeds belie them, and Don Juan scarcely has to go to the trouble of wooing her. Yet the change in her is perhaps not as great as it appears. Despite her professed hardness of heart, her opening speech gives plenty of clues to her latent sexuality. Its references to nature are full of hints of the tactile and sensual: the sea kissing the feet of the fisher-girls, the sun treading on the drowsy waves, the gentle combat of the water on the rocks, and the storks and turtle-doves nesting in her roof. She is subconsciously ready for passion, and there is no real inconsistency when she answers Don Juan's "Where am I?" with a clear invitation.

It is perhaps best, in delineating the character of Don Juan, to indicate first of all what he is not. Whatever later authors and the popular imagination may have made of him, in *El Burlador de Sevilla* he is not a great lover. He does not love any of his victims, not even with the sudden infatuation which in the *comedia* so often passes for love. He is not markedly sensual, and it does not seem to be beauty which chiefly stimulates him; he never admits to physical pleasure, nor lingers in the enjoyment of his conquests. He is not even abnormally highly sexed; his adventures do not follow one another with unnatural rapidity, since he makes long journeys in between—from Naples to Tarragona, from Tarragona to Seville; and if he is promiscuous, so is his friend the Marqués de la Mota, who although genuinely in love with Doña Ana, is quite at home among the Sevillian brothels. Indeed, far from being a symbol of abnormal sexual prowess, there is evidence that the author saw him as typical of the dissolute nobility of his day, to whom the play offered a stern warning.

If he is not a great lover, neither is he unusually attractive to women. He gains access to the two noble women only by pretending to be someone else. Aminta, the peasant girl whom he entices from her bridegroom on her wedding-day, dislikes and shrinks from him at first, and is only won over by promises of wealth and rank. Tisbea is the only one of the four to feel anything for him at all, and as has been shown, hers is a passion which he needs to do nothing to inspire.

The true keynote of his character is given in the title. He is not a lover but a *burlador*, a trickster.

> Burlar
> es hábito antiguo mío,   (Act I)

("Trickery is an old habit of mine"),

he declares, and

> el   mayor
> gusto que en mí puede h aber
> es burlar una mujer
> y dejalla sin honor.   (Act II)

("the greatest pleasure I know is to deceive a woman and rob her of her honour.")

He could not have existed without the code of *pundonor*. It is the fetish of feminine purity which stimulates him, and offers a challenge to his ingenuity. The more unapproachable the victim, the more savoury the adventure. Doña Ana attracts him more than the girls in the brothel, precisely because she is the beloved of his friend, who has just confided in him; Aminta because she is a still unpossessed bride. The eager Tisbea must have tasted rather flat; but he introduces the requisite note of mockery by stealing from her the horses on which he and his servant make their escape.

Much has been written about Don Juan's horses, which carry him on his vertiginous career. It is tempting to see them as sexual symbols, though it should be noted that it is always to carry him *away* from a woman that he has them made ready in advance. But there is no questioning the speed and urgency which he imparts to the play. This is a work with very few pause scenes. Don Juan is on stage for much of the time, always pressing the action forward:

> Esta noche he de gozalla.   (Act I)

("This very night I will possess her.")

> Gozarla esta noche espero;
> la noche camina.   (Act III)

(" I hope to possess her tonight; night is drawing on.")

This insistence on the swift passage of time where the fulfilment of his purposes is concerned, compared with its sluggishness in bringing death and judgement, gives rise to a powerful dramatic tension. "Esta noche he de gozalla" heightens the irony of "¡Qué largo me lo fiáis!"; and the night to which he repeatedly and impatiently looks forward, the darkness wherein he comes into his own—"Éstas son las horas mías" (Act III) ("These are my hours")—significantly foreshadows the long night of his damnation.

Along with this impatience go a recklessness and bravado which compel some admiration. Here his timorous servant Catalinón, whose name seems to imply cowardice, acts as a foil. Catalinón, unlike the typical *gracioso*, tries to restrain his master. He aligns himself with Tisbea and the libertine's father in reminding him of the reckoning to come, and is taunted for being a preacher. But his terror at the arrival of the stone guest throws into relief his master's courage. Don Juan has his own standards of honourable behaviour to which he scrupulously adheres. He assures the statue that his word as a gentleman is to be trusted; and Catalinón has earlier witnessed to his reliability, save only where women are concerned. The irony lies in his failure to realize that gentlemanliness and honourable behaviour extend to dealings with women as well as with men; and there is justice in the apparent paradox that it is his sense of honour, so inadequate and perverted did he but know it, which takes him to the rendezvous with the statue and destroys him.

The Don Juan of *El Burlador de Sevilla* is without any doubt an extraordinary and impressive creation, even if he is not the almost superhuman figure he has since become. Is there in the play we have been studying any warrant at all for this later concept? I think that there is; and that it is to be found in the powerful symbolism. Just as Tisbea's subconscious mind gives her away and belies her expressed scorn for love, so too the undertones of the play give it a significance beyond that which it was intended to have. When Tisbea tells Don Juan "Mucho fuego prometéis" ("You promise much fire"), her metaphor points ahead to the pangs she will suffer after her desertion; yet fire in the sense in which she means it, the fire of passion, is the more potent symbol. When Don Juan waits impatiently for the night, we are aware of the threat of eternal night hanging over him; yet it is the mystery and the magic of terrestrial darkness which we find more compelling. Much of the action of the play takes place in darkness, the darkness which lends itself to the deceptions of the "burlador". It is lit in turn by the candle of the King of Naples as he investigates the commotion in his palace, the torches of Don Gonzalo's funeral procession, and the flames in the chapel—all manifestations of the forces of order and authority which oppose Don Juan. Yet it is the fire in the darkness of human nature which we feel the play to be about, and which Don Juan himself has come to stand for. Much more emphatically than in *El condenado*, a positive human value has asserted itself in defiance of the author's intentions, and has clouded the message of the play. It is because of this implicit assertion that *El Burlador de Sevilla* has left so great a legacy to Europe.

Texts

Comedias escogidas, ed. J. E. Hartzenbusch, in *BAE*, Vol. 5 (Madrid, 1848).
Comedias, ed. E. Cotarelo, in *NBAE*, Vols. 4 and 9 (Madrid, 1906, 1907).
Obras dramáticas completas, ed. Blanca de los Ríos, 3 vols. (Madrid, Aguilar, 1946–58).

Critical Works

McCLELLAND, I. L., *Tirso de Molina. Studies in Dramatic Realism* (Liverpool, 1948).
Studi tirsiani, by GUIDO MANCINI and others (Milan, 1958).
Tirso de Molina (Madrid, 1949). (A collection of essays, many of them biographical, published by the Mercedarian review *Estudios*.)
VOSSLER, K., *Lecciones sobre Tirso de Molina*. (Originally given as lectures in Havana in 1938; published, with some useful biographical appendixes, Madrid, 1965.)

9

RUIZ DE ALARCÓN, GUILLÉN DE CASTRO, VÉLEZ DE GUEVARA, MIRA DE AMESCUA

WHILE Tirso de Molina was emphasizing the exaggerated and fervid elements in the *comedia*, his close contemporary Juan Ruiz de Alarcón y Mendoza was writing plays which in contrast often seem to breathe cool, refreshing common sense. It is a surprise to find what have emerged as basic conventions of the *comedia* being explicitly questioned and criticized. We have seen, for instance, how many plots depend upon untruthfulness; yet Alarcón writes a whole play, *La verdad sospechosa (Suspect Truth)*,[1] condemning this vice. *Comedia* gallants invariably appeal to the ladies by their looks; yet the hero of *Las paredes oyen (Walls Have Ears)*[1] is ugly. It is a conformist society which the Spanish dramatists paint; yet in *No hay mal que por bien no venga (It's an Ill Wind that Blows No Good)* Don Domingo de Don Blas cultivates eccentricities of dress and behaviour in the name of comfort and common sense, and convinces us that he is right. Minor disruptions of the accepted pattern are seen in isolated satirical comments on duels, disguised heroines, and servants who are in their masters' confidence and joke with royalty. Above all, it is Alarcón who gives most striking expression to a view of honour as more than a mere perquisite of birth:

> Sólo consiste en obrar
> como caballero, el serlo.
> ¿Quién dio principio a las casas
> nobles? Los ilustres hechos
> de sus primeros autores.
> Sin mirar sus nacimientos,
> hazañas de hombres humildes
> honraron sus herederos.

---

[1] Edited by Alfonso Reyes (Madrid, Clásicos castellanos, 1918).

Luego en obrar mal o bien
está el ser malo o ser bueno.

(*La verdad sospechosa*, Act II)

("Being a gentleman consists simply in behaving like one. What brought the noble houses into being? The illustrious deeds of their founders. Without regard to birth the exploits of humble men brought honour to their heirs. Therefore being great or small consists in acting well or ill.")

MARQUÉS: ¿ Vos sabéis
                que sois señor?
CONDE: Sé a lo menos
                que vos lo sois, y que soy
                vuestro hijo y heredero.
MARQUÉS: Pues no, no está en heredarlo,
                sino en obrar bien, el serlo.

(*El tejedor de Segovia*, Act I)

("You know that you are a nobleman?" "I know at any rate that *you* are, and that I am your son and heir." "You are wrong, nobility is not a matter of inheritance, but of behaviour.")

The force of contrast undoubtedly enhances the effect of these abnormalities. When we read further in Alarcón we find that they are the exceptions, and that the rule is a reliance on the conventions at times almost as tedious as that of Tirso. But there is a parallel with Tirso. Just as one can glimpse in the latter a gift for striking and individual characterization which the taste of his audience prevented him from developing, so it is now and then apparent that Alarcón has the ability to look critically at accepted norms and to create a lively comedy of manners. Had he written for a different public he might perhaps have been a Molière. It is probable that he did influence Molière. His best play certainly gave Corneille the plot of *Le menteur*, and prompted his well-known tribute: "Le sujet m'en semble si spirituel et si bien tourné, que j'ai dit souvent que je voudrais avoir donné les deux plus belles [pièces] que j'ai faites, et qu'il fût de mon invention." (*Examen du "Menteur."*)

The ability to step on occasion outside the conventions is closely linked with Alarcón's own personality and experiences. He was himself a permanent outsider. In the first place he was a colonial, born in Mexico in 1580 or 1581; trained as a lawyer; and only finally settling in Madrid about 1615. His transatlantic origin seems to have been a greater barrier to the life of the literary circles than Tirso's friar's habit. At all events he plays it down, and makes no use of it in his writings. More unfortunate, however, were his physical deformities—he was hunchbacked and pigeon-breasted—for which he was unmercifully lampooned by all his fellow men of letters. Some dignity of personality might perhaps have enabled him to live down his affliction; but it seems that a sense of social failure led him instead to over-compensate, and to make himself ridiculous in speech and behaviour.

Was this especially the case in his relations with women? There are certainly many satires on him as a would-be lover; and he never married, though he mentions an illegitimate daughter in his will. More telling is the figure of Don Juan de Mendoza (both names born by Alarcón himself), who in *Las paredes oyen* defeats two rivals for the heroine's hand despite his unprepossessing looks; and who, like the outlandish but ultimately triumphant Don Domingo de Don Blas, clearly represents some kind of self-justification—or wish—fulfilment —on his creator's part.

Alarcón's plays all seem to have been written in the decade following his arrival in Madrid in 1615. In 1625 he retired from the theatre, for unknown reasons, and obtained a government post in the Consejo de Indias, or Colonial Office, which he held until his death in 1639; his dramatic career thus presenting a curious chronological parallel with that of Tirso. But he wrote much less than any of his great contemporaries. He published only two *partes* or volumes of collected plays (1628 and 1634), containing twenty in all. Making allowances for the usual doubtful attributions, it seems that he cannot be credited with more than about two dozen plays.

His small output is one aspect of a restrictiveness, an avoidance of extravagance, of which we are often aware in Alarcón. Another is the use of homely realistic details which help him to keep his feet on the ground. We have seen that references to money and dress are commonplace in the *comedia*; but the garments mentioned are usually gorgeous, and the incomes dazzlingly high. Alarcón, on the other hand, makes his Don Domingo dress unfashionably, but with a view to comfort and convenience; and many of his characters show an unusual hard-headedness over money. When a house is being let, the rent is stated and also the fact that it is to be paid in advance. (There is also a mention of the likelihood of a new house being damp.) Inés of *El examen de maridos* (*Suitors under Scrutiny*), buying some jewellery privately to oblige a friend, stipulates that she must have it valued. The *gracioso* of *El tejedor de Segovia* (*The Weaver of Segovia*) allows for his breakages in calculating the wages due to him. It is fairly clear that Alarcón was preoccupied with money, and this may have been another consequence of his sense of social inadequacy. The frequency of his attacks on rapacious and venal women must certainly reflect the kind of sexual relationship which for him was normal. On the other hand, he does on occasion show an economic acumen which must have been rare in his day; as when García deplores the wearing of ruffs because of its effect on the balance of payments:

> Me holgara de que saliera
> premática que impidiera
> esos vanos canjilones.
> Que demás de esos engaños,
> con su holanda el extranjero
> saca de España el dinero,
> para nuestros propios daños.
>
> (*La verdad sospechosa*, Act I)

("I should welcome a regulation forbidding these stupid frills, for apart from their deceptiveness, the import of linen for them takes money out of the country which we can ill afford.")

Alarcón's handling of stock types is at times coloured by his own tendency to calculation. His heroines seldom share the zest and recklessness of their Tirsian sisters. Love drives them rather to mean and disloyal stratagems; or else they subordinate love altogether to self-interest: Jacinta of *La verdad sospechosa* is willing to consider another suitor when Don Juan's knighthood is slow in coming; but she wants to be sure of the new love before she is off with the old. The *graciosos* instead of abetting their masters tend to restrain and admonish them, and like Catalinón are frequently made mouthpieces of morality or prudence.

The question of moral teaching in the theatre of Alarcón is not a simple one. His attacks on specific vices—lying and slander respectively—in *La verdad sospechosa* and *Las paredes oyen* have distinguished him as the originator of moral comedy in Spain. Yet he is by no means always negative. There are numerous examples in his plays of staunch, upright figures, models of loyalty either to a friend, or to a sovereign threatened by conspiracy. Such characters, in whom the moral is exalted into the heroic, are to be found, for example, in *No hay mal que por bien no venga, El tejedor de Segovia, Los favores del mundo* (*The Favours of This World*), and *Ganar amigos* (*Gaining Friends*). In the last three of these plays their appearance is linked with a theme which was receiving increasingly frequent dramatic treatment, and which we have observed to play a significant part in Tirso's *La prudencia en la mujer:* that of the *privado*, or royal favourite. Alarcón's presentation of the theme is aimed not usually at the sovereign, but at the favourite himself, and carries a twofold lesson: the *privado's* special privileges imply special obligations; and he is more susceptible than most men to the mutability of fortune. It is clear that Alarcón, like Tirso, was writing with topical events in mind: the execution in 1621 of a former minister, Rodrigo Calderón, and the domination of the young Philip IV by Olivares; and that his plays on favouritism reveal some serious political thought. While he made no personal attacks on Olivares such as can be discerned in *Tanto es lo de más como lo de menos*, one speculates whether his having touched on a dangerous topic may have brought him under the same condemnation as Tirso, and may account for his retreat into silence together with the Mercedarian in 1625.

But the picture of Alarcón the moralist is not yet complete; for even in those plays which exalt a steadfast and noble character, a disturbing deviousness at times creeps in. The hero of *Ganar amigos*, returning good for evil, is consciously and deliberately acting in his own interests: virtue is the best policy. There is a strange moral equivocation in *No hay mal . . .* between the heroine's father, an excellent paterfamilias but a traitor to the King; and Don Juan, a spendthrift, gambler, embezzler and burglar, yet loyal, and ultimately rewarded with the heroine's hand. Alarcón's final marriages more than once strike one as unsatisfactory from the point of view of moral compatibility. Clariana, of *El tejedor de Segovia*, has for seven years been living in sin with the villain of the play; yet when the situation is rectified by a forced marriage and the convenient death of her lover she is thought a perfectly suitable bride for the exemplary Garcerán. Even in those plays most responsible for Alarcón's reputation as a moralist, something less than absolute rectitude seems acceptable. The father in *La verdad sospechosa* deplores his son's lies, yet wants to marry him off to an unsuspecting bride before his failing becomes generally known; and the ill-favoured Don Juan of *Las paredes oyen*, in order to make Doña Ana waver in her devotion to one of his rivals, stoops to the questionable manœuvre of pretending for a time to further the suit of the other. It is perhaps not unfair to suggest that, in his calculating disposition as in his looks, Don Juan de Mendoza is a mirror of his creator; and that the moral standards of Alarcón's theatre taken as a whole are no higher than those in the works of his contemporaries.

Alarcón is a better craftsman than Tirso. His plots are in general more carefully worked out, with convincing motivation leading to a real dénouement. He himself criticizes (*Las paredes oyen*, Act II) those dramatists who repeat their satire and their situations. His speeches are not over-long. His versification is meticulous, and there is even an occasional memorable or epigrammatic phrase; for example:

> El rostro feo
> les hice ver del temor.
>
> (*No hay mal. . .*, Act III)

("I let them see the ugly face of fear.")

One senses in the excellence of his technique less the instinctive skill and taste of a Lope de Vega, than the result of deliberation and effort; a further expression, perhaps, of a careful and calculating temperament. The only flaw from which his plays suffer with any regularity is the tendency common in thesis drama for the central concept to predominate, and for the plot and characters to be manipulated to fit it. Thus in *Los favores del mundo* the ups and downs of fortune follow one another with unnatural haste; and in *Las paredes oyen* Don Mendo's vice of backbiting has to be given an emphasis which the plot alone would not justify. In his anxiety for us not to miss the point, Alarcón will sometimes present a significant character from the outside, through the mouths of others, rather than allow him to reveal himself dramatically. When García returns from the University at the beginning of *La verdad sospechosa*, his father consults his tutor about the type of man the son has become, starting from the assumption:

> Que él tenga vicio es forzoso.
> ("It is inevitable that he should have some vice.")

It is, of course, not inevitable at all, apart from the fact that this is to be a play about one vice in particular; but the tutor has been given his cue for an exposé of the theme. After this superfluous beginning, it must be admitted that the thesis is well handled. García is given plenty of rope to hang himself through his own untruthful words, and Alarcón paints an excellent portrait of a compulsive liar or romancer, a man driven by an overwhelming need to impress.[2]

The development of conceptual or thesis drama, in the hands of Alarcón and others, marks the most important change which the *comedia* underwent in its later stages. Lope de Vega is always writing about real people; his dramas arise out of human situations. But his followers show an increasing tendency to start from an idea, a concept—whether this be a proverb, a moral

[2] See E. C. Riley, "Alarcón's *mentiroso* in the light of the contemporary theory of character", in *Hispanic Studies in Honour of I. González Llubera* (Oxford, 1959), pp. 287–97.

lesson, or a theological dogma—and to incarnate it in a play. This is a procedure in which it is manifestly difficult to attain complete dramatic success. The author of *El condenado por desconfiado* and *El Burlador de Sevilla* achieves it; Alarcón achieves it in *La verdad sospechosa*, but is less convincing elsewhere. It results eventually in a thorough modification of the dramatic vehicle. The everyday human stuff of drama becomes less and less important in its own right, until it finally yields to symbolism, and the end of a line of development is reached in the late theatre of Calderón.

It was doubtless in response to the popular demand for sensational action that Alarcón at times did violence to his own nature, forsook caution and common sense, and produced works as extravagant as any in the period. *La cueva de Salamanca* (*The Cave of Salamanca*) is a farrago of student escapades and necromancy. *El tejedor de Segovia*, similarly based on local legends, contains as we have seen some typical Alarconian traits, but also an overloaded plot involving duels, sieges, banditry, a heroine in male disguise and a sister who fails to recognize her brother, numerous reversals of fortune, and even a battle against the Moors.[3] *El Anticristo*, an astonishing mixture of allegory and horrific apocalyptic drama, is remembered above all for its disastrous opening night in December 1623. Two contretemps occurred: an actor required to be carried aloft by a *tramoya*, or piece of stage machinery, lost his nerve, so the heroine snatched his cloak and crown and allowed herself to be hoisted up in his place; and a bottle of foul-smelling liquid was spilt in the auditorium. Whether the authors of this practical joke were moved by a prior knowledge of the play's defects, or by simple hostility to Alarcón, one cannot tell; but certainly *El Anticristo* includes scenes worthy of third-rate pantomime, in which the nadir of the *comedia* would seem to have been reached.[4]

[3] The *BAE* volume of Alarcón contains *El tejedor de Segovia*, Parts I and II. Part II is the Alarcón play; Part I, even more wildly romantic, is spurious.

[4] For example, that in which a Christian and a Jew are debating which of their religions has produced more saints. They agree to take it in turn to name a saint of their own faith, and as they do so to pull out a hair from the

It would be unfair to let this stand as a last word on Alarcón. One might more fittingly end by applying to him, one of the most clear-sighted of the Golden Age dramatists, his own comments on the scorned but ultimately vindicated Don Domingo de Don Blas:

> Injusto nombre os ha dado
> la fama, que loco os llama;
> que mejor puede la fama
> llamaros desengañado.
>
> (*No hay mal. . .* , Act II)

("Reputation has dealt unfairly with you, calling you mad; it should rather speak of you as disillusioned.")

Of the many minor dramatists who exploited the demand created by Lope de Vega, I shall briefly consider three. Corneille's handsome acknowledgement of his debt to Alarcón has been noted, but he probably did a greater service to Guillén de Castro, for it is almost entirely as the author of the source of *Le Cid* that that dramatist is remembered. He was a Valencian, seven years Lope's junior, who began his career of playwright in his native city. The chronology of his plays can only be guessed at, but it seems reasonable to suppose that his romantic, novelesque dramas, with Central European settings and no concern for reality, are his earliest. Later he must have met Lope, during the latter's exile in Valencia, and by him been induced to give his work a Spanish content. He then writes plays with contemporary settings, in Valencia or Madrid, or borrows plots from Cervantes or from the Spanish ballads. From about 1618 until his death in 1631 he was living in the capital, and he published two volumes of plays there, in 1621 and 1625.

---

other man's head. The one to be left bald first will have lost the contest. They begin quietly: "Moses." "San Gonzalo." "Amos." The Christian quickens the pace with "The Twelve Apostles," and pulls out a whole lock of hair. The Jew retorts with "Jacob and his sons". Finally the Christian remembers "St. Ursula and the 11,000 virgins"—and pulls off the Jew's wig.

The two parts of *Las mocedades del Cid* (*The Young Cid*)[5] are based on the ballad versions of the hero's life, and it is the first part which corresponds to *Le Cid*. It is probably not generally known how much of Corneille is already there: not merely the famous "stances de Rodrigue" (at any rate three of them), with the corresponding "pena-Jimena" rhyme in the final couplets, but many speeches and scenes which the Frenchman did little more than translate. He did, admittedly, cut down the amount of material, because of the exigencies of classical drama and also, perhaps, with a surer dramatic sense. Guillén de Castro, like Juan de la Cueva, was reluctant to discard any of the material from his ballad source (which the audience knew and doubtless expected); Corneille is more compact and unified. But Castro has much more of the flavour of reality in his dialogue. Compare the two versions of the Count's reply to Rodrigo's challenge:

> J'admire ton courage, et je plains ta jeunesse.
> Ne cherche point à faire un coup d'essai fatal;
> Dispense ma valeur d'un combat inégal;
> Trop peu d'honneur pour moi suivrait cette victoire:
> A vaincre sans péril, on triomphe sans gloire.
> On te croirait toujours abattu sans effort;
> Et j'aurais seulement le regret de ta mort.
>
> (Act II, Scene 2)

> Quita, rapaz; ¿puede ser?
> Vete, novel caballero,
> vete, y aprende primero
> a pelear y a vencer;
> y podrás después honrarte
> de verte por mí vencido,
> sin que yo quede corrido
> de vencerte y de matarte.
> Deja ahora tus agravios,
> porque nunca acierta bien
> venganzas con sangre quien
> tiene la leche en los labios.
>
> (Act I)

("Get away, lad; what an idea! Be off with you, upstart knight, be off and learn first how to fight and to win, and then you can feel yourself honoured to be defeated by me, without making me sorry to have to kill you. Forget

---

[5] Edited by V. Said Armesto (Madrid, Clásicos castellanos, 1913).

your offences for the present, for vengeance through blood is no business
of one who still has his mother's milk on his lips.")

Note the colloquial tone of the Spanish, and the forceful physical
image in the last line, contrasting with the sophistication and
abstraction of the French. A detailed comparison of these two
plays would bring out very well the distinctive qualities of French
and Spanish drama, and especially the realism within convention
which is such a characteristic of the *comedia*.

The natural quality of his dialogue, more marked than in
any other writer of the period, is probably Castro's greatest
gift. It is equally apparent in plays with a contemporary setting
like *Los mal casados de Valencia*, where, despite a love intrigue
which by the end is as complicated as anything in Tirso, the
dialogue gives a painfully realistic representation of domestic
strife. In a memorable drawing-room scene where the quarrelling
couples sit down to play a parlour game, the brittle conversation,
the simultaneous outbursts and the short, sharp interjections
convey supremely well the tensions of two marriages nearing
breaking-point.

Yet the author's skill does not prevent this from being a loathsome play. It is not the mere picture of the breakdown of marriage
which makes it so, but the treatment of such a subject in a semi-
humorous, semi-cynical way. Flagrant adultery, suspected
homosexuality, importunate female desire, are all presented as
the stuff of comedy. There is a pretence of moral standards in
the lip-service paid to friendship, and in the final arrangements
which safeguard the marital honour of the two men; but what
this "honour" amounts to can be seen from the almost uniformly
dishonourable behaviour of most of the main characters, and
from Valerian's final admission in which he proves that he was
not a cuckold, but at the cost of proclaiming himself a murderer!

It is only worth dwelling so long on *Los mal casados . . .* to show
that the moralists were not entirely mistaken in their attacks
on the theatre, and to throw into relief the tremendous achievement of Lope, who, while rejecting outworn canons, admitting
the sensational, and giving full scope to men's weakness and

barbarism, could still create something human, satisfying and good. Guillén de Castro may fairly claim credit, however, for having at least discerned in the progress of a marriage a topic of dramatic interest. In a theatre where the great majority of plots lead up to final unions which we never see lived out, his dramatizations of marital conflict open the way for such later masterpieces as Lope's *El castigo sin venganza* and the great honour tragedies of Calderón.

Although only ten years separate the birth in 1579 of Luis Vélez de Guevara from that of Guillén de Castro, the effect of their drama is very different. Castro's work is unsophisticated and at times almost primitive; relatively little distinguishes *Las mocedades del Cid* from the plays of Juan de la Cueva. Vélez de Guevara, of an age with Tirso and Alarcón, like them exemplifies tendencies of the later theatre.

Most marked among them in his case is the increased elaboration of language. Vélez, an Andalusian from Écija, shared with the lyric poets of the south a love of colour and brightness, of precious objects, of decoration and conceits. This description of the tears of the heroine of *Reinar después de morir* (*Queen After Death*), unrealistically put into the mouth of the *gracioso*, clearly shows the influence of Góngora:

> Y en lluvias tan extrañas
> sartas de perlas hizo las pestañas,
> que en sus luces hermosas
> de perlas se volvían mariposas;
> y abrasándose en ellas,
> granizaron los párpados estrellas.   (Act I)

("And with such rare showers she made her eyelashes strings of pearls; but her lovely eyes turned the pearls into butterflies and burned them up in their brightness, so that her eyelids sent out hail-showers of stars.")

The interest in *culto* writing now begins to override Lope's criterion that characters should speak according to their social status, which had done so much to give the *comedia* its realistic flavour. This can have strange results. Two peasant couples figure in *La Luna de la sierra* (*The Moon-maiden of the Sierra*): one pair are conventionally rustic, even boorish, in their expression, but the second, though close relatives of the first, converse in involved language and figures of speech. Thus Antón, late home from the threshing because he has called round to milk the goats, assures his anxious wife of his love by a reference to the "grandson of the waters"—that is, Cupid, son of Venus, born of the waves.

This incongruity would not worry Vélez, because realism is no longer very important to him. The new interest in decorative elements for their own sake, like the tendency earlier observed for verisimilitude to yield to the presentation of a thesis or concept, makes for less realistic and more contrived intellectual creations. For Vélez, what he has to say is often of less interest than the way in which he says it. Hence his fondness for material which was already familiar, either in some other literary form or in the work of one of his dramatic predecessors.[6] He shares in a new vogue for the refurbishing of older plays. These re-workings, prompted by either moral or æsthetic considerations, are to play a major part in the later development of the theatre. We have already seen that our present text of *El Burlador de Sevilla* is probably such a *refundición*, and the same process will be responsible for most of the great works of Calderón. *La Luna de la sierra* is a fairly free reworking of Lope's *Peribáñez*. It has the same praise of domestic content, and the same spirited resistance to an aristocratic seducer. But Vélez sees fit to complicate the plot, and to heighten to the point of falsification both language and characters, making his heroine more of a finely-spoken Antona García than a Casilda. The conviction and the "rightness" of Lope's drama have gone.

[6] The Renaissance theory of Imitation, which governed the writing of lyric poetry in the sixteenth century, took it for granted that the poet's subject-matter would be taken from his predecessors, classical or modern; his only originality would be in his treatment of it. It is interesting to see the *comedia*, so recently criticized for its lack of literary standards, moving towards the norms accepted for other genres.

He is much more successful in his best-known play, *Reinar después de morir*.[7] This retells the old story of Inés de Castro, put to death by the King of Portugal because of her love match with his son, which stands in the way of a dynastic marriage, and exhumed when the son becomes King, so that his subjects may do homage to her dead body. This is one of the great love stories of the Peninsula, and had already inspired the two classical Nise plays of Bermúdez in the 1570's, and other works. Although this time Vélez seems to have had no immediate model for his play, it too comes unusually close to the classical pattern. In the simplicity of its plot, in its limited range of time and space, and above all in its contemplation of an action known to the whole audience in advance, it is unlike most Golden Age drama, and in particular the spectacular entertainment usually provided by Vélez. Compared with the irresponsibility which characterizes so many *comedias*, its honest and moving expression of emotion makes it a very adult play; it is a welcome change, for instance, to find the Prince explaining frankly to the Navarrese Infanta why he cannot marry her. In so far as it can be called a tragedy, it is almost a tragedy of fate in the ancient manner. There is, of course, a clash between the opposing forces of love and *raison d'état*; but a modern tragic concept would have required this conflict to be centred in the Prince, who in fact experiences no dilemma and is not at the heart of the action. Inés herself is so much a passive victim, and the grief-stricken King so insistent upon his helplessness, that the play is almost more elegy than drama. By his delight in imagery and his liberal use of songs, Vélez has transmuted the gruesomeness of the story into a wistful lyricism, full of the traditional note of Portuguese melancholy; and the country house where Inés lives and dies seems, in atmosphere at least, not far removed from the garden to which, a century earlier, Gil Vicente sent his Don Duardos.

This brief picture of Vélez de Guevara has given no idea of the quantity of his production, probably as extensive as Tirso's;

---

[7] Edited by M. Muñoz Cortés (Madrid, Clásicos castellanos, 1959).

of his fame in his lifetime, little short of Lope's; nor of the work by which he most deserves to be remembered, his witty satirical novel *El diablo cojuelo* (*The Devil on Two Sticks*). But it has perhaps sufficed to show in what ways he contributed to the development of the *comedia*, and how he prepared the way for Calderón.

Antonio Mira de Amescua, born in the mid-1570's, an Andalusian priest who was rebuked for spending more time among the literary coteries of Madrid than in his chaplaincy at Granada, also produced a far wider range of plays than can be examined here: religious dramas, comedies of intrigue and of manners, often with a strong realistic note. I shall consider chiefly his most distinctive quality, which is his moral seriousness. He himself, in his approbation of the twentieth *parte* of Lope's collected plays, states that the purpose of drama is to teach moral and political virtues. His own manner of doing this can be inferred from some of his titles: *La rueda de la fortuna* (*The Wheel of Fortune*); *El ejemplo mayor de la desdicha* (*The Most Hapless of Men*); *Próspera y adversa fortuna de Don Álvaro de Luna* (*The Rise and Fall of Don Álvaro de Luna*). Even more insistently than Alarcón he stresses the fickleness of fortune, particularly in the case of the *privado;* and once again the topical relevance is there. Álvaro de Luna is a figure who appears often in the literature of the 1620's, and for Álvaro de Luna we may nearly always read Rodrigo Calderón, whose earlier success and recent execution recalled the astonishing career of the great fifteenth-century minister. Mira's pair of plays on the subject, long ascribed to Tirso, are excellent portrayals of the pathos of downfall. In the first, the elder statesman Ruy López Dávalos is dismissed by the young Juan II to make way for his favourite Álvaro, and so great is the old man's veneration for the monarchy that the disgrace almost breaks him mentally and physically. Here as elsewhere Mira creates an effect of counterbalance: one man's rise is the measure of the other man's fall: while in the second play it is

Alvaro's own decline and death on the scaffold which point to the uncertainty of fame and fortune.[8]

The duality of "Próspera y adversa fortuna" was, of course, a commonplace of the time. It harked back to Petrarch's *De remediis utriusque fortunæ*, and echoed the Stoic motto *In utrumque paratus*. Mira preaches the essential neo-Stoic lesson, the need for equanimity in the face of all vicissitudes, far more emphatically than Alarcón, and in this shows how deep was his sense of his country's decline. Lope ignores it; Tirso and Alarcón make their political attacks, but seem to presuppose that an improvement is possible. Only Calderón, among the other dramatists, resorts like Mira to a philosophy born of despair.

One of Mira's plays must be examined in greater detail, so seminal was it for the period as a whole. This is *El esclavo del Demonio* (*The Slave of the Devil*),[9] whose title announces another drama of the sinner on a more than human scale. It is a *comedia de santo*, in which the hagiographical element is intertwined, as so often in the period, with a tiresome love intrigue. At the beginning of the play the Dominican Friar Gil is already renowned for his holiness. He comes upon a young man preparing to enter his lady's bedroom by means of a rope ladder, and utters a long admonition punctuated by the refrain

> Busca el bien, huye el mal, que es la edad corta,
> y hay muerte y hay infierno, hay Dios y gloria.   (Act I)

("Seek good, flee from evil, for life is short, and there is death and there is hell, there is God and glory.")

It is impossible not to be reminded of Tisbea's

> Advierte,
> mi bien, que hay Dios y que hay muerte.

The young man is dissuaded and goes off, but leaves the ladder behind; and Gil thinks "Why not, after all?" He makes use of it, and brings the girl down with him. The two of them take stock

---

[8] *La adversa fortuna de Don Álvaro de Luna* has been edited by Luigi de Filippo (Florence, 1960) and, under the title *La segunda de Don Aluaro*, by Nellie E. Sánchez-Arce (Mexico, 1960).

[9] Edited by A. Valbuena Prat (Madrid, Clásicos castellanos, 1926).

of their situation, and reach the apparently inconsequential deci-
sion, but one which accords with the psychology and logic of
the *comedia*, to go off to the hills as bandits. There they indulge
their appetite for crime.

> Tengo sed de pecados

("I am thirsty for sin"),

says Gil, showing, like Paulo, how the fallen saint is liable to become
the most abandoned sinner. One is tempted to write off *El
esclavo del Demonio* as derivative—until one realizes that it was
first printed in 1612, and that it must in fact have been Tirso
who copied Mira. And not only Tirso: Gil goes on to make a
Faust-like pact with the Devil, and the Devil rewards him, not
with possession of the woman he desires, but with her likeness
which turns into a skeleton in his arms; both these elements
were later to be made use of by Calderón. The beautiful woman
turned skeleton, who figures in legends of the period, is probably
the most perfect symbol of seventeenth-century disillusionment.
While Renaissance neoplatonism is still at times on the lips of
the poets, in their hearts they have learned that beauty is not
a path to God, but a sham and a snare; and Mira was one of the
first men in Spain to say so. This same disenchantment with the
life of the senses finds frequent literary expression in a trope
which sees the end of youth and beauty as dissolution into "earth,
smoke, dust, air and nothing". Góngora, Calderón, even the
sanguine Lope de Vega, all on occasion utter some version of this
despairing cadence. And again, it is in *El esclavo del Demonio*
that it makes one of its first appearances. Lisarda, like Gil, comes
to realize that

> La vida, el mundo, el gusto y gloria vana
> son junto nada, humo, sombra y pena.   (Act II)

("Life, the world, pleasure and vain glory, are but nothing, smoke, shadow
and pain.")

El esclavo del Demonio is by no means as powerful a work as the
theological dramas of Tirso, or others which were to follow; a
Spanish critic has called it, unchronologically, the younger

brother of the *Condenado*. Yet it opened the way for these master-pieces. It seems necessary to conclude that, both as author of the fine Álvaro de Luna tragedies and as one of the first to give dramatic expression to the *Zeitgeist* of seventeenth-century Spain, Mira de Amescua has never received his due meed of praise.

Mira and Vélez both died in 1644. To classify them neatly as followers of Lope and precursors of Calderón is to over-simplify; their careers overlapped with those of both giants. Yet their work, together with that of Tirso and Alarcón, exempli-fies so clearly the various modifications that were taking place, that it must be held to mark an important stage in the evolution of the *comedia*. It may be helpful to attempt a summary of these modifications.

There has been a slackening of the close link between style and content. A love of ornamentation has manifested itself, an interest in *culto* language and in complex intrigue unrelated to character, bringing with it a consequent diminution of realism. And this disruption of the harmony between matter and manner is but one aspect of a general breakdown of harmony, a disequili-brium, a loss of the sense of "rightness" and integration which informs so many of Lope's plays. Here, of course, Spanish drama-tists are sharing in the general mood of uncertainty and bewilder-ment experienced widely in Europe in the seventeenth century, as Renaissance expansiveness found itself once more fettered and frustrated; a mood whose literary expressions have often been designated "baroque". But in Spain this spirit was intensified by the country's catastrophic economic collapse and decline from greatness. The later *comedia* on the one hand reflects the national trauma in the violence of its action and in its exaggerated, un-natural characters; and on the other attempts to remedy it by throwing up two new modes. Moral drama, with its neo-Stoic teaching, offers a solution for this life; whilst theological drama, concerned primarily with the salvation of the soul, places the emphasis on the life to come, which is increasingly felt to be the only firm reality.

Texts

GUILLÉN DE CASTRO
MIRA DE AMESCUA
VÉLEZ DE GUEVARA
  Selected plays in *Dramáticos contemporáneos de Lope de Vega*, Vols. I and II, ed. Mesonero Romanos, *BAE*, vols. 43 and 45.
RUIZ DE ALARCÓN
  Comedias, ed. J. E. Hartzenbusch in *BAE*, Vol. 20.
  Obras completas, ed. Alfonso Reyes, 2 vols. (Mexico, 1957–9).
  Obras completas, ed. A. V. Ebersole, 2 vols. (New York, 1966) (a facsimile of the first edition).

10

CALDERÓN

SOMETHING clearly happened to the Spanish theatre in 1625. Not only did Tirso and Alarcón virtually cease writing then and turn to publication; Lope, who had been publishing his plays for some time, abruptly stopped, and after the appearance of his twentieth *parte* in that year, although the task was far from complete, turned instead to the issuing of religious poems. (One volume of these published in 1625 is dedicated, interestingly enough, to the wife of Olivares.) Whatever may be the full story behind the edict against Tirso, it seems fairly clear that 1625 was the year in which the views of the moralists finally prevailed to the extent that the *comedia* could henceforth only survive by coming to terms with them.

Certainly from the mid-1620's drama seems no longer to have been conceived simply as ephemeral popular entertainment. This is the age of *refundiciones*: not merely because by now it must have been difficult to find new stories, but also because a need was felt to improve, both morally and artistically, the less satisfactory creations of the earlier phase. By raising its own status, by acknowledging itself as an art, whose services, like those of painting, could be put at the disposal of morality and religion, the Spanish theatre ensured its survival for a further generation.

Don Pedro Calderón de la Barca, born in Madrid in 1600, an aristocrat and an intellectual, had had his first play put on in 1623; and it was above all he who, allying himself with the wanton *comedia*, made it respectable. He was destined by his family for the Church, and did eventually become a priest; though not until the age of 51, having meanwhile essayed the typical life

149

of a young gentleman, served in the army during the Catalan revolt of 1640, and written most of his best-known plays. The dating of his works, in so far as it is possible, depends mainly on records of performances, and from these it can be deduced that his most fruitful period was from about 1627 to 1640. The familiar painful experience of false attributions and mangled texts led him to begin publishing at an earlier stage in his career than either Lope or Tirso, and the *Primera parte* of his collected plays was brought out by his brother in 1636. Calderón's concern for the fate of his own writings has ensured that his theatre has come down to us almost in its entirety and in relatively trustworthy form. By a fortunate chance, less than a year before his death in 1681 he was asked by a friend to compile a list of all his plays. This list, which we may assume to be complete, survives, and shows him to have written 111 *comedias*. The texts of some hundred of these are still extant.

The neo-classicists whom Lope defeated are in some measure avenged by Calderón. There is of course no question of rigid Aristotelian precepts, or of any real modification of the *comedia* form. Calderón's classicism is a compromise, akin to the liberal classicism of his contemporary, the theorist González de Salas, who was presumably writing with some of Calderón's early works in mind. But his didactic preoccupations undoubtedly link him with El Pinciano and with Senecan moral tragedy, and the norms of his theatre are to a large extent those of this temporarily eclipsed genre.

Since his aim is less to entertain than to instruct, Calderón makes much more use than do his predecessors of familiar stories, and particularly those which acquire dignity from an origin in mythology or classical history, or a setting similarly distanced in time or space. Their main interest is not in the unfolding action itself, but in the theme which that action can be made to illustrate. The phrase "representable idea" which Calderón himself uses of one of his allegorical works, could well apply to the greater part of his production. It is largely irrelevant to look any longer for realism, whether in background, dialogue, or character portrayal; these aids to the suspension of disbelief were hardly Calderón's concern.

An elevated style was of course thought appropriate to classical drama, and while the theatre of Calderón by no means excludes humour and swift natural dialogue, its language is for the most part *culto*. But it still keeps the rhythms of Lope's *comedia*, with the old octosyllabic lines predominating; and this unexpected combination of exalted, seventeenth-century language with the short, simple lines which originally belonged to the popular poetry of the Middle Ages, is responsible for much of its characteristic flavour. Calderón is a fine poet; but what perhaps impresses the modern reader first in the diction of his plays is the element of artifice. The utterances of his characters, sometimes not even aware of each other's presence on the stage, will echo and balance each other like phrases in an operatic duet. Speeches will be given a pattern, one of the commonest being the enumeration of a series of images or analogies, recapitulated in the closing lines. Thus the Captain of *El Alcalde de Zalamea*, whose sergeant has marvelled at his falling in love at a single meeting, protests:

> De sola una vez a incendio
> crece una breve pavesa;
> de una vez sola un abismo
> sulfúreo volcán revienta;
> de una vez se enciende el rayo,
> que destruye cuanto encuentra;
> de una vez escupe horror
> la más reformada pieza;
> de una vez amor, ¿ qué mucho
> que, fuego en cuatro maneras,
> mina, incendio, pieza y rayo,
> postre, abrase, asombre y hiera?   (Act II)

("In one single instant a tiny spark is fanned into a blaze; in one single instant an abyss hurls out a sulphurous volcano; in one instant lightning strikes, destroying all it meets; in one instant the most ancient fire-arm spits out horror. Small wonder, then, that love, a fourfold fire with all the power of mine, blaze, fire-arm and lightning, should in one single instant overwhelm, consume, astound and strike.")

Calderón's education by the Jesuits is perhaps most immediately evident in those scenes where two characters faced with a dilemma, instead of discussing it in the rapid exchanges of natural dialogue, argue in long formal speeches, like participants in a medieval disputation. Clotaldo and Rosaura, anxious to recover the latter's honour (*La vida es sueño*, *Life is a Dream*), and Herod and Mariene, desperate to forestall a prophesied death (*El mayor monstruo los celos*, *The Monster of Jealousy*), all use the jargon of the debating chamber; and formulæ such as "The principle having been established", or "I concede the minor proposition", are common in the most varied contexts.

Calderón's florid style is a deliberate adoption of the cultured language of Renaissance lyric poetry, hitherto only sparingly used in the theatre. At his most characteristic he falls little short of the manner of Góngora, by whose classicism and richness of imagery he has clearly been influenced. There is the same piling up of metaphors—and not merely in the description, but even at moments of emotional crisis or in the heat of battle. There is the same kaleidoscopic vision which perceives in an object its affinity to so many others, that reality itself comes to seem shifting and uncertain. Particularly common in Calderón is the series of analogies for a single object, each one corresponding to one of the four elements, earth, air, fire or water.[1] Thus in the opening lines of *La vida es sueño* a bolting horse is described as lightning but for the flame, bird but for the colour, and fish but for the scales. A bright feather in a girl's hat is said to provoke a dispute between earth and air, as to whether it is a flower or a bird (*Casa con dos puertas*, Act I). Sometimes an object is given a metaphorical equivalent, and then even this is seen through the prism of imagination, and its reality fragmented and scattered among the elements: love is

> flecha
> bañada en venenos tales
> que salió del arco pluma,
> corrió por el viento ave,
> llegó rayo al corazón,
> donde se alimenta áspid. (*Casa con dos puertas*, Act I)

---

[1] See E. M. Wilson, "The four elements in the imagery of Calderón", *MLR* 31 (1936) 34–47.

("an arrow steeped in such poison that it left the bow like a feather, sped through the air like a bird, and struck like a lightning flash at the heart, where it now feeds like an asp.")

At times to the multiplicity of images Calderón prefers the development of one single one, as when the villain-hero of *El purgatorio de San Patricio* (*Saint Patrick's Purgatory*) is led on by the word "night" to speak of the brief tomb of sleep, a dark curtain drawn across the sky, mourning worn for the death of the sun, and obsequies sung by the birds of gloom. This seems at first to be a purely ornamental digression, inserted inappropriately into the factual account of a nocturnal escapade. Yet when it emerges that the adventure was the abduction and prostitution of a nun, the sacrilege and risk of damnation give significance to the insistence on darkness and death. Such use of what is now often called thematic imagery, where the sustained metaphors illuminate the meaning of a passage and sometimes even of a whole play, is a recurrent and striking feature in Calderón.

Calderón's dominant mode is rhetoric. He delights in learned allusions, figures of speech, verbal arabesques, parallelism and reiterations. Most of his plays contain long monologues, impressive as oratory, but indicative to a modern reader at least of defective dramatic technique. A modern style of acting is certainly inappropriate to them; but they seem to have delighted the audiences of their own day who, with an ear better attuned to language than ours, found grandiloquence far from distasteful.

El Alcalde de Zalamea[2] is probably the only one of Calderón's plays to which a criterion of realism is generally applicable. It represents something of a freak in his production. Many critics have assumed it to be a relatively late play, since in its depiction of soldiers billeted in a village it seems to draw on its author's own experience in the Catalan campaign of 1640. (Isabel's long monologue, in which she uses all the devices of rhetoric to tell her peasant father the story of her abduction and rape, seems quite out of place in this setting, but sprang

[2] Edited by Peter N. Dunn (Oxford, Pergamon, 1966).

from the need to give actors and actresses the kind of task they were used to by that time.) Calderón's *Alcalde de Zalamea* is based on a play of the same title attributed to Lope, and in action and spirit has much in common with the "comendador" plays. Here it is the aristocrat captain of the billeted troops who rapes the daughter of the mayor, and is punished by him, in his juridical capacity, with summary execution. Though its qualities of structure and atmosphere must not be overlooked, *El Alcalde* stands out from most other plays of the period in being a drama of character. As its title suggests, it is a play about a man, the mayor Pedro Crespo himself; a spirited and masterful though intensely human figure, of whom many facets are shown. He is seen as counsellor to his impulsive son, and gentle comforter of his wronged daughter; as sparring-partner to the gouty general, as suppliant for his daughter's honour, and relentless minister of justice. He is given a pronouncement on honour which has become a commonplace of Spanish ideology:

> Al Rey la hacienda y la vida
> se ha de dar; pero el honor
> es patrimonio del alma,
> y el alma sólo es de Dios.   (Act I)

("Life and possessions are at the King's disposal, but honour is the patrimony of the soul, and the soul belongs to God alone.")

This championship of an honour which is more than the worldly fetish of reputation must be borne in mind later when we approach the difficult question of Calderón's own view of the code.[3]

---

[3] For C. A. Jones ("*Honor* in *El Alcalde de Zalamea*", *MLR* 50, (1955, 444–9) and P. N. Dunn ("Honour and the Christian background in Calderón", *BHS* 37 (1960, 75–105, the theme of honour rather than the character of Pedro Crespo is the essence of the play. They rightly point out that a number of different attitudes to honour are embodied in the various characters of the play; but I question their suggestion that in Pedro Crespo Calderón is deliberately presenting a more humane and Christian view of honour, in contrast to the harsher approach of the husbands in the three honour tragedies which are to be studied later in this chapter. The situations are hardly comparable: there is a big difference between the rape of an innocent daughter and the suspected adultery of a wife; and Crespo does exact a bloody vengeance, even though he is at the same time the minister of justice.

With the exception of *El Alcalde de Zalamea*, Calderón's plays, like classical drama, portray aristocratic characters. Though they are still usually popular, at this stage, in the sense of being written for the public theatres and directed to the whole populace, that popular content which constituted so much of Lope's charm has gone. It is perhaps not unfair to take one of Calderón's less successful plays, *La niña de Gómez Arias* (*Gómez Arias' Girl*), as an illustration of what has been lost. It refashions a work of the same title by Vélez de Guevara; and it too resembles Lope's "comendador" plays in telling the story of a heartless philanderer and his punishment. Like *Peribáñez* it is based on a snatch of an old song:

> Señor Gómez Arias,
> doleos de mí,
> que soy niña y sola,
> y nunca en tal me vi.

("Señor Gómez Arias, have pity on me; for I am a mere girl and alone, and have never been in such a plight.")

Yet at the climax, when Gómez Arias sells his discarded victim to the Moors, and she utters the quatrain for which the audience has been waiting, it has none of the satisfying rightness in its context of Casilda's "Más quiero yo a Peribáñez. . . ". It contrasts almost jarringly with the courtly language and rhetoric at which she has already shown herself adept. She is, in any case, not the waif of the song, but a provincial society lady; and the play for over half its length is conventional love-and-honour comedy. It is admittedly very good comedy, with amusing situations skilfully contrived; but quite out of keeping with the simple pathos of the source. Calderón has not drawn the essential popular drama out of his traditional material, but has uncomfortably superimposed what he doubtless considered more artistic forms upon it. He fortunately seldom chose subjects so unamenable to his own characteristic handling.

He is not chiefly remembered as a writer of comedies, but he did write a number, and they still make excellent entertainment. They are ostensibly set in various Spanish towns, though the local colour is neither strong nor important. Lope's *Peribáñez* and Calderón's *Casa con dos puertas* are both set in the town of Ocaña; but in the one case the proximity of Toledo is a fact of some significance in the plot, whereas in the other the proximity of Aranjuez simply offers a pretext for some beautiful but extraneous descriptions of court life. These are primarily comedies of situation, whose appeal lies in their cleverly contrived plots, often shaped by balance and symmetry. Their cerebral nature is apparent in their reliance on external devices: the heroine of *La dama duende* (*The Fairy Lady*) baffles the hero by her mysterious comings and goings through a concealed door, while *Casa con dos puertas mala es de guardar* (*A House with Two Doors is Difficult to Guard*) gives the gist of the whole plot in its title. The intrigue is usually subtler than in Tirso's comedies, though the force of personality driving it forward may be less. Mischievous and impulsive heroines there are, but without the superhuman vitality of their Tirsian counterparts; and the new decorum prevents their donning male disguise to go out and recover a lost honour. (Rosaura of *La vida es sueño* is one of very few heroines to play such a part in Calderón's theatre.) Tirso's "disfrazada de varón" gives way to Calderón's "tapada", the woman who seeks adventure with her face intriguingly covered, shedding identity rather than taking on a new and masculine role.

But there are other heroines who do not scheme, whose behaviour is exemplary, and who become involved in intrigue through the indiscretion of others and the application of a rigid code of honour. These women are very unhappy, and it is in their persons and their dilemmas that the circle of brittle conventions is breached, and Calderonian comedy flows out to merge with a more serious genre. Thus Leonor of *No siempre lo peor es cierto* (*Things are not Always as Bad as they Seem*) might well have become a tragic heroine. She quite properly rejects the advances of Don Diego because she is already in love with Don Carlos. But Diego resents her apparent scorn, and a twisted sense of honour leads him to reveal his presence during one of Carlos' visits, so that she will know that *he* knows she has a lover. It will then be mutually, though tacitly, understood between them that there was a good reason for her refusal of him, and he will not have lost face. This is all very well for Diego, but it is ruinous for Leonor. Despite her assurances of innocence Carlos now rejects her, since *his* honour will not allow him to love where there is any suspicion of relations with another man. A long chain of typical adventures, concealments and overheard conversations brings everything right in the end; but Leonor's initial plight as a helpless pawn between rival men is not very different from that of other heroines for whom it leads to tragedy.

Calderón has perhaps been popularly remembered above all as the author of three powerful plays in which the code of honour forces a man to kill his wife, because she is, or appears to be, compromised by the attentions of another man. In *A secreto agravio secreta venganza* (*Secret Revenge for Secret Dishonour*)[4] and *El pintor de su deshonra* (*The Painter of his Own Dishonour*),[4] the woman has agreed to an arranged marriage, having been mistakenly informed that the man she loved was dead. He then returns to pester her and imperil her reputation, and the husband for the sake of his own good name must kill them both. Leonor of *A secreto agravio* does eventually give some encouragement to her former suitor. Serafina of *El pintor* resists hers even after he has abducted her; until, shaken by a nightmare, she momentarily drops her defences and lets him take her in his arms. But the degree of guilt in the wife is almost immaterial; the very fact of another man's attentions, even if they are unwelcome, endangers the husband's honour. When the still innocent Serafina is abducted, it is the loss of honour that her husband and his friends lament, when one might have expected them to be more concerned over her whereabouts or her safety. The third play is *El médico de su honra* (*The Doctor of his Own Honour*).[4] Here Mencía

---

[4] Edited by A. Valbuena Briones (Calderón, *Dramas de honor*, 2 vols., Madrid, Clásicos castellanos, 1956). *El médico de su honra* is also edited by C. A. Jones (Oxford University Press, 1961).

has loved the King's brother, but aware that rank made her

> para dama más
> lo que para esposa menos   (Act I)
> ("equally too good for a mistress and not good enough for a wife"),

has accepted the hand of Gutierre. After a chance encounter the Prince starts to pursue her again. She never wavers in her rejection of him, but is merely misguided in the manner of it, so that Gutierre has reason to think his honour may be at risk. It is no more than a risk, but it is enough; Mencía must die. This time no vengeance can be taken on the would-be lover (the only main character with any real guilt, as opposed to misjudgement), since his royal blood makes him immune. Indeed, as the text foreshadows and as the audience would know, he goes on after the play is finished to overthrow his brother and become King of Castile.

A number of different aspects of the code of honour are touched on in these plays. There is the impossibility of taking vengeance on the King, in whom all honour resides, or one of his blood, often expressed in the period in the formula "Del rey abajo ninguno" ("No one beneath the King [shall insult me]"). There is the close association between honour and noble birth, succinctly indicated in another formula: "Soy quien soy" ("I am who I am") is a phrase often on the lips of these troubled wives. There is the principle referred to in the title of *A secreto agravio secreta venganza*, that since honour depends on public esteem, dishonour becomes greater the more widely it is known; and the role of Don Juan, a minor character in this same play, illustrates two further aspects: the obligations of friendship and the fact that in obeying the law of honour one may still fall foul of the law of the land.

But it is honour in the marital relationship which constitutes the essence of these plays and offers the most poignant dramatic situations. Calderón does not spare our emotions. We feel the almost unbearable tensions of the wives and their terror as they face undeserved death. In each case the husband rails against an unjust and inhuman code which, ignoring his own decency, makes him helpless to avoid dishonour, and drives him to murder in order to remedy it. And yet he does each time commit the murder, in anguish but with a sense of duty done; and each time in closing scenes which seem to parallel the royal ratifications of Lope's "comendador" plays, the King or local ruler tells him he was right.

Some such exoneration by supreme authority is of course necessary to get round the fact that all these husbands have broken the law of the land, since none of their wives have been found *flagrante delicto*, which situation alone would legally have justified the taking of life; and with this as the last word, it is not surprising that generations of readers have believed that Calderón too endorsed the code of honour. Many would still maintain this view. But in recent years a different interpretation has been suggested by Professor E. M. Wilson,[5] and supported by other British critics. May not Calderón be saying in effect: "Be guided by *pundonor* if you like, but look at the injustice and inhumanity to which it can lead"? Several features of the plays can be adduced as evidence for this interpretation, but even as regards the question of royal approval alone there are strong grounds for it.

It is clear from the rest of his theatre that Calderón did not necessarily believe that kings were always right. The idea of kingship undergoes a marked change in Golden Age drama, a change which reflects both increasing dissatisfaction with the Hapsburg monarchy in Spain, and the evolution of political thought in Europe as a whole. In Lope's theatre the idea of the divine right of kings is very strong; but in the drama of Calderón —during whose lifetime an English king would be beheaded by his subjects—kings are only too fallible, whether they be historical figures like Henry VIII (*La cisma de Ingalaterra, The English Schism*) and Herod (*El mayor monstruo los celos*), or fictional entities such as Basilio of *La vida es sueño*. The King is no longer

---

[5] E. M. Wilson, "La discreción de Don Lope de Almeida", *Clavileño* 2 (1951) 1–10, and "Gerald Brenan's Calderón", *BC* 4 (1952).

the viceroy of God, the minister of divine justice among men. Kingship is wholly of this world, merely one of many parts which men are called upon to play on earth, one of the dreams from which they will awaken after death.

The key to the understanding of Calderón's honour plays would thus seem to be the existence of a double scheme of values: the worldly code, which the King embodies and must support, and a higher standard, which shows up the inadequacies of the first. The actual words in which the husbands bewail their involuntary loss of honour are significant: one speaks of an "unjust law", another of the "mad laws of this world, the tyrannical error of men". If one aspect of the code earns these epithets, can they not also apply to that which follows from it, the obligation to shed blood?

It so happens that Calderón has elsewhere left proof that he did not consider *pundonor* the ultimate criterion of right behaviour. There is a clear, if crude, illustration of the double jurisdiction in an early *auto sacramental*, *La devoción de la misa* (*Devotion to the Mass*), where Pascual is torn between the obligation to hear Mass and the duty to protect the honour of his lady. His choice of the former is approved by an angel, who assures him that being a Christian comes before being a gentleman. And the superiority of Christian values is much more movingly and convincingly shown in a later example of the same genre. Calderón sometimes takes the plots of his own plays as material for these allegorical works, one such case being *El pintor de su deshonra*. In the *auto* of that title God is the husband and the offending wife is Human Nature; but here her husband does not kill her, he pardons her.[6]

In the attempts which have been made to dissociate Calderón from a harsh and un-Christian moral code, another dramatist has perhaps not received his due. Tirso de Molina made very little dramatic use of these sterner aspects of *pundonor*, and advised

[6] The different solutions in the two versions of *El pintor* were first pointed out as long ago as 1937 by A. Valbuena Prat in his *Historia de la literatura española*.

extreme caution in their application in real life. His hero in
El celoso prudente suspects his wife's infidelity and is prepared to
kill her, but prudently investigates and finds her innocent. He
too, while still in doubt, deplores the laws of honour, in terms
more outspoken than any found in Calderón:

> ¡ Ay, leyes fieras del mundo,
> de las de Dios embarazo! (Act III)
> ("Oh savage laws of this world, an impediment to the law of God!")

Here is a clear enunciation of the idea of a higher and lower
moral standard; and it is repeated elsewhere in Tirso:

> Venganza, sólo sois vos
> ley del mundo sin prudencia;
> ley de Dios sois vos, clemencia.
> (*Escarmientos para el cuerdo*, Act II)
> ("Vengeance, you are but the law of the imprudent world; you, mercy,
> are the law of God.")

Although Calderón is not as unequivocal as this in his honour
plays, he does seem to hold a similar view of a heavenly versus
an earthly set of values; and as I have shown elsewhere,[7] since
we know that he borrowed other material from *El celoso prudente*,
it is likely that his ideas on *pundonor* were at least partly shaped
by his reading of Tirso.

Whatever the moral attitude underlying them, Calderón's
honour tragedies are all fine examples of stage entertainment.
Of the three, *El médico de su honra* is perhaps the richest in its
dramatic texture. Its sub-plot which concerns Gutierre's earlier
relationship with another woman serves to characterize him and
to illumine still more the cruelty of excessive scruple in matters
of honour, as well as to advance the main action. Settings play
their part in the build-up of tension, whether in the disastrously
overheard conversations in the King's sumptuous Moorish
palace in Seville, or in Gutierre's unexpected return and furtive

---

[7] Margaret Wilson, "Tirso and *pundonor*: a note on *El celoso prudente*",
BHS 38 (1961) 120–5.

entry into his own garden after dark; while few climaxes could be more spine-chilling than the revelation in the early morning light of a hand imprinted in blood on Gutierre's door, followed by the sight of Mencía's bloodless corpse. Gutierre must of course keep his possible dishonour secret, and so he coldly devises for Mencía an end which looks accidental, allowing her to bleed to death through the apparent negligence of a physician. Hence the title of the play and the conceit sustained through many of its scenes; for Gutierre argues that his honour is sick, that he is the physician who must cure it, and that the only remedy is a blood-letting. This conceit is little more than adumbrated in Calderón's source play, an earlier *Médico de su honra* ascribed to Lope; it is developed in Tirso's *El celoso prudente*; but only Calderón carries it through to the point where the imagery of bleeding becomes central to the play.

Nor is this obvious imagery, to which the playgoer's attention is directed by the title, the only kind of which Calderón makes use. The darkness in which much of the action takes place serves not only as atmosphere but as symbol. Gutierre, availing himself of darkness to spy on his wife, admits his aberration:

> Mato la luz, y llego
> sin luz y sin razón, dos veces ciego.   (Act II)

("I will put out the light and grope my way in doubly blind, lacking light and lacking reason.")

Honour necessitates secrecy, which is ensured by darkness, and so he again puts out the light as he leads the blood-letter away from his wife's death-bed. Moreover, since he more than once describes Mencía as the sun, these incidental extinctions point to the fact that in killing her he is putting out the very light of his life. He loves Mencía. Calderón is perhaps not able to convince us of this as intimately as Lope convinces us of the love of Peribáñez for Casilda, but Gutierre himself says so repeatedly, and believes it. He loves her more than he has loved any other woman; yet honour requires him to sacrifice her and to marry the less loved Leonor. An opposition between love and honour runs through the play. "El amor te adora, el honor te aborrece" (Act III) ("Love adores you, honour abhors you") he writes to Mencía; while she has earlier summed herself up in the simple statement: "Tuve amor y tengo honor" (Act I) ("I had love, now I have honour"). Her honour is a "mountain of ice", the fire of her former love for the Prince is shut away in "prisons of snow". The old Petrarchan commonplaces are thus given new life. It is possible to trace an equation between honour, cold, darkness and death, to which are opposed love, warmth, light and life; and to see the imagery of the play as this time not merely decorative but thematic, reinforcing its action and its lesson, and greatly enriching its poetic texture.

Although Calderón frequently refashions the work of earlier playwrights, the range of his serious dramas is rather different from that found in Lope. He still draws repeatedly on legend and history, but less exclusively on the legends and history of Spain. His desire for a moral and respectable theatre founded on authority leads him to take more stories from antiquity and other sources similarly remote in time or space, which have in common their suitability as moral exemplars. As Dr. Albert E. Sloman has shown, his *refundiciones* are all carried out in such a way as both to improve artistically on the original, and to point a clearer moral lesson.[8]

Events of a mere century earlier, but set in a distant land, offered him perfect material for his needs in *La cisma de Ingalaterra*.[9] This is straightforward historical drama, in which a simple reporting of the facts is enough to warn against the surrender to lust which damages Henry VIII, and the graver, because spiritual, sin of excessive ambition in Ann Boleyn and Wolsey. It is also fine, compassionate human drama, realistic in its portrayal of character and relatively sober in expression. Another

[8] Albert E. Sloman, *The Dramatic Craftsmanship of Calderón* (Oxford, 1958).
[9] See A. A. Parker, "Henry VIII in Shakespeare and Calderón. An appreciation of *La cisma de Ingalaterra*", *MLR* 43 (1948) 327–52.

play of the same early period[10] gives a constructive example
of a virtue, indicated in its title: *El príncipe constante*.[11] Fernando
of Portugal, brother of Henry the Navigator, is the constant prince
who in imprisonment, degradation and martyrdom by the
Moors never wavers in his Christian faith. Constancy is perhaps
not a very dramatic quality, allowing by itself for little development or complexity in the action. But Calderón guards against
a too unilinear plot by introducing Fénix, the Moorish princess,
as a counterpoise to Fernando. She is beautiful, like the flowers
in the garden where she sits with her ladies, and feels horror
at the prophecy that she will one day be "the price of a dead
man". But the captive Fernando reminds her that the flowers
will soon die; and when she, captive in her turn, is exchanged
as ransom for the dead body of the Prince, the prophecy is
fulfilled, and ephemeral beauty set at its true value. Unlike
La cisma, this is a very stylized play, full of lyrical interludes,
pattern and rhetoric. The long rousing speech delivered by
Fernando while he is dying of disease and starvation is a striking
instance of Calderón's lack of concern for realism. The play is
also one of Calderón's most openly didactic. Constancy is described in terms taken from St. Thomas Aquinas and is early
equated with Stoic equanimity:

> en un ánimo constante
> siempre se halla igual semblante
> para el bien y el mal.   (Act I)

("A constant spirit always shows the same face to good and ill alike.")

The flowers find "both cradle and grave present in the bud"
(Act II); and this neo-Stoic insistence on the swift approach of
death, and the need for detachment from worldly values, becomes

[10] Parker thinks *La cisma* too good to be an early play, but N. D. Shergold
and J. E. Varey have shown ("Some early Calderón dates", *BHS* 38, 1961,
277) that payment for a performance of a play of this title was made in 1627.
There seem to be no strong grounds for believing that this was *not* Calderón's
play, especially as it is more naturalistic in technique than works known to
date from a later period.

[11] See E. M. Wilson and W. J. Entwistle, "Calderón's *Príncipe constante*:
two appreciations", *MLR* 34 (1939) 207–22; and A. E. Sloman, *The Sources
of Calderón's "El príncipe constante"* (Oxford, 1950).

increasingly urgent as Fernando nears his earthly end.

> Hombre, mira que no estés
> descuidado: la verdad
> sigue, que hay eternidad;
> y otra enfermedad no esperes
> que te avise, pues tú eres
> tu mayor enfermedad.
> Pisando la tierra dura
> de continuo el hombre está,
> y cada paso que da
> es sobre su sepultura.   (Act III)

("Man, pay heed, follow the truth, for there is eternity to come; and do not wait for sickness to warn you, for you yourself are your own greatest sickness. Man continually treads the hard earth, and every step he takes is on his grave.")

There is a romantic wistfulness about the garden scenes, and the attraction of natural beauty is most poignantly felt. But its equation, in a startling baroque juxtaposition, with the stinking body of Fernando, makes it clear that no Platonism can be countenanced. Only those spiritual qualities which survive death are worthy of regard.

Woman is, for Calderón, more appropriately associated with other virtues than beauty. In telling the story of Coriolanus in *Las armas de la hermosura* (*Beauty's Weapons*),[12] he alters the historical period so as to make his hero's betrothed one of the Sabine women. She thus already represents a reconciliation between hostile peoples, and is given the further role of peacemaker between the estranged Coriolanus and his fatherland, preaching that forgiveness is nobler than vengeance. One feature of Calderón's style which is very marked in this play and elsewhere is the use of hyperbole, often on a cosmic scale. Not only is the violence of the action described in exaggerated terms, but a character experiencing strong emotion will invoke the whole universe to express it. Thus Veturia calls not only on the gods, but on the heavenly bodies, the four elements and their inhabitants, and all the physical features of the earth to give her patience.

[12] See the essay on this play by A. A. Parker, "History and poetry: the Coriolanus theme in Calderón", in *Hispanic Studies in Honour of I. González Llubera* (Oxford, 1959), pp. 211–24.

Herod, of *El mayor monstruo los celos*, repeatedly exaggerates his rage and grief to cosmic proportions:

> Soy epílogo y cifra
> de las miserias humanas.

("I am the limit and the sum of all human misery.")

> ¡ Oh caigan, oh caigan
> sobre mí mares y montes!

("Let seas and mountains overwhelm me!")

> Esferas altas,
> cielo, sol, luna y estrellas,
> nubes, granizos y escarchas,
> ¿ no hay un rayo para un triste?   (Act II)

(" Lofty spheres, heavens, sun, moon and stars, clouds, hails and frosts, can you not spare a thunderbolt to despatch an unhappy man?")

This is a play which uses the old device of prophecy and its fulfilment to give it structure: although Herod loves his wife passionately, she will be killed by his dagger. The resulting action is undistinguished; but the theme of the play, enunciated in its title, is well sustained. Herod is so consumed by love for his wife that he cannot bear the thought of another man possessing her, even after his death, and gives orders that if he should die in battle, she must be killed too. The honour plays have sometimes been compared to *Othello*, but Herod's overmastering passion offers a far closer parallel to the frenzy of the Moor. When reproved for his excesses he retorts:

> Cuando amor no es locura
> no es amor.   (Act I)

("When love is not madness it is not love.")

But of course he is wrong: a passion so possessive that it denies the loved one even the right to live is indeed madness, but it is insane jealousy rather than love. Even marital love can become warped and sinful, if the passions are not controlled by a true respect for the other's personality and freedom.

It is easy to see how Calderón uses his historical subjects for the moral lessons they may be made to convey; but I hope that something of the wisdom and profundity of his teaching is also apparent. Wolsey, Henry and Ann are clearly in error; Fernando is a straightforward example of neo-Stoic constancy. Yet even *El príncipe constante* is more than a simple parable;

and a few years later Calderón goes beyond clear cases of right
and wrong to show that principles normally upheld by decent
men—military power, marital love, or family honour—can
themselves represent a distortion of values. Moral confusion,
adherence to the wrong set of values, is, as A. A. Parker has
justly shown, the keynote of most of Calderón's great dramas.[13]

His religious plays show a comparable increase in depth and
complexity. The early *Purgatorio de San Patricio* is a derivative
play, based on an old legend and borrowing also from other
comedias. Like Tirso's Enrico, its main character introduces
himself with an appeal to the Devil, and boasts of his many
crimes, yet clings to the Christian faith. Like Mira de Amescua's
Gil, he wants to go on living in order to sin more; but passes
after conversion from one extreme of the moral scale to the other:

> Yo soy Ludovico Enio:
> temblad a mi nombre todos,
> que soy monstruo de humildad,
> si fui de soberbia monstruo.   (Act III)

("I am Ludovico Enio: let all tremble at my name, for I am a monster of
humility, who was once a monster of pride.")

Ludovico is the simple type of the Christian sinner, drawn
in exaggerated strokes. Although at one point he spurns God's
mercy, his faith enables grace to work on him to the extent of
granting him a vision of death, which converts him; after
which he is able to expiate his sins in "St. Patrick's Purgatory",
an awesome cave in an Irish mountain-side. The setting of much
of the play is strange and farouche, to match his character, which
is described in terms of the globe:

> Soy un abismo de culpas
> y un piélago de furor,
> soy un mapa de delitos,
> y el más grave pecador
> del mundo.   (Act III)

("I am an abyss of sins and an ocean of fury, I am a map of crimes and the
greatest sinner in the world");

but the legendary purgatory also serves as a device whereby

[13] A. A. Parker, "Henry VIII in Shakespeare and Calderón", *MLR* 43
(1948) 338.

Calderón can present as happening on earth events which allegorize the death and purgation of a sinful believer.

Elsewhere Calderón resorts to supernatural occurrences to
prolong the action after the main character's death. The Constant
Prince appears in glory to spur on the Portuguese army, and to
leave the audience in no doubt that his steadfastness has been
worth while. An ending which at a first reading seems less
acceptable is that of *La devoción de la Cruz* (*Devotion to the Cross*).[14]
Another wicked man, a bandit and habitual murderer, pays for
his crimes with death. But he is miraculously restored to life
for just long enough to enable him to make his confession and
save his soul, this special grace being accorded him because of
his lifelong devotion to the symbol of the Cross. There is much
more than this to the plot, which turns on undisclosed identity,
and the profligate's love for the woman who, unknown to either
of them, is his twin sister, and like himself has a birthmark in
the shape of a cross on her breast. A masterly account and interpretation of the play has been made available by Professor
Parker.[15] He reminds us that it is a mistake to apply any lingering
criteria of realism to the action of such a work, but shows that
in its theme it can still be a convincing expression of human and
divine truth; for Eusebio's crimes arise ultimately from the
mistaken values of his father, who through unwarranted concern
for his honour had repudiated his innocent wife and left his
newborn son to be a foundling; while to this parental harshness
is opposed the unfailing mercy of God, of which the Cross is
the visible symbol.

I am convinced that Parker's interpretation is the true one;
yet modern readers have repeatedly failed to find it for themselves,
and have been revolted by a play which seemed to suggest that
eternal salvation could be won by the superstitious veneration
of a symbol. There is a real difficulty here. If Calderón's intention
was to preach love and mercy, why did he not make his lesson

---

[14] Edited by A. Valbuena Prat (Calderón, *Comedias religiosas*, Madrid,
Clásicos castellanos, 1930).
[15] See *The Approach to the Spanish Drama of the Golden Age* (London, 1957).

unambiguously clear? Eusebio has shown no mercy to his victims; his respect has been only for the outward form of the Cross; the explicit lesson of the play is that enunciated in the title and repeated twice near the end:

> Tanto con Dios alcanza
> de la Cruz la devoción.
> ("So much can devotion to the Cross win from God.")

This has understandably been described as fetishism. But of course fetishism is a word which has no meaning to the believer in the revered object, for whom it is no empty form but one charged with spiritual significance. Calderón would almost certainly not have understood that any differentiation could be made between the outward form and the inner realities it stood for. Trained to think sacramentally, he would, like many Spaniards today, unquestioningly identify the material object of devotion with its spiritual associations, and see no need to clarify his lesson any further. If, moreover, the play was written in celebration of some religious feast, possibly that of the "Cruz de mayo", or Invention of the Cross, on 3rd May, then the emphasis on the outward form would be perfectly natural. I am not aware of any independent evidence that this was the case, but the play does seem to me to have an affinity with the *autos sacramentales* written for the feast of Corpus Christi and exalting the Blessed Sacrament, in which devotion to the outward forms of the Sacrament naturally implies adherence to all the spiritual realities they incarnate.

Eusebio, like Ludovico Enio, owes something to *El esclavo del Demonio*; but in the careful chain of cause and effect which this time explains his character and his career, Calderón shows the intellectual maturity to which he had attained during the second decade of his dramatic activity. *El mágico prodigioso (The Prodigious Magician)*[14] also copied Mira de Amescua's play, this time in its dramatization of a pact with the Devil; and again the notion is handled with far more subtlety and persuasiveness.

---

[14] Edited by A. Valbuena Prat (Calderón, *Comedias religiosas*, Madrid, Clásicos castellanos, 1930).

Cipriano, a student in third-century Antioch, is groping towards a knowledge of the true God. The Devil tries to defeat him in argument (and for once Calderón's scholastic disputatory style is entirely appropriate), but fails. He then tempts him with the sight of the beautiful Justina, and this time succeeds so well that Cipriano agrees to sell his soul for her. Justina is beginning to love Cipriano too, and the Devil plays on her emotions with haunting voices urging "amor, amor", and suggestive images of love: the nightingale, the clinging vine, the faithful sunflower. But Justina is a Christian, and knows she must resist. She invokes the help of God—and the Devil is beaten. He cannot now give Cipriano the real Justina, but only her likeness, which turns into a skeleton in his arms. This is the moment of Cipriano's awakening. He realizes the deceitfulness of the Devil, and the power of Justina's God, whom he recognizes as the deity he has been seeking. He embraces her faith, and goes with her to a martyr's death.

In one respect at least this is an unusually satisfying version of the Faust theme. The possession of a beautiful woman is a constant feature of the story, but it is more often one episode among many in the hero's enjoyment of power. Even Helen of Troy, symbol though she be of all sexual delight, is only incidental in the career of Marlowe's Faustus. In *El mágico* the female element is fully integrated, to the extent that Justina becomes the very pivot of the action. The scene of her temptation is a magnificent climax. Innumerable plays use music as an embellishment, but Calderón here incorporates it into the very stuff of his drama. In such near-operatic scenes as this one is reminded of the ritual origins of drama; and their emotional impact must have had great power to involve the audience at a non-rational level. Where Lope had used realism as a means of securing the audience's participation in his fictions, Calderón prefers stylization; but the distancing effect this might have is amply counteracted by the æsthetic and sensuous appeal of his richly textured plays. As with the music and incense, the action and symbolism of the Mass, they address themselves to the whole hearer, not his intellect alone; and their great popularity in their day must have been due at least as much to their ritual power of catharsis as to the force of their moral teaching or the intellectual beauty of their devising.

Justina shows that free will, aided by divine grace, is always strong enough to resist temptation, but it is in Cipriano that the real anagnorisis takes place. He must learn, like Fénix, that beauty is subject to death and decay. He must mistrust his deceiving eyes, which show him the loveliness of the flesh, and see only the enduring skeleton. The senses spread illusion, but he must awaken to the disillusionment or *desengaño*, which is the essential mood of seventeenth-century Spain. For Peribáñez and Casilda love, work, home, honour and religion were all strands in the one fabric of life; now the unity is gone, and love of a woman can no longer seem of a piece with love of God. Instead there is a baroque duality, a cleavage and opposition between body and soul, illusion and reality. *El mágico prodigioso* is one of the great seventeenth-century dramas of *desengaño*.

A greater drama still in the eyes of many critics is *La vida es sueño*,[16] generally regarded as Calderón's masterpiece. It owes its fame in part to its diffusion through early German critics and its influence on Grillparzer, and even more to the unusual breadth of its conception. It contains no specifically Christian teaching, and Prince Segismundo, bewildered by his experiences and struggling towards a *modus vivendi*, is easily seen as an allegory of Man, constantly seeking to understand the meaning of life. Yet analysis shows it to be entirely in harmony with Calderón's other moral dramas.

Its story is a complex one, since main action and sub-plot are closely intertwined and cannot be narrated separately. Rosaura has been seduced by Prince Astolfo of Muscovy, and has followed him to Poland, dressed as a man, hoping to induce him to restore her honour by marriage. There she stumbles on the remote prison where King Basilio has caused his son Segismundo

---

[16] Edited by Albert E. Sloman (Manchester, 1961).

to be brought up, to avert the disasters foretold by his horoscope. This had prophesied that Segismundo would be a monster who would bring civil war to the kingdom and trample his father's grey hairs underfoot. He has been given a tutor, Clotaldo, to bring him up, but is still a wild and passionate creature, resentful of his imprisonment and prompt to respond with violence to any frustration. Basilio feels some compunction at his treatment of his son, and decides to put him to the test. He is to be drugged and brought unconscious to the palace, where he may prove himself fit to rule after all. If not, he can return as he came, and will think that his brief taste of freedom was merely a dream. Basilio will then effect a marriage between his niece and nephew, Estrella and Astolfo, and bestow the kingdom on them.

Clotaldo, meanwhile, has realized that he is Rosaura's father, and is therefore responsible for her honour and under an obligation to do all he can to marry her to Astolfo. He brings her to the palace and gets her appointed lady-in-waiting to Estrella. Segismundo is now in the palace too, and the sight of Rosaura arouses his lust. After other manifestations of lack of control, it is his assault on Rosaura and his attempt to murder Clotaldo when he comes to her defence that finally convince Basilio that the experiment has failed. Segismundo must go back to the tower.

There he is prepared to accept Clotaldo's explanation that it was all a dream, but the unsettling experience has robbed him of certainty. In a famous monologue he voices something like utter weariness and disbelief. One seems to hear echoes of Macbeth's "Life's but a walking shadow . . . a tale told by an idiot", in

> ¿ Qué es la vida? Un frenesí.
> ¿ Qué es la vida? Una ilusión,
> una sombra, una ficción,
> y el mayor bien es pequeño;
> que toda la vida es sueño,
> y los sueños sueños son.   (Act II)

("What is life? A frenzy. What is life? An illusion, a shadow, a fiction, and the greatest good it offers is but small; for the whole of life is a dream, and dreams are only dreams.")

Yet even as he says this he doubts his own scepticism, for one of his memories seems undeniably real. He had, for the first time, loved a woman, and this was a new experience he could hardly have dreamed. But whether the palace was a dream or not, he had lost its freedom and its delights through his uncontrolled behaviour, and so comes to realize that, in whatever uncertainty about life, it still pays to do what is right:

> No se pierde
> obrar bien, aun entre sueños.   (Act III)
> ("Doing good is not wasted, even in dreams.")

This moment marks the beginning of his conversion.

Though the episode is closed for Basilio, it is not so for his subjects, who having learned of the existence of a crown prince now demand that he shall be acknowledged. An army marches to the tower to free Segismundo, battle ensues, and the King does indeed come to kneel at his son's feet, expecting annihilation. But Segismundo has learned his lesson. A third meeting with Rosaura has given him the chance to overcome his lust and confirm his adherence to the principle of "obrar bien". He restores his father to the throne, marries Rosaura to Astolfo, and gives his own hand to his cousin Estrella. The three encounters with Rosaura have thus provided the occasion and framework for Segismundo's growth from a brute to a rational moral being; and he, by making himself fit to rule, has thwarted the marriage of Astolfo and Estrella and brought about the restoration of Rosaura's honour.[17]

It will be seen that the play is not merely an allegory. All these characters, even Segismundo, are individuals with their own stories, some of which have no wider relevance. The sub-plot concerning Rosaura and her honour has certainly not the wide universal significance of Segismundo's search for reality; and some of its episodes, such as Estrella's jealousy and a tussle over a portrait, bring the play down abruptly from its high philosophical level. Here, as in analogous episodes in *El mágico prodigioso* and *El mayor monstruo*, Calderón is speaking to his

[17] See A. E. Sloman, "The structure of Calderón's *La vida es sueño*", *MLR* 48 (1953) 293–300.

seventeenth-century Spanish audience through the dramatic conventions it knew; just as Tirso introduces *comedia* intrigue into his biblical dramas, to the slight detriment of their enjoyment by most modern readers.

One of the themes of the main action seems similarly irrelevant today, but is in fact resolved in such a way as to transcend its temporal limitation. Segismundo's horoscope is of great importance, not merely, as in so many prophecy plays, as a device to set the plot in motion and bring it to a neat conclusion, but because through it Calderón gives serious teaching on the influence of the stars. It is the old orthodox lesson of Aquinas, that the stars incline but do not compel. Segismundo reiterates it in his last long monologue of the play, but adds moral depth by making an object-lesson of his father's mistake. By depriving his baby son of the civilizing influences of home and society, Basilio had only confirmed him in his brutishness, and brought about the very situation he had hoped to avert. This was not the way. We cannot forestall events; we can only so regulate our conduct in the face of them as to minimize their dire effects, and as far as possible to bring good out of evil. Even if we no longer take our horoscopes seriously, few of us would question the wisdom of this attitude towards the future.

But it is, of course, the theme of the title which has made this play so widely known. "La vida es sueño" is perhaps not quite so straightforward a statement as it first appears, and we owe much of our present understanding of the work to a penetrating analysis by Edward M. Wilson.[18] There is an apparent contradiction in Segismundo's reflections at the end of Act II: if the *whole* of life is a dream, there is no point in any of it, not even in doing good; good done in dreams is as much of an illusion as all the rest. Moreover, the idea of dreaming itself presupposes that at other times the dreamer is awake, and able to recognize his past dream as such; if the whole of life were a dream, we should have no means of recognizing that it

---

[18] E. M. Wilson, "*La vida es sueño*", *RUBA* 4 (1946) 61–78.

was one. But Segismundo does not really believe that the whole of life is a dream. He already has an inkling of a more lasting reality in his love for Rosaura. His problem is to distinguish between dream and waking, between illusion and reality—to become *desengañado*, in fact; and this he has already begun to do in this same great monologue:

> Sueña el rico en su riqueza
> que más cuidados le ofrece;
> sueña el pobre que padece
> su miseria y su pobreza; . . .
> y en el mundo, en conclusión,
> todos sueñan lo que son,
> aunque ninguno lo entiende.   (Act II)

("The rich man dreams the wealth that brings him care; the poor man dreams his poverty and want; . . . and in short, everyone in the world dreams what he is although none realizes it.")

Dreams *what* he is, not *that* he is. Man's existence itself is not illusory, but only the ephemeral trappings of it (of which, be it noted, kingship is given as an example); the awakened dreamer will know the one from the other.

Calderonian style is seen at its richest in this play, and thematic imagery again reinforces the lesson. Segismundo in his tower is alternately "a living corpse", "a live skeleton", "a man among beasts and beast among men"—an embryo creature not yet put to the test of living in the world. The tower is an abode of darkness, set in a savage landscape. From there he is born into the "dream" of the palace, but the true awakening to light, the rebirth of conversion—"to give birth" is in Spanish "dar a luz"—comes only with *desengaño*. This for Calderón is not the negative, despondent thing that "disillusion" suggests to us, but a constructive process of enlightenment. It is to "la luz del desengaño" that Segismundo's journey from his dark tower leads him.

La vida es sueño is seen to be another play about moral confusion and the search for right values, but one whose scope is not this time limited to any one sphere of human conduct. It certainly has a special relevance to princes and rulers, who are shown that they must subordinate their own desires to the common good, but it is also a didactic drama for everyone, with the simple, comprehensive lesson "obrar bien". And it is even more than this. Segismundo in his frustration and bewilderment is also a perfect artistic expression of baroque anguish. "The Renaissance delight in new human potentialities was necessarily followed by a sharper sense of the contrast with the unchanging limitations of human existence."[19] This is one explanation given for the pessimism of much of early seventeenth-century English literature, but do not Segismundo's experiences in the palace offer an exact analogy to it? And since many men in all centuries must undergo something of the same blind groping towards an understanding of life, it is not difficult to see the dreaming prince, for all his closeness to his author and his author's day, as a symbol of mankind. That Calderón also saw him as such is shown by the *auto sacramental* which he was many years later to base on his play.

Texts

Comedias ed. J. E. Hartzenbusch, in *BAE*, Vols. 7, 9, 12, 14.
Obras completas (Madrid, Aguilar).
    Vol. I: *Dramas*, ed. L. Astrana Marín (1933).
    Vol. II: *Comedias*, ed. A. Valbuena Briones (1956).
    Vol. III: *Autos sacramentales*, ed. A. Valbuena Prat (1952).

Critical Works

HESSE, EVERETT W., *Colderón de la Barca* (New York, Twayne's World Authors Series, 1967).
SLOMAN, A. E., *The Dramatic Craftsmanship of Calderón* (Oxford, 1958).
Critical Essays on the Theatre of Calderón, ed. B. W. Wardropper (New York, 1965).
    (A useful collection of recent important articles, including three referred to in the notes to this chapter: those by C. A. Jones and P. N. Dunn on honour in *El Alcalde de Zalamea*, and that by E. M. Wilson on *La vida es sueño*, here given in an English version.)

---

[19] R. G. Cox, "A survey of literature from Donne to Marvell", in the *Penguin Guide to English Literature*, Vol. 3, ed. Boris Ford (1956), p. 46.

11

CALDERÓN *(continued)*
ROJAS ZORRILLA, MORETO

IN 1644 Philip IV's Queen died; and scarcely had the theatres reopened after the customary period of mourning when the death of Prince Baltasar Carlos, heir to the throne, caused them to be closed again. This closure lasted from 1646 to 1649, during which time many actors left the stage altogether. The *corrales* never quite recovered from this long interruption. Their heyday was over, and though they continued in existence into the eighteenth century, they are of little further interest for the history of Spanish drama.

But there was by this time a third theatre in Madrid.[1] It too was public in so far as the populace was admitted to it, but it was in fact the King's own theatre, situated in the royal palace. From the Middle Ages the performance of masques, pageants and eventually plays had been a regular feature of court life, and a tradition of lavish spectacles of this kind had grown up side by side with that of the simpler *comedia*. By the 1620's a special salon had been set aside for them in the old palace, and when the great new Buen Retiro palace was built for Philip IV in what is still today the Retiro Park, a theatre was incorporated in it. It was called the Coliseo; and its auditorium copied such *corral* features as the lateral boxes and the *cazuela*. Apparently even the *corral* habits of arguments and catcalls were deliberately encouraged for the amusement of the royal spectators.

The stage of the Coliseo, however, was not like those of the *corrales*, but one such as is usual today, with a proscenium arch

[1] For all the material on theatres and staging in this chapter see N. D. Shergold, *A History of the Spanish Stage* (Oxford, 1967).

177

and curtain, a backcloth, and wings. This type of stage had been introduced from Italy by Cosme Lotti, a brilliant stage designer and *metteur en scène*, who worked for Philip from 1626 until his death in 1643. In addition to painted scenery he also made great use of stage machinery, through which he seems to have been able to achieve astonishing effects of movement and scenic transformation. The story of the actor in Alarcón's *Anticristo* who refused to fly makes it clear that simple stage machines or *tramoyas* were already in use in the *corrales* by 1623. They became increasingly popular there, but could never compete with the far more elaborate contrivances of Cosme Lotti and his successors at the court theatre.

Theatrical performances were renewed in 1649 in honour of Philip's second marriage, and for the rest of the century, apart from an interruption after Philip's own death in 1665, the Coliseo was the scene of sumptuous spectacle plays put on for royal birthdays and other occasions, and also of *comedias* from the everyday repertory of the *corrales*. Its superior facilities attracted a large paying public, and it had first claim on the services of actors, who quite often had to dishonour their other commitments when they were summoned to perform in the palace. This unfair competition undoubtedly contributed to the decline of the public theatres.

The break of the 1640's was matched by a similar interruption and change of course in the career of Calderón. His participation in the Catalan campaign at the relatively advanced age of 40 suggests that he may already have been feeling unsettled. The long closure of the theatres no doubt made him review his position, and in 1651 he took the step planned for him so long before, and became a priest. Thereafter he wrote no more for the *corrales*. The output of his last thirty years consists entirely of *autos sacramentales* for the feast of Corpus Christi, and court plays, mainly on mythological subjects, for the royal theatre.

Calderón served his apprenticeship to court drama with Cosme Lotti himself in pre-Coliseo years, and there is a record of their collaboration in *El mayor encanto amor* (*The Witchcraft of Love*), elaborately staged on the lake in the Retiro Park in the summer of 1635. This play tells the story of Ulysses and Circe, and the latter's enchantments offer plenty of scope for the achievement of startling effects through the use of stage machinery. A palace appears and disappears, men step out of tree-trunks, turn into swine, are swallowed up by the earth; Iris comes down from heaven on a rainbow; hail falls. The original conception was that of Lotti, who devised the entertainment chiefly as a breath-taking spectacle for which Calderón was merely to provide suitable dialogue. Calderón objected to this and asserted the primacy of the text; but he did incorporate many of Lotti's proposed effects, and it is clear that we get a very inadequate impression of the work if we consider the printed text alone.

The same is true of the score of mythological dramas which Calderón wrote after 1651. In them the *comedia* as a genre is stretched to its limits. They retain the three-act structure and the varied verse forms, and since they were performed by the regular acting companies they inevitably employ stock types. Their *graciosos* are perhaps their closest link with the *comedia* of Lope, providing humour now by their very incongruity in a mythological setting. Merlín of *La estatua de Prometeo* (*Prometheus' Statue*)[2] steps right outside mythology to make quips about coachmen and grumble like a typical Golden Age servant about his wages and his inadequate meals. But these plays have, not merely as decoration but as something integral to them, a complexity of staging quite alien to the old *comedias*. As their subject-matter draws further away from reality their scenery becomes more elaborate and realistically painted. Frequent scene changes occur, and stage directions give some indication of what could be achieved by *tramoyas*: "A rock opens." "Minerva and Prometheus fly on a tree trunk." "Venus and Cupid fly on the backs of swans." "A volcano erupts, throwing out dense smoke." Flight, and the appearance of gods in the air, are common occurrences which clearly presented no difficulties. These same gods often emphasize their divinity by uttering their lines in recitative

[2] Edited by C. V. Aubrun (Paris, 1958, 2nd ed., 1965).

rather than in speech. Music, like staging, is no longer an adjunct but integral to the work. The repetition of musical refrains often stresses a theme or lesson; and so much of *Eco y Narciso* is sung that parts of it seem more opera than play. Patterned and symmetrical movement also contributes to the whole, so that these works come almost to constitute a genre of their own, to which scenic, operatic and choreographic elements belong as essentially as the text itself.

But even if the mere reader loses much of the magic, the texts will usually still repay his study. In the earlier plays of the group, such as *La hija del aire* (*The Daughter of the Air*) which dates from 1653, he will find a richness of poetic texture unsurpassed anywhere in the *comedia*. Menón's speech describing the beautiful Semiramis whom he has found hidden in a cave (*La hija del aire*, Part I, Act II) contains no fewer than thirty-three images. Among them are the usual trite metaphors of gold and ivory, rose and lily, coral and pearl, but there is more density of meaning in the "golfo de rayos" ("ocean of lightning flashes") which is her hair; and one can also find a more significant, thematic use of imagery in the way in which Menón keeps returning to the idea of society and the body politic to convey the conjunction of Semiramis' features. The separate locks of her loose-flowing hair are a rebellious republic; the hair usurps the dominion of the brow; the black eyes are Ethiopians reigning in the Alps, but reigning barbarously since they kill for the sake of killing; the mouth is the court of the soul. In this way Menón points the contrast between the woman's beauty and the wild, uncivilized state in which she has grown up, and suggests the necessity for the submission to social order which is one of the main themes of the work.

Until fairly recent years it would have seemed strange to talk about the themes of Calderón's mythological dramas, or to suggest that they were anything more than spectacular fantasies. But we now know that once the classical legends had become common currency in Renaissance Europe, they quickly acquired allegorical interpretations. The Counter-Reformation treated mythology as it treated the arts, not with puritanical abhorrence, but cunningly manipulating it for its own ends.[3] Calderón, much of whose earlier theatre was already an exhortation to faith and morality, was now as a priest supremely well fitted to tell the old stories in a new and moral way. It has been demonstrated that his mythological plays coincide closely with his earlier dramas in their didacticism;[4] and that the source material has again often been reworked in such a way as to underline the moral lesson.[5]

Even the actual themes which the myths are made to express often echo those of his better-known plays. *Fieras afemina amor* (*Love the Tamer*) depicts the humbling of Hercules, and exalts the feminine principle of love over masculine strength as does *Las armas de la hermosura*. *La hija del aire* coincides with *La cisma de Ingalaterra* in its condemnation of ambition and lust, and with *La vida es sueño* in its lesson that a monarch must curb his desires. There are strong reminiscences of the latter play also in *Eco y Narciso*. Narciso's mother has brought him up in isolation so as to avert a prophesied fate; and it is shown through him as through Segismundo that parents must give their children the freedom to grow up in society and live for themselves. The mythological dramas are by no means a mere coda to Calderón's secular theatre, but rather the recapitulation of his major themes in a different key.

The great festival of Corpus Christi, one of the main holidays of the year, had been celebrated from medieval times by pageants, tableaux and displays. These gradually became more dramatic, and by the early seventeenth century had evolved into a new and peculiarly Spanish genre, the *auto sacramental*. This was a one-act allegorical play, teaching some moral or doctrinal lesson

[3] See J. Seznec, *La survivance des dieux antiques* (London, 1940).

[4] W. G. Chapman, "Las comedias mitológicas de Calderón," *RLit.* 5 (1954) 34–67.

[5] Gwynne Edwards, "Calderón's *La hija del aire* in the light of his sources", *BHS* 43 (1966) 177–96.

which could be related to the complex of beliefs connected with the feast, and always leading up to public display and adoration of the Sacrament. The Corpus *autos* became a regular institution in Madrid, so important that the Town Council was responsible for their organization. This involved commissioning a dramatist to write them, choosing the best actors to play in them, and arranging for their performance in the city squares, first before royal and official audiences and then to the general public.

Because of the employment of professional actors, *auto* roles often corresponded to the stock types of the *comedia*: the part of Beauty, for instance, would be taken by the actress who normally played heroines, and Wit, or the Peasant, might be conceived of as a *gracioso* role. The use of professionals also constituted a public patronage which was of great financial assistance to the companies chosen to act, and indirectly benefited the *corrales*.

The fact that the *autos* received several performances in different parts of the city meant that the scenery for them must be mobile. It was actually constructed on carts which could be wheeled into position; but such were the mechanical possibilities available by the time of Calderón that the stage directions to some of his *autos* suggest scenic effects as startling as those achieved in the Coliseo. Music similarly contributed to the total effect, which appealed strongly to ear and eye, and not to the intelligence alone. Calderón himself, prefacing an edition of his *autos* in 1677, warns the reader that "the printed page can by itself convey neither the sound of the music nor the spectacle of the staging". The performance of the *auto* was a ritual, involving the total response of the spectator at all levels.

The keynote of the earlier *autos sacramentales* was usually simple piety. One man remembered almost entirely for his contributions to the genre is the Toledan priest José de Valdivielso, who died about 1638; and his works are popular, easy, and full of God's tender love for sinners. Lope and Tirso both wrote *autos*, though without any striking achievements. A curiosity of Tirso's is *Los hermanos parecidos* (*The Identical Brothers*), written for a well-known pair of actors who were twins; one of them played Man and the other Christ who assumes the likeness of Man and suffers in his place.

But the *auto sacramental* in its developed form is above all the work of Calderón. He was writing *autos* from the 1630's, and every year from 1648 received the commission for the two to be performed in Madrid; so that for the last thirty-three years of his life the field was his alone. The resulting body of some seventy works is an achievement almost as monumental as that of his dramas.

Given the obligation to turn out two *autos* a year over so long a period, it is surprising that he repeated himself so little. The range of subjects he contrived to put to allegorical use is remarkably wide. There was fairly obvious material to hand in Bible stories (*Primero y segundo Isaac, Las espigas de Ruth*), or parables similarly easy to relate to the idea of the Eucharist, such as *La siembra del Señor* (*The Lord's Sowing*) and *La viña del Señor* (*The Lord's Vineyard*). Slightly more manipulation was needed for classical myths, (*Psiquis y Cupido, El divino Orfeo, Andrómeda y Perseo*); though as in the case of the mythological dramas, the common practice of giving a moral interpretation to classical legends made the process a natural one. Calderón was of course writing *autos* and mythological dramas at the same time, and in both manner and content his works in the two genres are sometimes quite close. *Los encantos de la culpa* (*The Charms of Sin*) like *El mayor encanto amor* dramatizes the story of Ulysses and Circe, and illustrates Calderón's skill in making *autos* out of his own plays. The case of *El pintor de su deshonra* has already been quoted, and a further example is *La vida es sueño*. In all these works the drama has been cleverly accommodated to the new genre, each main character being given his allegorical counterpart; and the *auto* may well illuminate the meaning of the play, as in the closer analysis of the waking-dreaming opposition which we find in the later *Vida es sueño*. Another of Calderón's frequent devices was to allegorize some topical event, such as the building of the Buen Retiro in *El nuevo palacio del Retiro*, the mid-century celebration of a Holy Year in *El año santo de Roma*, or the conversion of Queen Christina of Sweden in *La protestación de la fe* (*The*

Protest of Faith). And there are too *autos* which start from an abstract idea, rather than from any given story.

Whatever the allegorical vehicle, it is always related at the end to the Sacrament in whose honour the feast is being held. Sometimes the link is easy and natural; the complex of ideas surrounding the Mass—offering, sacrifice, redemption, transubstantiation, communion—was rich enough for Calderón to be able to connect a wide range of subjects with it. Occasionally the relevance is forced. Calderón himself draws attention to the weakness in this respect of *El gran teatro del mundo* (*The Great Theatre of the World*). This is a beautiful dramatization of the old metaphor, in which God, the theatrical manager, allots parts to his various actors who are to play them as best they can, being rewarded accordingly at the end. But when he invites them to his feast after the performance the allegory breaks down, since they are by that time off the stage, that is, out of the world, and the Sacrament is something for this world alone. Very often the adaptation of the story to the sacramental ending requires a leap forward in time to the Christian era. The same thing had happened in Gil Vicente's *Auto de la Sibila Casandra*, where Old Testament figures come to kneel at the end before a Christmas crib; and in many medieval works, such as the twelfth-century Play of Daniel from Beauvais, in which the search for variety had led dramatists to herald Christmas with other Bible stories, somewhat tenuously linked at the close to the Nativity. This serves as a reminder that Calderón is still cultivating an essentially medieval form. His *autos sacramentales* are the last in an unbroken line of *autos* stretching back to the early Christmas and Easter plays; and their purpose is still the same: to bring the Church's teaching to life for the people by presenting it in dramatic form.

Calderón seems to have begun by limiting himself to facets of this teaching strictly connected with his eucharistic theme. Thus in the early *Cena de Baltasar* the story of Belshazzar's feast and profanation of the sacred vessels of the Temple is used to warn the faithful against making their Communion in a state of sin.

Soon, however, the lessons range wider, and the didactic content of the *autos* becomes an important element distinct (though not entirely separate) from both the surface allegory and the sacramental ending. Two main types of lesson are found: the vast doctrinal exposition covering the whole story of the Creation, Fall, Incarnation and Redemption (*La vida es sueño* and *La viña del Señor* are examples); and the exhortation to right behaviour.

With the moral *autos* we are back on well-known ground. They warn against the same confusion of values, and preach the same *desengaño*, as do the dramas. They insist on the deceptiveness of the senses. One recurrent variant on this theme is the inability of sight, smell, touch and taste to perceive in the Host anything more than bread; only hearing, instructed by faith, can recognize the Body of Christ. There is the same anguished awareness of the lure of earthly beauty; the long speeches of the Circe figure in *Los encantos de la culpa* are perhaps some of the most voluptuous hymns to sensuous pleasure in the whole of Calderón's theatre. The stoicism of *El príncipe constante* is echoed in *No hay más fortuna que Dios* (*There is no Fortune, only God*),[6] and the central metaphor of *El gran teatro del mundo* is itself a Stoic idea, taken from Epictetus. The title of the play to be acted in the world-theatre, and the only prompt the actors are allowed, is "Obrar bien, que Dios es Dios" ("Do right, for God is God")—the same "obrar bien" which the reimprisoned and bewildered Segismundo had come to discern as the only reality. And the King, whose role is just a part to be played like any other, with no lasting validity outside the theatre, further confirms Calderón's view of an earthly and a heavenly scheme of values, and the great fallibility of kings.

Here as in the dramas Calderón's teaching is austere. Only rarely is there room for tenderness. When the Soul is led astray by Sin, Pleasure and Deceit in Valdivielso's *Hospital de los locos* (*The Madhouse*), the result is a jolly romp; and she comes back tearfully like a naughty child to her loving parent. In

[6] Edited by A. A. Parker (Manchester, 1949, 2nd ed., 1962).

Calderón the temptations are more insidiously powerful, the sins more deliberate and grievous, the warnings and the exhortations sterner. This is moral teaching for a nation in decline.

Calderón's typical stylizations of speech and movement are fully in place in this allegorical and highly intellectual drama. If the splendours of his language pale somewhat in his later years, the allegories are, if possible, more carefully worked out and the thought more profound. Just as the combination of simple medieval verse forms with Renaissance language and imagery creates a strong personal flavour in Calderón's writing, so the survival of a form of medieval church drama right up to the Age of Reason, and its enrichment with seventeenth-century staging and thought, constitute a peculiar national phenomenon. The *auto sacramental* is an offspring of the *comedia* as remarkable and as Spanish as its parent.

With the death of Calderón in 1681 Spain's Golden Age was at an end. He had kept alive in the drama until that late date an excellence which had long since vanished from every other sphere of national activity. For fifty years he was the Colossus of the theatre. It is an anticlimax to turn from him to his lesser contemporaries; but two of them at least were very popular in their day, and can still claim consideration.

Francisco de Rojas Zorrilla was born in Toledo in 1607, and seems to have devoted most of his relatively short adult life to the theatres of Madrid. He wrote for court and *corral*, he essayed most genres from comedy of intrigue to tragedy, and it was his death in 1648 that left Calderón in sole command of the *auto sacramental*. It used to be regularly repeated that his best play was that alternatively entitled *Del rey abajo ninguno* (*None Below the King*)[7] or, from the name of its hero, *García del Castañar*. But the American scholar Raymond R. MacCurdy has shown that the authorship of this play, like that of some fifty of the eighty-odd ascribed to Rojas, is uncertain.[8] In any case

[7] Edited by F. Ruiz Morcuende (Madrid, Clásicos castellanos, 1917).
[8] *BC* 9 (1957) 7 ff.

its merits are questionable. It is a very derivative play, whose rustic hero has about him something of Peribáñez and something of the "villano en su rincón", and is faced with an honour problem akin to that of the "médico" Don Gutierre. He has reason to believe that the King himself has designs on his wife; and since no vengeance can be taken on the King, prepares to kill the dearly loved and unquestionably innocent Blanca so as to keep his honour intact. But "del rey abajo ninguno"—as soon as he learns that the lecher was not the King but a nobleman of his suite, he runs his sword through him and Blanca is spared.

For a modern reader to feel the tragedy of *El médico de su honra* involves a considerable effort to understand and accept unfamiliar attitudes; for him to suspend disbelief in *Del rey abajo ninguno* is virtually impossible. Instead of the series of mostly minor human errors which, within the given social framework, build up Calderón's tragic situation, there is here nothing but black and white; a "case" of honour rather than a credible human drama. García is only free to draw his sword on a nobleman because he and Blanca are not real peasants but nobles living under an assumed identity; and the fiction and contrivance are further emphasized by this typically seventeenth-century instance of misleading appearances.

We owe to MacCurdy a truer picture of Rojas as a dramatist excelling chiefly in tragedies of revenge. He takes up this Senecan strain from Juan de la Cueva and produces vigorous, well-constructed works like *Morir pensando matar* (*Killers Turned Victims*),[9] where in Act I the initial offence is given and the vengeance planned; in Act II that vengeance is executed and the counter-revenge set in motion; and the murderers themselves die a violent death in the final act. Rojas like Calderón often goes to the ancient world for his tragic stories, and he is perhaps at his best in *Lucrecia y Tarquino*:[10] a play of schematic characterization, but remarkable for its brief shaft of perception that Lucretia's hubris may have been the cause of her downfall;

[9] Edited by R. R. MacCurdy (Madrid, Clásicos castellanos, 1961).
[10] Edited by R. R. MacCurdy (Albuquerque, 1963).

for was it perhaps her very insistence on her own modesty and purity that acted as the spur to Tarquin's desire?

The use of symbols in this play—a stricken white dove for Lucretia, a broken glass for her husband's honour—is heavily underlined. Rojas is content to employ the old dramatic devices, and to copy most of Calderón's tricks of style (though without excess). His work lacks subtlety, and his tragedies rarely convey the complexity of life. Yet he is a competent playwright and dramatizes with verve and vigour, his women characters being particularly assertive. Critics have pointed to his occasional feminism, and unusual solutions of honour problems from the woman's point of view.

His insistence on woman's right to a husband of her own choice, or none if she prefers, is echoed by his contemporary Agustín Moreto y Cabaña (1618–69); and both treat the theme on occasion in conjunction with a new development of the comedy of manners. A father has arranged that his daughter shall marry for family or financial reasons a man who on acquaintance turns out to be quite unsuitable. Isabel, of Rojas' comedy *Entre bobos anda el juego* (*Not as Stupid as You'd Think!*),[7] declares with spirit that whatever her father says she will not marry the impossible Lucas. Inés, of Moreto's *El lindo Don Diego* (*Don Diego the Dandy*), [11] is slightly more submissive, but puts to her father what is clearly the Church's teaching on the matter:

> Cuando yo he de estar
> pronta siempre a obedecer,
> no me debieras mandar
> cosa en que puedo tener
> licencia de replicar.
> Y si me da esta licencia
> el cielo, y tu autoridad
> me la quita con violencia,
> casárase mi obediencia,
> pero no mi voluntad.   (Act I)

---

[7] Edited by F. Ruiz Morcuende (Madrid, Clásicos castellanos, 1917).
[11] Edited by N. Alonso Cortés (Madrid, Clásicos castellanos, 1916).

("Although it is always for me to obey you, you ought not to give orders in a matter in which I have the right to freedom of choice. And if you exert your authority so rigorously as to deprive me of that right bestowed by heaven, my obedience will submit, but not my will.")

Her sister is even more outspoken:

> La elección no ha de ser
> de quien no fuere el peligro.
> El riesgo de un casamiento
> que si se yerra es martirio,
> ha de ser el escogello
> de quien se obliga a sufrillo.   (Act I)

("It is for the person who runs the risk to make the choice. An unhappy marriage is martyrdom, and no one should subject another willy-nilly to the risk of having to endure it.")

The seriousness of such statements, which momentarily recognize marriage as more than the tying up of the loose ends of a plot, does not pervade the whole play. In both *El lindo Don Diego* and *Entre bobos* we know that all will come right in the end, and the heroines' resistance is merely incidental to the main point, which is the outrageousness of the suitors. Lucas is gruff, dirty and boorish, Diego is a ridiculous fop. Both recall Alarcón's portrayal of exaggerated tendencies in *La verdad sospechosa* and *No hay mal que por bien no venga*—as with Alarcón's Don García their enormities are described by a servant before they are allowed to reveal themselves—but in them eccentricity is developed to the point of caricature. These plays point to the growing popularity of what came to be known as the *comedia de figurón*, a type of comedy based on an outlandish central character. Examples are rare before the 1630's, but its vogue, once established, continued on into the eighteenth century.

Not only do Moreto and Rojas Zorrilla coincide in the use of certain motifs, they are broadly comparable in output and scope. Both attempted most dramatic genres, including the *comedia de santo*, in which they can be as violent and extreme as any of their predecessors. But whereas Rojas is outstanding in tragedy, with Moreto it is the witty, urbane comedy which predominates. His *gracioso* parts are usually strong, and some of his comic scenes a real delight. One may instance the climax to Act II of *El desdén con el desdén* (*Disdain to Conquer Disdain*),[11] where Diana is watching the Count Carlos and his servant walk in her garden. Carlos is with great difficulty feigning indifference to Diana, and somehow manages to keep on talking about the flower-beds while the *gracioso* holds a dagger to his head to stop him turning round and responding to her siren song.

Diana's progression in this play from coldness to pique, and then to love and heartbroken jealousy, is very well conveyed. While it would be out of place to look for any great depth of characterization in these passing diversions, they do show a measure of interest in personality which gives them perhaps a little more substance than the comedies of Calderón.

They chiefly coincide with the latter in their characters' exaggerated punctiliousness over honour. A gentleman accepts a challenge to a duel so as not to seem a coward, rather than offer the simple explanation which would make the duel unnecessary; a lady refuses to hear the explanations of her apparently unfaithful gallant, since to do so would be to admit that she had been hurt and so to lose face (*El lindo Don Diego*). Suitors must persevere with their wooing even when it is hopeless, since to concede rejection means loss of prestige; while the object of their attentions must steer an almost impossibly narrow course: if she is too casual she will insult them, if she is too gracious she will compromise herself (*El desdén con el desdén*). Moreto's heroines, fanatically concerned with propriety, are even further removed than Calderón's "tapadas" from the transvestite gadabouts of an earlier age.

Many of Moreto's plays are reworkings, and the adaptation often consists of a scaling down, and a moving away from exaggeration towards something nearer normality and respectability. *El lindo Don Diego* is based on Guillén de Castro's *Narciso en su opinión* (*A Narcissus in his Own Eyes*). As in the source, the heroine is freed from the attentions of the fop by his being made to think he has a chance of a match more befitting his great beauty; and the central episode is still the implausible (and very

[11] Edited by N. Alonso Cortés (Madrid, Clásicos Castellanos, 1916).

funny) impersonation of a countess by a lady's maid. But this time the favoured young man remarks on the impropriety of such a thing, and refuses to be involved in the scheme. In the field of serious drama, a play with a story taken from antiquity, *Antíoco y Seleuco*, has the same initial situation as Lope de Vega's *Castigo sin venganza*; but whereas in Casandra Lope paints a woman in love, Moreto's Stratonice never forgets that she is a queen. The word "decoro" is repeatedly on her lips. Indeed all the characters behave with decorum and generosity, and the play has a happy ending. (It also lacks any real dramatic tension, and is rather dull.)

One sees in Moreto a slighter and a less critical Alarcón. He too appealed to French taste—Molière based *La Princesse d'Élide* on *El desdén con el desdén*; and his plays continued popular with his own countrymen when a new century and cultural influences from across the Pyrenees were starting to bring the old *comedia* into disfavour.

Texts

MORETO, *Comedias escogidas*, ed. L. Fernández-Guerra, *BAE*, Vol. 39.
ROJAS ZORRILLA, *Comedias escogidas*, ed. Mesonero Romanos, *BAE*, Vol. 54.

Critical and General Works

CASA, F. P., *The Dramatic Craftsmanship of Moreto* (Cambridge, Massachusetts, 1966).
FRUTOS CORTÉS, E., *La filosofía de Calderón en sus autos sacramentales* (Zaragoza, 1952).
KENNEDY, R. L., *The Dramatic Art of Moreto* (Philadelphia, 1932).
MACCURDY, R. R., *Francisco de Rojas Zorrilla and the Tragedy* (Albuquerque, 1958).
PARKER, A. A., *The Allegorical Drama of Calderón* (Oxford, 1943, reprinted 1968.
SHERGOLD, N. D., *A History of the Spanish Stage* (Oxford, 1967).
SHERGOLD, N. D. and VAREY, J. E., *Los autos sacramentales en Madrid en la época de Calderón, 1637–1681. Estudio y documentos* (Madrid, 1961).
WARDROPPER, B. W., *Introducción al teatro religioso del Siglo de Oro* (Madrid, 1953).

12

ASSESSMENTS

THE death of Calderón in 1681 provides a closing point for this study. Little of any originality was contributed to the *comedia* after that date. Francisco de Bances Candamo (1662–1704), a poet of some delicacy and imaginative power, brought these qualities to a handful of plays, but leans as heavily on Calderón for his dramatic concepts as on Góngora for his metaphors. His treatise *Teatro de los teatros de los pasados y presentes siglos*,[1] written between 1689 and 1693, surveys the development of the drama up to that time, and is interesting as the only piece of dramatic theory from the age dominated by Calderón.

The spate of *refundiciones* continued, and early in the eighteenth century produced another version of the Don Juan story, Antonio de Zamora's *No hay plazo que no se cumpla ni deuda que no se pague* (*All Accounts Must be Settled, All Debts Paid*). This was the second of Spain's three major dramas on the subject, and it remained popular until supplanted in the Romantic period by José Zorrilla's *Don Juan Tenorio*. Already in Zamora interest in the protagonist and the plot has quite ousted any theological lesson; and although his work is by no means dull, it exemplifies the way in which attention is being turned from the substance of what earlier dramatists had to say, to the external and more trivial aspects of their work. The vogue is now for the comedies of Moreto and others like them, with an especial fondness for the *comedia de figurón;* or for empty rehashes of the more horrific plots of Calderón and his predecessors, with eye-catching and ear-splitting scenic effects doing duty for any real dramatic content. With no adequate renewals of the old forms such as Calderón himself had achieved in his day, they became irretrievably debased.

[1] An edition by D. W. Moir is to be published shortly by Támesis Books.

There were moreover Bourbon kings on the throne of Spain from 1700, and French taste was beginning to prevail. Spanish culture, even at its best, came to seem rude and provincial. The barbarousness to which Lope light-heartedly admitted in his *Arte nuevo* was now imputed to him in all seriousness, and plays which so conspicuously failed to observe the good manners of literature were thought to be making Spain a laughing-stock. Religious drama seemed the most *outré* of all. Not only had no one come forward competent to succeed Calderón in the field of the *auto sacramental*: the genre itself was despised as primitive, and the beauty and poignancy of its allegories ceased to have any appeal in an age of reason. The performance of *autos* was suppressed by royal decree in 1765. From that time on the drama-tists of Spain tagged along behind those of France. Only with Valle-Inclán and García Lorca in the twentieth century were authentically Spanish voices heard again.

Meanwhile the *comedia* had had its echoes in other parts of Europe. Long before the time of Zamora, probably even in Tirso's own lifetime, Don Juan had appeared in Italy in Cicog-nini's *Convitato di pietra*. This was followed by the French versions of Dorimon and Villiers, and these in turn led to Molière's *Don Juan* (1665). Molière's debt to *El desdén con el desdén* and Corneille's to *La verdad sospechosa* and *Las mocedades del Cid* have already been noted. The first French dramatist to make extensive use of the *comedia* was Rotrou, who among many borrowings from Lope based his play of martyrdom *Saint-Genest* (1647) on *Lo fingido verdadero* (*Pretence Turned Truth*), and whose *Venceslas* (1647?) looks back to Rojas Zorrilla's *No hay ser padre siendo rey* (*One Cannot Be King and Father Too*). He was followed by Boisrobert, Scarron, Thomas Corneille and others; though as the vogue for romantic drama gradually gave way to that for outright comedy or tragedy, it was increasingly the Spanish comedies of intrigue which these latter writers laid under contribution.[2]

When the English courtiers returned from France at the

[2] See E. Martinenche, *La comédie espagnole en France de Hardy à Racine* (Paris, 1900).

Restoration, they brought with them a taste for the kind of play they had been seeing there. The dramatists writing for the newly reopened English theatres borrowed freely from across the Channel—and so indirectly from Spain. Spanish ancestry has been traced for a number of Restoration comedies: thus *An Evening's Love, or The Mock Astrologer* by Dryden is borrowed from *Le feint astrologue* by Thomas Corneille, which in turn goes back to Calderón's *Astrólogo fingido*; while *La verdad sospechosa* gave rise, via *Le menteur*, to an anonymous *The Mistaken Beauty, or The Liar*. Many Spanish plays were known too without the intermediary of French. Dryden read Spanish, and borrowed textually from *El príncipe constante* for *The Indian Emperour*. Translations of Calderón comedies appeared on the London stage, some of them suggested, it seems, by Charles II himself. Digby rendered *No siempre lo peor es cierto* into English as *Elvira*; Pepys in 1664 attended a performance of *Worse and Worse*, which is Calderón's *Peor está que estaba*. Wycherley more than once adapted Calderón: *El maestro de danzar* for *The Gentleman Dancing Master*, and *Mañanas de abril y mayo* (*April and May Mornings*) for *Love in a Wood*. Moreto's popularity in his own country was also reflected in the pillaging of his works by minor English dramatists.[3]

What interest the Restoration writers in their Spanish sources are mainly the external paraphernalia of situation and plot: the endless subterfuges, letters, concealments and overheard conversations that keep the action moving; the spirit has been transformed. Not merely is Restoration comedy much bawdier than its Spanish or French originals, it lacks the supposition of seriousness which still underlies the intrigues of Moreto and Calderón. Their characters, through all their improbable escapades, sincerely seek happiness, and they seek it for the most part within the narrow limits of correct behaviour. The figures of Wycherley and Congreve are playing a cynical game of love,

---

[3] See Allardyce Nicoll, *A History of Restoration Drama, 1600–1700* (2nd ed., Cambridge, 1928). On Dryden's debt to *El príncipe constante* see N. D. Shergold and Peter Ure, "Dryden and Calderón: a new Spanish source for *The Indian Emperour*", *MLR* 61 (1966) 369–83.

in which nothing is barred, and the only goal is amusement. *The Way of the World* makes fun of Lady Wishfort worrying about her "decorums". For Diana of *El desdén con el desdén* "decoro" is the necessary and unquestioned framework of behaviour within which her love for Carlos must be contained; and the process nearly breaks her heart.

The Spanish plays imitated elsewhere in Europe in the seventeenth century did not for the most part belong to the central tradition of the *comedia*, but to somewhat more marginal modes: the comedy of manners of Alarcón and Moreto, the comedy of intrigue of Moreto and Calderón. Lope's and Calderón's great dramas were either unpopular or unknown abroad. Spanish neglect of them in the eighteenth century kept them in oblivion; and when they did eventually arouse interest again, it was in an entirely new quarter.

It seems to have been the German writer and critic Ludwig Tieck who through his translation of *Don Quixote* brought Spanish literature to the notice of his friend August Wilhelm von Schlegel. Schlegel went on to read the Golden Age dramatists, and in his enthusiasm for what he had discovered, planned with Tieck a series of translations of the plays of Cervantes, Lope, Calderón and Moreto. In the event the translations were Schlegel's alone, and were limited to works of Calderón. They appeared in two volumes of *Spanisches Theater* (1803 and 1809), and Schlegel later wrote an enthusiastic essay in praise of Calderonian drama. Other Calderón translations, by J. D. Gries, fired the interest of Goethe. The very exoticism, richness and theatricality which had repelled the eighteenth century now became a decisive influence on the æsthetic ideas of the German Romantics, and for the first time the *comedia* was seriously considered as literature.[4]

In 1822 Goethe published a short essay on *La hija del aire*,[5] interesting not least for the mere fact of its treating a play which only

[4] See Werner Brüggemann, *Spanisches Theater und deutsche Romantik*, Vol. I (Münster, 1964). A second volume is promised. Also Svana L. Hardy, *Goethe, Calderón und die romantische Theorie des Dramas* (Heidelberg, 1965).

[5] Published in *Goethes Sämtliche Werke*, Jubiläums-Ausgabe, Vol. 37 (Stuttgart and Berlin, 1902), pp. 213–16.

a full century later was to receive proper recognition. Goethe praises it as a drama of human passions with a minimum of supernatural intervention, and undistorted by the Catholicism which, as he sees it, so often forced Calderón to present reason as unreason. That is, he fails to recognize the essential unity of Calderón's theatre, and the way in which Christian, historical, mythological and other stories are all made to serve as vehicles for the same moral truths. But if he still applies a criterion of realism to the content, he appreciates the play's rhetoric and sophistication. His similes "ballet-step" and "minuet-like" anticipate by many years the general recognition of these aspects of Calderón's art.

So far it was all Calderón. The rediscovery of Lope in German-speaking lands came a little later. Grillparzer based his *Jüdin von Toledo* (finished 1855) on Lope's *Paces de los Reyes* (*The Royal Reconciliation*), and praised him in a series of *Studien zum Spanischen Theater* written mainly in the 1830's and 1840's. And it was this latter decade which saw the first major work of criticism on the Spanish drama, A. F. von Schack's *Geschichte der dramatischen Literatur und Kunst Spaniens* (3 vols., 1845–6).

By this time the Spaniards had been driven to look afresh at their own dramatic heritage. Golden Age plays found their way on to the stage again, sometimes in nineteenth-century *refundiciones;* but the ultimate enthusiastic acceptance of the *comedia* is due principally to one man: Juan Eugenio Hartzenbusch. He was himself a dramatist in the romantic manner, and was also director of the National Library. He edited large numbers of the plays of Tirso, Lope, Calderón and Alarcón for the big new series of the *Biblioteca de autores españoles*; and these first modern editions, though imperfect, are still for a great many plays the only ones easily available. In their day they introduced the works of the dramatists to the reading public, and opened the way at last to their critical evaluation in Spain.

The middle of the nineteenth century was largely the age of the regional novel, and it is the values of this somewhat cosy genre that the Spanish critics of the period tend to prize most in the *comedia:* realism, "Spanishness", the vitality and goodness of simple country people. Lope's staunch peasants and Tirso's sparkling heroines, the humour of the *graciosos* and the fresh charm of the scenes of country life—these are what win most approval. Lope in particular is seen as the mouthpiece of the nation, presenting his fellow countrymen to themselves. Calderón is admired for the robustness of Pedro Crespo and the philosophical grandeur of *La vida es sueño*, but not for much else. Those qualities in him which appealed to the German Romantics are once again out of fashion. Menéndez y Pelayo, the great man of letters of the turn of the century, edited fifteen volumes of Lope's plays for the Spanish Academy (1890–1913), with introductions which still stand as worth-while criticism; but in his *Calderón y su teatro* (an early work, written in 1881), while admitting the grandeur of the conceptions, he dismisses rhetoric as bombast, and laments the lack of convincing characterization, local colour and human truth, thus showing his very imperfect understanding of Calderón's aim and manner.

His work of editing and criticism was continued in the early twentieth century by Emilio Cotarelo, particularly for the plays of Lope and Tirso. The rehabilitation of Calderón in Spain has been due mainly to Ángel Valbuena Prat. This great critic's surveys in his *Literatura dramática española* (1930) and *Historia de la literatura española* (1937) showed a sensitive awareness of plays and dramatists that had previously been overlooked; and his *Calderón* (1941) first gave adequate recognition to the fact that a deliberately schematic and stylized drama, and a patterned and richly textured diction, might have a peculiar æsthetic beauty of their own. His later *Historia del teatro español* (1956) deals mainly with Golden Age drama, but on the basis of recurrent themes.

By the time of the Second World War Spanish had become a subject of study in a number of universities outside Spain, and a new body of professional academic critics was coming into being. Some of these turned their attention to the *comedia*, and found it to be of more than parochial interest. Particularly in Great Britain, where students of the Elizabethan and Jacobean theatre had pointed the way to the understanding of a drama remote from nineteenth-century realism, the approach first adopted in the 1940's by W. J. Entwistle, A. A. Parker and Edward M. Wilson, and quickly taken up by Albert E. Sloman and other younger colleagues, has resulted in an important revaluation of the *comedia*. Most of the work of this "English school", as it has been called, has been published in article form; and it has been concerned mainly with the theatre of Calderón.

Its chief contribution has been to underline the importance of theme. Recognizing the beauty of Calderón's stylization, as Valbuena had done, the British critics have gone on to analyse the reasons for it and have shown how Calderón presents action and character, not as dramatic absolutes, but always so as to bring out an underlying theme or lesson. He thus emerges fully as a moral and didactic dramatist, and the essential unity of his serious drama is seen. Parker's statement in 1948 that "*confusión* . . . in various forms is the keystone of nearly all Calderón's *comedias*" was an important new critical insight; and the validity of the new approach had been well demonstrated two years earlier in Wilson's analysis of *La vida es sueño*. In one sense this cut the play down to size, showing it to be not strictly a *comedia filosófica*, more grandiose and universal in conception than the religious or historical dramas, but yet another play about moral confusion and the search for right values. In another sense it brought out its true greatness, demonstrating the artistry with which main action, sub-plot and all the individual characters are made to serve the moral theme. Other articles, as already indicated, aim to show that the honour plays too fit into the same pattern, and present no real inconsistency in Calderón's moral outlook.

In 1957 Professor Parker indicated the general direction of the new criticism in an important pamphlet, *The Approach to the Spanish Drama of the Golden Age*. This was originally given as a lecture, and the compression necessary for that purpose has resulted in some generalizations which are perhaps open to question. But it enunciates fundamental principles, and must be taken into account by anyone who wishes to understand the *comedia*. Parker argues that the Spanish dramatists subordinate character to action, and action in turn to theme; that the unity of a play is to be seen in its theme rather than its action, since even if the action is multiple all the plots will illustrate the same theme; that this theme will be a moral lesson, emphasized by the fact that guilty characters suffer according to the principle of poetic justice;[6] and that plots are constructed on the basis of dramatic causality, so that by following the action back along the chain of effect and cause, the reader can arrive at an understanding of the moral lesson. These points are illustrated by analyses of some major plays.

While Parker's approach to a play is usually through its action, other critics have begun to make close studies of the actual texts, and this has led to an examination of the imagery of many *comedias*. As already stated, it is now recognized that imagery can be not merely decorative but also thematic, carefully chosen so as to illuminate and emphasize still further the theme of the play. Among a number of recent studies illustrating this point, Sloman's analysis of the imagery of *La vida es sueño* in his edition

[6] The principle of poetic justice, though it does frequently obtain, is perhaps not as binding as Parker here suggests. I shall later mention some plays by Lope and his contemporaries in which it seems not to apply; and even in Calderón one might instance the case of Mariene of *El mayor monstruo los celos*. Not only has she not deserved her death, she refuses to save her life by the sinful means of fleeing from her husband with another man, explicitly stating that if she must die it shall be through his fault and not her own, for it is better to die innocent than to live guilty.

Parker does moreover in a later essay ("Towards a definition of Calderonian tragedy", *BHS* 39, 1962, footnote on pp. 225, 226) suggest something rather different, limiting the idea of poetic justice to "the fact that there is no moral guilt without suffering of some kind, and no suffering without some degree of moral guilt", and making an exception for innocent victims of another's wrongdoing. The exception is a very big one (and would of course cover Mariene). The limitation, with its rider that there is no necessary proportion between the degree of guilt and the degree of suffering, seems to move away from the idea of justice, and to take us back to something not very different from the Aristotelian *hamartia*.

of the play (Manchester University Press, 1961) is perhaps outstanding.

The spate of *comedia* criticism has gone on, some of it building on the foundation laid by the British reappraisal, some of it maintaining an independent standpoint. In France probably the chief but by no means the only contributions have come from C. V. Aubrun. Scholars in America have perhaps earned gratitude most by their labour of textual study which has established facts on which æsthetic assessments can rest. One thinks of the work of Morley and Bruerton on the chronology of Lope's theatre, and subsequently that of J. H. Arjona on orthoepy as a guide to the authorship of disputed plays; or Ruth Lee Kennedy's dating of a number of plays by Tirso, and her study of the growth and decline of Tirso's friendship with Lope. But there have been too the valuable literary analyses of Bruce W. Wardropper, Arnold G. Reichenberger, Gerald E. Wade and many others. In Britain, in addition to those to whose work I have referred specifically in earlier chapters, T. E. May, Peter N. Dunn, Daniel Rogers, Victor Dixon, C. B. Morris, A. I. Watson and others have made significant contributions.

We are still far from any definitive view of the *comedia*, and while the ferment of criticism continues it is only possible for me to make a few provisional and subjective comments on it. My indebtedness to a great deal that has been published in the last twenty-five years will have been clearly apparent; but it seems to me that two kinds of error have sometimes been incurred. The first is that of over-interpretation. With the new awareness that there is much more in the *comedia* than met the eyes of its earliest critics has come a tendency to look too hard, and to see subtlety and significance in a great deal that is merely the conventional stock-in-trade of popular entertainers. In this connection it is worth remembering the extent to which the dramatists sometimes labour their points in order to drive them home. Secret motives are nearly always explained in asides, omens made conspicuous. When Calderón uses the trick of speeches intended to be understood differently by different hearers, he repeats

them afterwards to make sure that we have got the point.[7]
There is a moment early in Act III of *La prudencia en la mujer*
when Tirso for once seems to be using a powerful poetic association, letting the freedom of the hunt suggest the young king's
emancipation from his mother; but he goes on to explain the
relevance, and the directness of its impact is lost. Audiences
are clearly not credited with very much acumen. Of course
this does not mean that we are wrong to see anything in the plays
that would not have been obvious to them, but it should put us
on our guard against seeing too much.

The second error is that of over-simplification. When one tries
to isolate and convey the peculiar qualities of the Spanish *comedia*,
there is a temptation to present it as being more of a piece than
it actually is, blurring the important evolution which took place
in the 1620's and 1630's. Certain American critics have written
of both Lope and Calderón as representatives of the Baroque; I
see their theatres as so different, apart from externals of form,
that the same label could not possibly be attached to both. In
Britain the tendency has been to analyse the Calderonian system
and then project it back on to Lope. It is true that even with
Lope there was room for advance from the nineteenth-century
view of him as the natural instinctive mouthpiece of his age.
Thanks to such perceptive studies as the articles of E. M. Wilson
and Victor Dixon on the imagery of *Peribáñez*, we now have a
much truer picture of Lope the artist, in whose work literature and
life were wonderfully fused. But it seems to me a mistake to see
his theatre, or even that of Tirso, as necessarily conforming to
principles which have been found to underlie the work of
Calderón. Lope made no secret of his own principle: to please
his audience. This he would surely be more likely to do by the
telling of a story than by the presentation of a dramatic metaphor
or "representable idea". I agree with Mr. R. D. F. Pring-Mill
in seeing Lope primarily as a dramatist of action, and finding
no need to postulate moral themes in his plays (which is not of

[7] e.g. Leonor's sonnet at the end of Act I of *A secreto agravio secreta venganza*,
and the half-overheard conversation in Act II of *La hija del aire*, Part I.

course to deny that the normal moral standards of the *comedia* apply there).[8] The fact that so many of his titles are proper names (*Peribáñez y el Comendador de Ocaña, Fuenteovejuna, El Caballero de Olmedo, Castelvines y Monteses, Los Tellos de Meneses, El Duque de Viseo*), whereas Calderón more often chooses attributes of behaviour or moral apothegms (*El príncipe constante, El médico de su honra, La vida es sueño, El mayor monstruo los celos*), suggests that in Lope the main interest is in people rather than in values. For me at any rate the reading of too much system into his theatre tends to obscure his humanity.

There has been disagreement among the critics over the important question of tragedy in the Golden Age. The fact that a great many plays follow the principle of poetic justice is probably largely responsible for the common assertion that there is no Spanish tragedy. The concept of a prevailing justice and moral order is often held to be incompatible with tragedy, which is "a protest against the unjust ordering of the universe in the name of a concept of justice evolved by man himself and unsanctioned by any transcendental system. Tragedy occurs when there is a conflict between man's innate sense of justice and the gods."[9] It is frequently maintained that true tragedy, that which seeks to arrive at an understanding of the human condition and a reconciliation between man's aspiration and the forces that frustrate it, can only arise in a climate in which faith and

[8] R. D. F. Pring-Mill, Introduction to *Lope de Vega (Five Plays)*, translated by Jill Booty (New York, 1961). Mr. Pring-Mill seems to me to put the danger of over-simplification very well: "The trend in recent criticism has certainly been to see Lope de Vega as more subtle than earlier writers thought he was, but I should be reluctant to sacrifice his freshness and spontaneity and the vigor of his exultant theatricality in order to turn him into something more akin to Calderón.

"Both Lope de Vega and Calderón did what they did supremely well, but they did different things within the framework of the *comedia* which Lope had created, and they set about achieving their purposes in very different ways —Calderón with cerebral ingenuity, and Lope with a direct and keen-edged thrust which can get blunted by too detailed scrutiny. The old-fashioned contrast between them does deserve to be perpetuated, for it is much more than merely a convenient pedagogic device." (p. xxxvi.)

[9] Anthony Hartley, reviewing T. R. Henn's *The Harvest of Tragedy* in the *Manchester Guardian*, 16th October, 1956.

scepticism are in equilibrium. If scepticism predominates, it is pointless to look for any meaning in the universe. If faith predominates, the answers are already known; drama can illustrate them, but it cannot lead the spectator into an apprehension of any truth not already revealed to him. Christian tragedy, on this showing, is an impossibility. Whatever happens to the protagonist is only provisional, as the whole of this life is provisional. He knows the rules, and if he adheres to them, *sub specie æternitatis* all will be well. Such considerations have been applied to Golden Age drama by a number of writers, of whom Erich Auerbach is typical:

> It turns the world into a magic stage. And on that magic stage . . . a fixed order reigns, despite all the elements of adventure and miracle. In the world, it is true, everything is a dream, but nothing is a riddle demanding to be solved. There are passions and conflicts but there are no problems. God, King, honor and love, class and class decorum are immutable and undoubted, and the figures neither of tragedy nor comedy present us with questions difficult to answer.
>
> (*Mimesis*, translated by Willard Trask, New York, 1957, p. 292.)

It is tempting, and even legitimate, to judge Golden Age tragedy according to our modern concepts, and by this standard it may sometimes be found wanting. If we are invited to make moral judgements on a character we are automatically distanced from him to some extent, and cannot fully identify ourselves with his sufferings. We do not then experience as a personal catharsis what many would regard as the essence of tragedy, the sense of reconciliation, the acceptance that brings release, the final affirmation of order in life, high as the price of it has been. A moral standpoint takes us away, too, from the modern postulate of an amoral inevitability: the sense that these things must happen, because life is like that; and from Hegel's concept of tragedy as a conflict between mutually incompatible forces, both of which are nevertheless good. The stronger the moral emphasis in a play, the less likely is that play to exemplify what now seems to many the purest kind of tragedy.

It is probably more fruitful, however, to look at Golden Age drama against the background of its own period. Hegel, and most subsequent theorists, have written with Greek tragedy in mind; Calderón and his contemporaries still looked back to Seneca. Elizabethan and Jacobean tragedy in England has the same ancestry, and it too takes a moral viewpoint for granted.[10] Its themes are often very close to those of the theatre we have been studying. Chapman treats the fall of favourites, as does Mira de Amescua; Middleton shows sinfulness leading to damnation, as does Tirso de Molina; Tourneur preaches other-worldliness, as does Calderón.[11] Its aim is not an Aristotelian catharsis but an emotional disturbance; it arouses the emotions in order to work through them upon the will. At its best it goes beyond this, to an exploration in artistic terms of the problem of suffering, and a quest for meaning in it; but its tragic situations, even those of Shakespeare, always arise out of the existence of moral evil.

A not dissimilar view of Spanish tragedy at its best has recently been put forward by Parker in another important essay, "Towards a definition of Calderonian tragedy" (*BHS* 39, 1962 223–37). In this an analysis of *La devoción de la Cruz, El pintor de su deshonra* and *Las tres justicias en una* (*Three Justices in One*) leads him to find the key in the concept of diffusion of responsibility. A protagonist may be justly punished for his misdeeds, but the responsibility for them may not be his alone; it may be shared by a number of other characters in the play. The guilt of parents may be particularly strong; by their conduct during their son's early years, or even before his birth, they may have predisposed him to behave in a certain way, and unknowingly contributed to his disaster. (Here Calderón seems to be expressing those strong personal feelings about the father–son relationship to which Parker has rightly drawn attention elsewhere.[12]) But minor characters, even down to the servants, may also have their part to play in the final catastrophe. Over and above his own

[10] See M. C. Bradbrook, *Themes and Conventions of Elizabethan Tragedy* (1st paperback edition, Cambridge, 1960), pp. 75, 76.

[11] See Irving Ribner, *Jacobean Tragedy. The Quest for Moral Order* (London, 1962).

[12] A. A. Parker, "The father–son conflict in the drama of Calderón", *FMLS* 2 (1966) 99–113.

guilt, therefore, the protagonist may justifiably have that bewildered sense of being the victim of uncomprehended forces outside himself, which can make of him a true tragic hero.

Nor is an ultimate vision of some kind of meaning lacking, for Parker shows Calderón to be presenting in dramatic terms a widely-experienced truth about human nature: that our self-regarding actions cannot be limited in their effects, but have repercussions on the lives of others; that we are all members one of another, and that "the solidarity in wrong-doing of each one of us with the whole of humanity makes us sharers in the afflictions of human life". This is a tragic view of life but also a Christian one, and it refutes the idea that there can be no such thing as Christian tragedy. It also means that "the Spanish drama of the Golden Age, through Calderón, has a contribution to make to the theory of tragedy and to tragic drama which should no longer be so consistently ignored".

To this important view of Spanish tragedy a few further comments may be added. Calderón does not speak for all his predecessors, and if, as I believe, the moral element is less strong in them and the principle of poetic justice less closely adhered to, a few of their works may be found to conform even to a modern idea of tragedy. Schopenhauer would have certainly recognized *La venganza de Tamar* as belonging to one of his three tragic modes, that in which the action springs from a monstrous or perverse character. Tirso is at great pains to build up a picture of Amnon's abnormality, so as to make his wickedness less stark than it is in the Bible story. In Mira de Amescua's studies of the fall of great men, though sins of ambition, pride and envy are observed, the main tragic agent is, as so many of their titles suggest, a fluctuating and amoral Fortune. Vélez de Guevara's *Reinar después de morir* presents a case in which the victim is, in terms of the play, entirely blameless. If she had not been so upright she would have suffered less. If she had had a mere liaison, or been willing to admit any irregularity in her marriage, she would have lost the Prince but she need not have died. Her very insistence that she had behaved correctly makes her death inevitable. Here surely is the Hegelian conflict of good with good: an innocent woman's life must yield to the imperative of *raison d'état* and the pledged word of a king. In Lope's *Caballero de Olmedo* the pattern of right and wrong is so confused that no clear line of moral thought emerges. Alonso's rival was wrong to kill him, especially since Alonso had saved his life in the bull-ring; but he had behaved correctly in his wooing of Inés, which Alonso had not. Alonso was wrong to employ a go-between and witch; but as a stranger in Medina he had no other obvious means of access to Inés, and he himself as he dies blames not his recourse to Fabia but his foolhardiness. It seems to me that, as so often, Lope was concerned not to think the matter out logically, but simply to convey the complexity—in this case the tragic complexity—of life.

As far as the unmistakably moral tragedies are concerned, I would suggest that they often lack one element which would have left their status in no doubt; namely some clear anagnorisis, some adequate recognition of their guilt on the part of those ultimately responsible for the catastrophe. It is suggested that *La devoción de la Cruz* is the tragedy not of the brigand Eusebio, who is saved, but of his father Curcio, to whose excessive scruples all the action can be traced, and who is punished by the death of his two sons. Yet Curcio's last words are a threat to kill his daughter, and show how far he still is, even at the end, from any recognition of his own responsibility for her situation too, or of the need for fatherly forgiveness.

Similarly in the honour plays, one looks in vain for any realization on the part of the husbands that though the code may have forced them to act as they did, they were transgressing a higher code and should suffer for it. Gutierre immediately contracts a new marriage—not entirely welcome to him, it is true, but scarcely a punishment or an occasion for the recognition of guilt. Juan Roca the *pintor* does expect vengeance to be taken on him, but instead even the relatives of the murdered pair tell him he was right.

Herod of *El mayor monstruo los celos* is one of the few Calderonian protagonists to recognize his guilt for what has happened and feel himself unfit to live. Although his stabbing of Mariene is accidental, he rightly blames his own jealousy for her death, and throws himself from a high tower into the sea. This solution, possible for a pagan, was not of course available in the case of Spanish characters, who in killing themselves would have committed the damning sin of theological despair. Even Herod, we are told, is "desesperado y confuso" when he does it. His suicide is not the sublime and reconciling act that Othello's is, performed in ultimate clarity of mind; it is merely the last of his moral errors. As Kenneth Tynan has stated, "anyone who arrives at self-knowledge through desperation is the raw material for a great play".[13] This is the meaning of anagnorisis. But neither Curcio, nor Gutierre, nor Juan Roca, nor even Herod, arrives at true self-knowledge; it is left to the audience to make the pilgrimage for them.

Is this enough? The problem is well illustrated by the comments of two critics on Lope's *Castigo sin venganza*. At the end of this play the Duke shows no recognition of the fact that his own conduct has brought the tragic situation into being. His last words are of satisfaction at the grim stratagem that has enabled him to allow revenge to masquerade as justice. Arnold G. Reichenberger, in "The uniqueness of the *comedia*" (*HR* 27, 1959 303–16), states that "the tragic potentialities in the character of the Duke seem never to have occurred to Lope. . . . Magnificent, truly tragic possibilities have been left untapped." Parker, in *The Approach to the Spanish Drama of the Golden Age*, maintains that the play *is* a magnificent tragedy, with the truly tragic figure of the Duke at its centre. These assessments are not in fact as far apart as they seem. Parker argues that "we must look not only at explicit comments, but also at implications and practical consequences"; and this is just what Reichenberger has done. His arrival by this means at an awareness of the tragic potentialities would amount for Parker to the recognition of the play as a great tragedy. But Reichenberger asks, I think

[13] Kenneth Tynan, *Bull Fever* (London, 1955), p. 49.

justifiably, for *some* explicit comment. One does not require all blame to be fairly and squarely apportioned in the text, or we should have a mere morality play; but neither can one be left fully satisfied by a work which makes a final statement apparently in contradiction to what the action can be shown to imply.

I think it is possible to detect in *El castigo*, and perhaps even more in Calderón's honour plays, a hint of conformism, a reluctance on the part of the dramatists to break away from convention if need be, and follow their insights wherever they may lead. It was, I think, the same conformism as that which held back Tirso from the full development of his powers of individual characterization, and Alarcón from the creation of a thoroughgoing comedy of manners; and in the final assessment it must be counted against the *comedia*. Parallel with it is the conformity in language. This is not to deny the qualities of naturalness in Lope and brilliance in Calderón; and there can of course be something very satisfying about the expected image in the appropriate place, as there is about the inevitability of a Handel cadence. But those endless references to the phoenix, those stereotyped descriptions of facial beauty in terms of coral and pearls, those fanciful metaphors that are *de rigueur* whenever dawn or dusk are mentioned, even in the most matter-of-fact contexts—all these become very tedious, especially when so seldom redeemed by a line of genuine poetry.

But I hope it will have been apparent how much there is to be said on the other side. The Spanish *comedia* is a substantial and significant field of European literature that deserves far wider recognition than it has ever received; and it is very much to be hoped that recent translations of some major plays, and even more the steady increase in the number of people who read Spanish, will result in its being given something nearer its true valuation. Early critics usually saw tragicomedy as Spain's chief contribution to the European stage; and I certainly know no other drama that can claim such masterpieces in this genre as *Fuenteovejuna*, *Peribáñez* and *El Alcalde de Zalamea*. The wicked may suffer in them and the good triumph, in something like story-book fashion, but it *is* a triumph—a manifestation of human dignity and courage put to a great test and proclaiming its worth. Recent studies of the moral and theological plays have brought out their artistry and their wide relevance, and many may now feel that it is in this field that Spanish drama makes its most individual contribution. It is certainly no longer possible to see them as Goethe did, as the irrational propaganda pieces of a sectarian interest; or to deny that they too, in their less naturalistic manner, present truths about humanity, and are still capable of guiding our explorations into the labyrinth of life.

ABBREVIATIONS USED

BAE	*Biblioteca de Autores Españoles*
BC	*Bulletin of the Comediantes*
BH	*Bulletin Hispanique*
BHS	*Bulletin of Hispanic Studies*
BRAE	*Boletín de la Real Academia Española*
FMLS	*Forum for Modern Language Studies*
HR	*Hispanic Review*
MLR	*Modern Language Review*
NBAE	*Nueva Biblioteca de Autores Españoles*
PMLA	*Publications of the Modern Language Association of America*
RF	*Romanische Forschungen*
RFE	*Revista de Filología Española*
RLit.	*Revista de Literatura*
RR	*Romanic Review*
RUBA	*Revista de la Universidad de Buenos Aires*

SOME MODERN ENGLISH TRANSLATIONS

Collections

The Classic Theatre, ed. Eric Bentley, Vol. III, *Six Spanish Plays* (New York, Doubleday Anchor, 1959). Includes translations by Roy Campbell of Cervantes, *The Siege of Numantia;* Lope de Vega, *Fuenteovejuna*; Tirso de Molina, *The Trickster of Seville*; and Calderón, *Love After Death* and *Life is a Dream*.

Lope de Vega (Five Plays), translated by Jill Booty (New York, 1961). Contains *Peribáñez, Justice Without Revenge, The Knight from Olmedo, Fuenteovejuna* and *The Dog in the Manger*.

Calderón: Four Plays, translated by Edwin Honig (New York, Mermaid Dramabooks, 1961). Contains *Secret Vengeance for Secret Insult, Devotion to the Cross, The Mayor of Zalamea* and *The Phantom Lady*.

Calderón: Six Plays, translated by Denis Florence MacCarthy with revision by Henry W. Wells (New York, Las Américas Publishing Co., 1961). Contains *Life is a Dream, The Wonder-Working Magician, The Constant Prince, The Devotion of the Cross, Love After Death* and *Belshazzar's Feast*.

Spanish Drama, ed. Ángel Flores (New York, Bantam Books, 1962). Includes Lope de Vega, *Fuenteovejuna*; Tirso de Molina, *The Rogue of Seville*; Alarcón, *The Truth Suspected*; and Calderón, *Life is a Dream*.

Single Works

Calderón, *Life's a Dream*, translated by F. Birch and J. B. Trend (Cambridge, 1925).

Calderón, *The Surgeon of his Honour*, translated by Roy Campbell (Madison, 1960).

Calderón, *A House with Two Doors is Difficult to Guard*, translated by Kenneth Muir (*Tulane Drama Review* VIII, No. 1, 1963, pp. 157–217).

INDEX